D1751041

BARTLETT WORKS
ARCHITECTURE BUILDINGS PROJECTS

Building design, architectural education, film direction, furniture design, architectural journalism, landscape, history and theory, arts and architecture policy, video production, website design, completed projects and works-in-progress by the Alumni, Faculty and Friends of the Bartlett School of Architecture, UCL

Published by August Projects Ltd,
in association with the Bartlett School of Architecture, UCL
Distributed by Cornerhouse
Printed in England by Trichrom
ISBN no. 1-902854-23-3
Copyright ©2004 August Projects and
the Bartlett School of Architecture, UCL

EDITORIAL BOARD:
Laura Allen
Iain Borden
Peter Cook
Peter Gibbs-Kennet
Rachel Stevenson
Tim Wray

DESIGN:
Ninety Seven Plus

IMAGE CREDITS

All images have been supplied by the relevant contributors. Unless otherwise stated below, images are reproduced courtesy of the practices and individuals under whose names they appear. Every effort has been made to acknowledge appropriate image sources and authors, and any omissions or errors notified to us will be corrected at the first possible opportunity.

Dulwich Pool House: Huffon+Crow
32 Murray Mews: Tim Bysted
Great Notley School: Tim Soar
Broadgate Club West: Richard Bryant
Jubilee School, CASPAR Housing: Tim Soar
Work/Learn Zone: Niall Clutton
Cloth Hall Street: Putler/3DD
Clearwater Yard: Tim Soar/Matt Chisnall
Dalston Lane: Tim Soar
RIBA Headquarters photograph © Nicholas Kane
Stonebridge Health and Community Centre model photographed by Roderick Coyne
Mancunian Way Footbridge: Photec
Dominican Monastery, Lille: René-Jacques
Takahata House: Takeo Dec / Akira Koyama
Tree House Apartment, Grand Central Bar and Museum of Modern Art, Oxford: Leon Chew
National Centre for Popular Music: Graham Gaunt
CowParade image © CowParade
SmartSlab™ image © Smartslab™
'The Pleasure of Treasure' and 'King's Cross Journey' images courtesy of Artangel and Richard Wentworth
Venus exterior: Paul Tyagi, interior: Dennis Gilbert
Cargo Fleet Visualisations: June Raby
San Michele Cemetery: Alessandra Chemollo/ Richard Davies
Kunsthaus Graz Bix images © realities:united
Drop House, Voss Street House, Fordham White Hair and Beauty Salon photographs: Tim Brotherton
'Inside the Whale' image: Balaenoptera Musculus, Blue Whale reproduced courtesy of the Natural History Museum
Albion Riverside Development: images by Hayes Davidson
Selfridges Birmingham: Richard Davies/Soren Aagaard
Selfridges Foodhall Manchester, Comme des Garçons Tunnel, Wild at Heart at the Great Eastern, Vogue Table, Marni London: Richard Davies
Isobel's Treehouse: Bob Sheil
City Learning Centre: Morley Von Sternberg
The Eden Project Education Resource Centre image © Michael Dyer Associates
Battersea Power Station photograph © Smoothe
Great Glass House Internal Landscape: Peter Culley
Elm House: Paul Smoothy/William Hodgson
Wellcome Trust Headquarters: GMJ
Berkeley Tower Penthouse: Paul Grundy
Faith Zone photograph © Peter Cook

Tottenham Hale Station and Crystal Palace Park photographs: Morley von Sternberg
North Greenwich Underground Station: Dennis Gilbert
Hayling video stills courtesy of the artist FC Kahuna and Skint Records
Nature is Ancient video stills courtesy of the artist Björk and One Little Indian Records
Thames Barrier Park: Martin Charles
Microflat, Microlife, Martello Tower, FLO houses photographs © Smoothe
Microlife photographs: Paul McGill
Architecture Week: Augustus Casely-Hayford. Reproduced courtesy of the Arts Council
Scents of Space photographs: Sam Brocks/Pletts Haque
EDF Trading Interactive LED Wall: Chris Gascoigne/VIEW
Bolton Gardens: Jonathan Pile
'Alice's Pillow Books': etching 'Disturbed Earth' by Oona Grimes
RIBA Journal pages reproduced courtesy of *RIBA Journal*
Spire of Dublin: Barry Mason Photography
Minamiyamashiro School: Katsuhisa Kida
National Assembly for Wales: Eamonn O'Mahony
Barajas Airport aerial view rendering: Melon Studio
Ourtown Story: © Grant Smith
Tribunal de Grande Instance interior: Vincent Montiers, exterior: Christian Richters
Lloyd's Register of Shipping photographs: Katsuhisa Kida/Dennis Gilbert
1&2 Waterside: Daniel Wright
Torro Espacio model: Eamonn O'Mahony
The Cross: Nicholas Kane
Veritas Headquarters: Carlos Dominguez and SBT
95 Queen Victoria Street: Sean Corrigan
Salvation Army Headquarters: image by Virtual Artworks (London)
'Treehouse' and 'Floating Retreat' reproduced courtesy of *Wallpaper** magazine
Urban Renaissance Programme film © Yorkshire Forward
Architecture Today cover reproduced courtesy of *Architecture Today* magazine.
The Line of Lode Miners Memorial and Visitors Centre: Sam Noonan
Summer Stage photographs: Robert Barker
Esplanade images from DP Architects Pty Ltd, photographer: Hidetaki Mori
Port Tawe Footbridges: Nick Wood

LIST OF CONTRIBUTORS: 01 **ACQ**, 02 **ADAMS & SUTHERLAND**, 04 **AHMM**, 10 **ALLIES & MORRISON**, 11 **ALSOP**, 16 **ARCA**, 17 **ARCHIDESIGN**, 18 **ART2ARCHITECTURE**, 19 **ASHTON PORTER**, 21 **ATELIER KO**, 22 **AZHAR**, 23 **BLOCK**, 25 **BLUSTIN HEATH**, 26 **IAIN BORDEN**, 28 **BRANSON COATES**, 28 **MICHAEL BROWN**, 29 **JASON BRUGES**, 30 **CAMPKIN, PENNER & RENDELL**, 32 **CHANCE DE SILVA**, 33 **CHIPPERFIELD**, 34 **COOK & FOURNIER**, 39 **COOK WITH PÉREZ ARROYO + HURTADO**, 40 **DECQ-CORNETTE**, 42 **DILLER + SCOFIDIO**, 43 **TOM DYCKHOFF**, 44 **EMULSION**, 44 **EVENT**, 47 **FEATHERSTONE ASSOCIATES**, 49 **FLETCHER PRIEST**, 50 **ADRIAN FORTY**, 52 **FOSTER AND PARTNERS**, 58 **FUTURE SYSTEMS**, 64 **STEPHEN GAGE**, 66 **GENERAL LIGHTING AND POWER**, 68 **GHAHREMANI + KOHN**, 70 **GLAS**, 70 **GOLLIFER LANGSTON**, 71 **GRIMSHAW**, 72 **CHRIS GROOTHUIZEN**, 72 **GUSTAFSON PORTER**, 74 **CHRISTINE HAWLEY**, 78 **WAYNE HEAD**, 79 **LOUIS HELLMAN**, 81 **JONATHAN HILL**, 83 **WILLIAM HODGSON**, 84 **ANDREW HOLMES**, 86 **HOPKINS**, 90 **HÛT**, 91 **IMAGINATION**, 92 **DARYL JACKSON**, 93 **JESTICO + WHILES**, 94 **EVA JIRICNA**, 95 **PATRICK KEILLER**, 97 **L&V KIRPICHEV**, 97 **LAB-7**, 100 **THE LIGHTHOUSE**, 102 **CJ LIM/STUDIO 8**, 106 **JOHN LYALL**, 108 **LYNNFOX**, 110 **MARCOSANDMARJAN**, 113 **RICK MATHER**, 114 **NIALL MCLAUGHLIN**, 118 **BRIGID MCLEER**, 118 **MIRALLES TAGLIABUE**, 121 **NAAU**, 122 **NOODLEJAM**, 123 **OLIVEIRA ROSA**, 125 **ORMS**, 126 **PASTINA MATTHEWS**, 126 **PATEL TAYLOR**, 127 **PENOYRE & PRASAD**, 128 **PÉREZ ARROYO + HURTADO**, 130 **PHAB**, 132 **PIERCY CONNER**, 135 **ALICIA PIVARO**, 136 **PLETTS HAQUE**, 137 **PRINGLE BRANDON**, 138 **PROJECT ORANGE**, 139 **JOHN PUTTICK**, 141 **PEG RAWES**, 142 **JANE RENDELL**, 144 **RIBA JOURNAL**, 145 **RICH MARTINS**, 145 **IAN RITCHIE**, 149 **RICHARD ROGERS PARTNERSHIP**, 155 **SATELLITE DESIGN WORKSHOP**, 156 **SCOTT BROWNRIGG**, 156 **SHEPPARD ROBSON**, 161 **DEBRA SHIPLEY MP**, 162 **SIXTEEN*(MAKERS)**, 164 **SOM**, 164 **SOFTROOM**, 170 **SPACE SYNTAX**, 172 **NEIL SPILLER**, 174 **SPRINGETT MACKAY**, 175 **SQUINT/OPERA**, 176 **STORP_WEBER_ARCHITECTURE**, 178 **MARK SWENARTON**, 179 **JERRY TATE**, 179 **TECHNIKER**, 181 **TEMPLETON ASSOCIATES**, 182 **TESSERA**, 184 **THARANI ASSOCIATES**, 185 **STEPHEN TIERNEY**, 186 **TRANSIENT**, 188 **UNIVERSITY OF SOUTH AUSTRALIA**, 189 **UFO**, 190 **USHIDA FINDLAY**, 194 **VELVET AIR**, 196 **WAG**, 197 **INGALILL WAHLROOS**, 198 **WHAT**, 199 **WHITE PARTNERS**, 200 **MICHAEL WILFORD & PARTNERS**, 201 **WILKINSONEYRE**, 203 **TIM WRAY**

ACKNOWLEDGEMENTS

Bartlett Works would not have been possible without the help and contributions of a great many people – far too many to thank individually here. Particular thanks however are due to all of the practices and individuals that have contributed and allowed us to reproduce their drawings, photographs, images and words. Thanks to all those who have researched and gathered information on our behalf, especially to those who have patiently returned to their archives when we have come back asking for more facts, figures and pictures. We must also acknowledge Peter Gibbs-Kennet, whose idea this project was, and the essential contributions of Nick Barley at August and Belinda Moore at Ninety Seven Plus, for their creative input and expertise in helping realise the finished book.

This publication has been generously supported by Foster and Partners, Sheppard Robson, White Partners Limited, the Bartlett Architecture Society and the UCL Friends Programme.

The Bartlett Architecture Society is an association of former students, staff and friends of the Bartlett that supports the activities of the School. We welcome new members: for more information please write to the Bartlett Architecture Society, the Bartlett School of Architecture UCL, 22 Gordon Street, London, WC1H 0QB.

The Friends Programme is UCL's annual giving programme. Every year, thanks to the generosity of alumni and staff, the UCL Friends Programme supports a variety of projects throughout the UCL community, which may otherwise have gone unfunded.

The UCL Friends Programme is keen to ensure that grants reach departments right across the UCL constituency and is happy to be associated with projects and initiatives which promote the innovation, expertise and talent within UCL.

Thanks also to the Bartlett's other supporters: Lowe & Partners Worldwide, Altro, T. Brewer and Company Limited, Concordmarlin, Gradus Limited, LSA Projects representing Gustafs of Sweden with Hurrel Interiors and Sound Research Laboratories Limited.

FOREWORD

It was a pleasure to be asked to introduce this book.

Gaining a higher education qualification is a great individual achievement. But of more lasting importance is the use graduates make of that foundation in building a lifelong career which is of benefit to them as individuals and to society as well.

This is especially true in the case of architecture, one of the most diverse educations available, leading to a working life of great variety and length, which can be enjoyed in a number of different and exciting settings both at home and abroad.

This volume gives us a glimpse of the contribution architecture can make to society through the eyes of staff and former students at one institution.

Certainly, the achievements illustrated here should reinforce our confidence in the importance of investing in higher education for the ultimate benefit of us all.

Rt Hon Margaret Hodge, MBE, MP, Minister of State

IAIN BORDEN

In 2000, we published the *Bartlett Book of Ideas* – a celebration of nearly a decade's worth of student work in the Bartlett School of Architecture at UCL. Stuffed to the gills with design projects and texts of every manner of interest, obsession and perspicacity, *BBI*, as we have now come to call it, acted as simultaneous celebration, record and crib-book – a place where we (and other schools of architecture and practices around the world) could turn for a sense of recollection, pride and sheer surprise at what really good architecture students are capable of achieving.

Except, of course, this could only ever be the start of the story. Once out in the world, where we know for a fact it has been gutted and devoured by thousands, *BBI* begged the question as to what these graduates have gone on to pursue in their later lives. Are they now architects? If so, what is the architecture that they are now dreaming, designing and building? Who are they working for? And in which parts of the world? Or if not architects, in what other fields of creativity are they practising? – from journalism and literature, to furniture and video design, to politics and policy formulation... ?

Similar questions need also to be asked of our own staff, for what we expect of our graduates we should surely expect of ourselves. What kinds of buildings are being designed, artistic projects created, books and exhibitions produced? The realm of academia is no longer an ivory tower, and Bartlett staff are as keen as Bartlett graduates to have an impact in the more public worlds of clients, readers, users and audiences. In following up *BBI* with *Bartlett Works*, it was clear we had to address these issues as well.

In asking these questions, we also quickly realised that it would be wrong to maintain that there is always some kind of direct connection between the world of education and the world of practice. More often than not, a student's final Diploma project does not bear any immediate relation to the buildings that he or she first works on when in an office – an eel farm designed here will hardly ever lead to an eel farm in practice, and even a speculative office building here will rarely lead to an equivalent project after graduating. Rather, what architecture students experience at the Bartlett will, we hope, be a unique kind of learning and, it must be said, inspiration to get out there and achieve something architectural, whatever that might be. We teach – and the students learn – a particular 'basic' set of knowledge, from the principles of technology and environmental design, to significant historical dates and facts, to drawing techniques and software packages, to rules of management, business and ethics. These are all important. Yet even more important is that students for themselves develop all manner of less definable skills, things like intelligence and intuition, creativity and invention, dissection and synthesis, interpretation and speculation, problem-spotting and solving, rigour and obsession, and the courage and independence to enquire, take risks and be unpredictable. It is these kinds of qualities which we believe our graduates display in abundance, and it is these qualities which we hope are bearing real fruits in the world of architecture, however that world is being realised.

Bartlett Works, then, is most definitely not a collection of projects which we as the Bartlett can in any way claim to be 'ours'. Instead, this is a kind of tracking of paths pursued, careers developed, buildings built, texts published and projects completed by those who have been (and often still are) connected with the School. If, by and large, we only mention the contribution of Bartlett graduates and staff to the projects included in *Bartlett Works*, it is not to claim that they are solely responsible for them, or to diminish the role of other design team members, engineers, surveyors, artists, clients and everybody else involved, whom we do not have space to acknowledge fully. We are highly indebted to all the practices, institutions and individuals whose work this actually is, and inordinately grateful to everyone involved for their efforts, patience and participation. Many, many thanks.

Now that one comes to peruse the final volume, seeing all that it contains, I am much encouraged and highly stimulated by the rich range of achievement on display, from architectural practices of all kinds, shapes and sizes, from those working in a team or who prefer to go it alone, from those designing, writing or politicking, and from those who produce buildings, ideas, sounds, visions and texts. Much more than just being about people from the Bartlett, this book offers a cross-section of the great range of projects that are being produced in contemporary architectural practice – in the widest sense of the term. Whereas many books on the subject only feature the buildings of the most well-known of architects, *Bartlett Works* also highlights projects that might otherwise go unnoticed. Looking at all of these projects together – from the big to the small, the famous to the unknown, the expensive to the small-budget – one gets a very real sense of the extraordinary degree of ingenuity and perspicacity involved, for these are real acts of research, ones which truly test the creativity of their designers to their limits, transform corners of the world as it is encountered in everyday life, and collectively constitute the rich depth of architectural endeavour. Above all, I am pleased to be constantly surprised by all that our graduates and staff do. One of the great things about being in an architecture school is that one never quite knows what is going to happen next, and *Bartlett Works* more than fulfills this tradition. Long may it continue.

Iain Borden, Director of the Bartlett School of Architecture, UCL

PETER COOK

It has long been established that some of the best architectural conversations and some of the wittiest and most intelligent processes of design go on in London. Some of the most provocative and intriguing people in the business enjoy meeting our students at the Bartlett because there seems to be a continuous trail of new ideas and new interpretations coming forth from student work.

The British strength seems to thrive through its famous great engines of design: Fosters, Rogers, Grimshaw, Hopkins: now joined in international reference by Hadid, Alsop and Chipperfield. Even if it is arguable that Spain, Holland, Austria or Switzerland have in recent times displayed a proportionally greater number of independent young architects, the creative power of the 'engines' is undeniable.

Tracking the works of our recent graduates for this book revealed a healthy situation out there. It was a fascinating exercise in mapping: who is where – and with whom? Which of the 'name' architects is wise enough – or bold enough – to entrust millions of somebody's money in a contrivance that was driven by some up-to-the-minute thinking? Safeguarded, perhaps, by that very strength of the engine and its collective expertise, some of these offices have a similarity to the present-day Bartlett: internally competitive, externally thrusting and identifiable. With the added power of the London tradition of inventive engineering: its structural wizards, gadget boffins, environmental explorers (many of whom come and go into the school and are therefore already 'friendly faces'), the resultant work is often recognisably 'cutting-edge'.

In the face of such power, how does the new, two-person band emerge? Yet it does, by stealth, by some piece of the engine splitting-off, by finding a corner of the market that may simply be less profitable for the big office. This book is full of companies that you might only have heard of once, but will hear of again. The British scene seems poised to attack the Spanish, Dutch etc. and a disproportionately large number of the attackers came out of the Bartlett. That same set of foibles: energy, intelligence, inventiveness (laced with a touch of arrogance without which architects can rarely survive) that render our graduates so attractive to the engines – may it be the same set that can enable them suddenly, one day, to take off?

Regeneration is necessary if we are to remain a discussible architectural country. Looking outside we can ask the question: did SOM in the States or Behnisch in Germany really manage to reinvent themselves? Does the nature of architectural practice not need to reinvent *itself*? Will the future of architecture be some new set of co-operative activities? The 'artiste' along with the production expert? The inventor with the cataloguer? Take a closer look at the stories as well as the illustrations within this book. Think on the hybrids, the in-between state of much that they do. Relish those who move outside conventional so-called 'practice': their books, films, exhibitions, or chairs still have much to say about architecture.

Bartlett Works is more than just a pointer to those who may have already acknowledged that the Bartlett can think, draw and dream. It suggests that it works because it thinks and it makes, often applying as much thought to the logic of process and understanding of 'stuff' as to obvious mannerisms. This is a very British strength, and one that we consciously inculcate to our (now) increasing number of non-British students.

More than this: through the book there are teams of designers of varying ages. The 'name' architects have generously permitted us to winkle out and spell out those of our graduates who are making the projects. I am sure that this will have its own reward and act as an attraction for more bright people to go to good offices.

So the sum of the book is a certain kind of collective culture: sniffing, investigating, honing, commenting – then back to sniffing again, with stuff that is the result of a certain shared optimism. It is well known that most Bartlett people are bright and resourceful, so now we make a document that can be read as a series of case-histories/the first of a flood of projects/a weird 'network'. From inside the School, we send out a message to *them* also: *you* are an essential part of *us*: you are our reference as much as you (often) say we are yours.

Peter Cook, Chairman of the Bartlett School of Architecture, UCL

ACQ

01

The partners of acq all worked together at Richard Rogers Partnership before forming the practice at the height of the dot com boom. The emerging and rapidly growing new media companies provided the bulk of our early workload. We completed quick-turnaround fit-outs for companies such as Clickmango and Sportal alongside short-listed competition entries for the new parliament in Liechtenstein, a housing scheme in Collyhurst, Manchester and for Channel 5 Television. We believe that it is possible to pursue the unusual, and get the stuff built. All the practice's work, whether commercial, residential or competition schemes, seeks to balance practical and economic concerns with dynamic, eye-opening design.

Hal Currey

Dulwich Pool House, London
Domestic refurbishment
Budget: £500,000
Completed: December 2001
Hal Currey: architect

We transformed a normal dilapidated 1950s house in South London into an inspiring light-filled space to be enjoyed by a large family with an informal lifestyle. Solid structures (stairs for example) have been cut away to allow light to flow through the previously austere upper levels. The ground floor is reconceived as three distinct internal and external zones: a substantial living area with floor to ceiling glass wall, a swimming pool courtyard framed by coloured walls with an integral fireplace, and a garden courtyard beyond, centred around a lawn.

32 Murray Mews, Camden, London
New build house
Budget: £200,000
Completed: 2002
Hal Currey: architect

A new house for my family and I, built in Murray Mews, a street already featuring many individually designed houses by architects including Edward Cullinan and Norman Foster. Large areas of glazing coupled with voids maximise natural daylight and create a sense of spaciousness in a tight site. If desired, at a later date voids could be in-filled to create new living and sleeping spaces. The house is constructed as a steel frame (exposed at roof level), with a zinc rainscreen at first- and second-floor levels, and resin-coated plywood cladding to the ground floor.

02 ADAMS & SUTHERLAND

Will Adams Centre, Bloors Wharf, Rainham, North Kent ▼
RIBA international competition winner
Estimated cost: £900,000
1997 (unbuilt)
Graeme Sutherland: co-designer

I have taught in the Year 1 studio at the Bartlett since 1993. In 1997, after winning the Will Adams Centre competition, I set up in practice with Elizabeth Adams. Our work ranges in scale from urban regeneration and landscape design to smaller projects for voluntary organisations and schools. We aim to articulate and answer social needs. We are involved both in initiating and developing projects, and consider collaboration with users an integral part of our creative process. A precise reading of the physical and social context underpins the development of our spatial ideas. Highlighting overlapping or complementary uses of space, a number of projects have a dynamic 'in-between' quality: defining the work as open and fragmentary rather than finite.

Graeme Sutherland

This winning entry in an RIBA and Kent Architecture Centre competition for the sustainable reuse of a heavily contaminated wharf and adjacent fields on the tidal Medway Estuary included proposals for a new educational and recreational building with bird-watching and astronomical facilities. A 'constructed' landscape of flint banks and enclosed gardens is 'laid' onto the existing wharf surface to heighten the sense of place, forming the site for a new building and relating the land to the estuary. Adjacent fields are transformed into reed beds and a willow coppice, creating a new inland marsh habitat. This landscape allows sustainable occupation of the wharf, producing fuel to run a power plant and cleansing all drainage. The 'Light Field', a grid of fibre optic points linked to sensors around the estuary, provides a register of its unseen life, such as the passage of migratory birds overhead or the movement of ships, and shifts the scale of the wharf.

In 1998 we were appointed to investigate the feasibility of developing the wharf, but due to lack of political support no further work was commissioned.

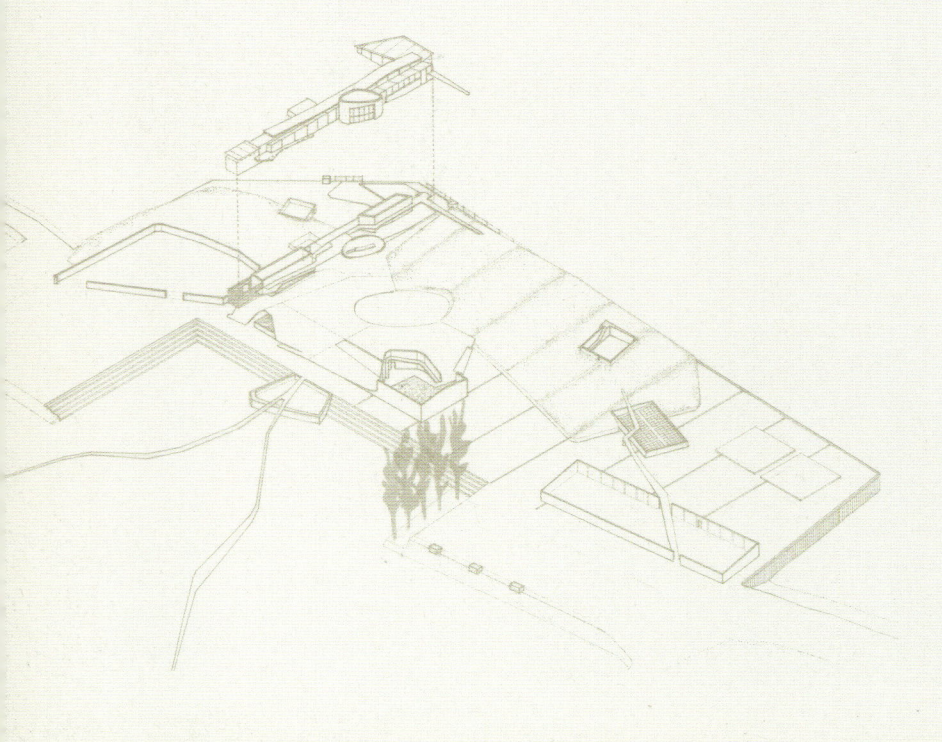

Evergreen Adventure Playground, Hackney, London
Community playground
Cost: £200,000 (including sponsorship and contributed labour)
Completed: 2000
Graeme Sutherland: co-designer and contract administrator

Evergreen Play Association has provided a supervised play facility for children in the Holly Street Estate in Hackney for over 20 years. In a part of London with few safe open spaces, the playground is a wild oasis. With the redevelopment of the estate, a design strategy was developed for a 'landscape of play' in which the ground is a continuous spatial field onto which a series of interrelated elements are placed. 'Skydens', tree walkways and a pole forest create a circuitous play journey. The new structures also provide integrated access to a full range of experiences for children with disabilities. Through the lengthy evolution of this project a strong collaborative relationship was formed between the design team, the play workers and children. Since reopening, the playground has become a model of play provision, enjoying a huge increase in popularity.

04 ALLFORD HALL MONAGHAN MORRIS

Allford Hall Monaghan Morris, commonly known as AHMM, has a unique shared history with the Bartlett. Over the past 20 years, we have been first students, next teachers and now also employers of Bartlett students, thus establishing a continuing and developing relationship which we are proud to enjoy.

All four partners – Simon Allford, Jonathan Hall, Paul Monaghan and Peter Morris – completed their Diploma at the Bartlett in the 1980s, undertaking our 'Fifth Man' project as a collaborative effort. From here came the idea to work in professional life as a quartet, first at BDP and shortly after in our own practice. Over the past decade we have continually extended the range of buildings we have constructed – from medical practices, offices and social housing to transport interchanges, pool-houses and lofts, as well as ephemeral art collaborations, exhibition pavilions and theoretical propositions. The office is enacting a multifaceted yet coordinated form of architectural endeavour, concerned not only with architecture as object and design but also as a way of engaging with the city and landscape, responding to clients and users, collaborating with engineers and artists, and, indeed, as a way of practising architecture itself.

It is unsurprising that one of the many arenas which AHMM have operated within is that of teaching, with Simon and Paul running first Unit 5 in the BSc and then Unit 10 in the Diploma programme. Through this and other routes, a myriad of Bartlett students have gone on to work in the AHMM office, adding to the diversity of our work in a multitude of different ways. We name here but a few of these individuals and the projects they have worked on.

05

Private House, North London ▶
New build house
Completion: September 2003
Joe Morris: project architect

This new family home in the St. John's Wood Conservation Area is configured around a double-height open-plan living space, onto which more private family areas (kitchen/family room, swimming pool and playroom) connect. A first-floor gallery overlooking this space connects children's bedrooms with the master bedroom suite. The mosaic-tiled elevations are punctured with window openings that take their proportions from the fenestration of the surrounding period properties. The split-pitch lead roof responds to the surrounding rooflines, whilst allowing in more light.

◀ Walsall Bus Station, West Midlands
New build bus station
Budget: £4.7 million
Completed: July 2000
Ceri Davies: assistant architect

Won in an RIBA-run international competition, our design provides an enormous roof gathering up the programme within a single perimeter. The elliptical form, punctuated by a series of large conical rooflights, is impressive both in scale and shape, provoking local comparisons with a moonbase, a giant Frisbee, and a visiting flying saucer. In addition the project has restructured a major part of the centre of Walsall, including the formation of a new public square – and is thus not just architecture but also urban improvement and civic amenity.

Great Notley Primary School, Essex ▶
New build school
Budget: £1.25 million
Completed: September 1999
David Archer: project architect

Won in an international competition, this model school demonstrates energy-efficient and sustainable principles within a standard public sector budget. The school is an Egan Demonstration Project and a show project for The Design Council. It features a unique combination of a triangular plan (to minimise wasted circulation space), sedum roofs and a real-world attitude to materials selection. The school has received an RIBA Award for Architecture and Millennium Product Status. In June 2000 it was given the Royal Fine Arts Commission Award for education buildings.

06 ALLFORD HALL MONAGHAN MORRIS

Jubilee School, Tulse Hill, London
New build school
Budget: £4.5 million
Completed: July 2002
Susan Le Good: project architect

This new community primary school, nursery and 'Surestart' base includes a Special Educational Needs facility for hearing-impaired pupils that will become a centre of excellence for their education. The sustainable design was developed after wide local and specialist consultation. A rectilinear composition is brazenly dominated by an almost blank front elevation with a massive cantilevered roof. We worked with artist Martin Richman to create a number of colouristic modulations, from hard glazed bricks in the entrance to cheek walls painted in purples and pinks.

Peabody Trust Housing, Raines Dairy, London
New build housing
Budget: £8 million
Completed: December 2002
Karen Stirlock: project architect

This experimental venture for the Peabody Trust, providing shared ownership homes and live/work spaces, uses prefabricated construction techniques to maximise quality by utilising off-site construction under factory conditions. The scheme is built following modular principles developed into a prefabricated and standardised architecture. Three six-storey blocks are arranged around a central access core. Two front blocks house 41 two-bedroom apartments above eight live/work units. The rear block comprises eleven three-bedroom family apartments.

Broadgate Club West, London
New health club
Budget: £2 million
Completed: December 1998
Susan Le Good: architectural assistant

Broadgate Club West stands out from the normal pop-in and pump-up buzz of a conventional gym; the modernist hotel elegance of the reception yields to the traditional gentleman's club-like changing rooms, while the rawer techy atmosphere of the exercise zone is screened from the calmness of the adjacent bar. The architecture works with the club's marketing, incorporating surface-oriented tactics that directly wed manipulations of space and material with urban presence and promotion – most notably a coloured and illuminated spine wall runs the length of the scheme, dictating the character of the spaces.

CASPAR Housing, Birmingham
New build housing
Contract value: £2.3 million
Completed: December 1999
Demetra Ryder Runton: project architect

This scheme for the Joseph Rowntree Foundation, providing low-cost rental accommodation for keyworkers, posits a unique prototype for urban living: two identical blocks eight metres apart and each housing 23 single-bedroom apartments are conceived as individual structures, with a courtyard between protected from extremes of weather by end-glazing and a simple oversailing glazed umbrella roof with open sides. Access to apartments is by way of private bridges (not shared decks), reached by two staircases and a lift within the glazed screens.

07

Union Square, London ▲
New build mixed-use development
Budget: £18 million
Completion: 2006
Morag Tait: project architect

Containing office, housing and retail facilities, this mixed-use scheme in Union Street is an exercise in urban as much as architectural design; extending further south London's 'Bankside triangle' focused regeneration of Southwark. The development acts as a new counterpoint to Tate Modern, the Millennium Bridge, Globe Theatre and Thames Path to its immediate north. A new urban square and an elegant residential tower form the focus of the design. Café and retail units face the square at ground level, with residential spaces, both for sale and affordable housing.

08 ALLFORD HALL MONAGHAN MORRIS

Work/Learn Zone, Millennium Dome, London
Exhibition pavilion
Budget: £2.5 million
Completed: December 1999
Tony Martin: project architect

For one of the most distinctive pavilions in the Millennium Dome exhibition, AHMM collaborated with Tim Pyne's company WORK. The content is predicated upon the concept of 'Lifetime Learning', exploring the duality of 'Work' and 'Learn'. The result was an elegant shed, animated with gigantic, alternating billboard triptychs. Each of the three exterior images represents a different aspect of British life: print works of the *Financial Times* for working, rows of books for learning, and a typical countryside-park setting for something quintessentially British.

Cloth Hall Street, Leeds
New build retail and apartment building
Budget: £6.5 million
Completion: August 2003
Rob Burton: project architect

This proposed building sits on an important triangular site in Leeds, next to Cuthbert Brodrick's elliptical Corn Exchange and the White Cloth Hall. Four storeys of residential apartments wrap around a private first-floor level courtyard with retail units below. The design draws inspiration from the prevalent Victorian brick warehouses and ceramic faience of the surrounding shopping arcades. Robust external elevations using smooth hard bricks are made more dramatic through a chameleon-like mutation from yellow through green to blue, played out along the large facing panels.

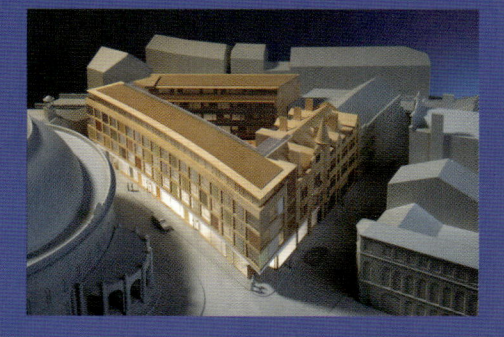

Peabody Trust Housing, Dalston Lane, London ◂
New build housing/retail
Contract Value: £1.87 million
Completed: June 1999
Jenny Lovell: project architect

This building contains 18 two-bedroom flats and six one-bedroom flats set back above a plinth of retail units. Bedroom windows are punched in the north façade facing Dalston Lane, whose enormous chequerboard surface pattern creates a bold colouristic insertion into an otherwise drab and gritty neighbourhood. South-facing living and dining spaces open on to deep balconies at the rear. The low-level street elevation comprises glass and steel-framed retail frontages contained at each end by deep-blue glazed brick flank walls. Folds in the brickwork form entrance points to the flats.

Clearwater Yard, Camden, London ▴
New build speculative office building
Budget: £1.85 million
Completed: June 2002
Scott Batty: project architect
Charlotte Harrison: architectural assistant

The site for this small office, just off the busy Camden High Street, demanded a reconciliation of several seemingly contradictory oppositions: private and public, bustle and rest, dynamism and calmness, security and openness, anonymity and publicity. Three blocks with fully glazed façades overlook a central courtyard that leads into a main reception space. The central core behind houses the lift, staircases and unisex toilets with a communal hand-wash fountain, seen as the real social heart of the development.

10 ALLIES AND MORRISON

Bob Allies and Graham Morrison established Allies and Morrison in 1984. The practice has completed a diverse range of award-winning architecture, landscape, interior design and conservation projects. Current projects include a new headquarters for the BBC, the restoration of the Royal Festival Hall and masterplans for the redevelopment of major brownfield sites at King's Cross and Cricklewood in London, and the city centre of Sheffield.

Sidgwick Site Masterplan and Institute of Criminology, University of Cambridge
Masterplan and new build
Completion: 2004
Jenny Lovell: masterplan design development, Institute of Criminology job architect

Our masterplan for the Sidgwick Site, initially developed by Sir Hugh Casson in the 1950s, with later additions by Foster and Stirling, seeks to bring together a number of disparate buildings, bringing cohesion to this key Arts & Humanities Campus through built and planted forms and a series of open courtyards.

The Institute of Criminology will sit four storeys above ground within a landscaped court. Accommodation includes seminar rooms, general teaching space and the Institute's world-renowned library collection on the ground and first floors. The façade has been developed as a unitised system that will be brought to site in fully glazed three-square-metre panels.

Royal Institute of British Architects Headquarters, Portland Place, London
Refurbishment
1996-present
Helena Thomas: project architect for current works

The new bookshop was our first completed project as house architects for the RIBA headquarters. The bookshop was expanded by 105 square metres to occupy the whole of the Weymouth Street frontage. The main sales area is conceived as a single volume and restores G Grey Wornum's original 1932 open plan design. The removal of the previous sales desk and entrance screen has also allowed the cross axis of the formal entrance hall to be re-established. Other completed projects include the refurbishment of the Florence Hall and Jarvis Hall. Design of the Council Chamber, Members Room and Bar is underway.

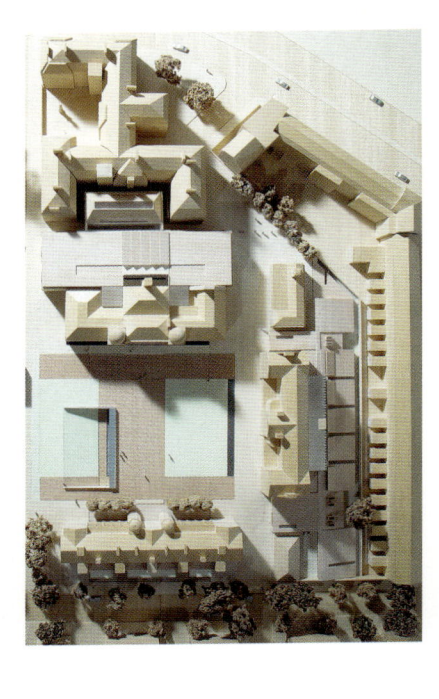

Chelsea College of Art and Design, Millbank, London
Redevelopment of listed building
Completion: 2004
Vicky Thornton: project associate

We are remodelling and extending the Grade II listed former Royal Army Medical College to provide a new home for the Chelsea College of Art and Design, which is currently housed in four separate sites. Incorporating a new gallery and with Tate Britain (which we also refurbished and extended) next door, the site has the potential to become the centre of a vibrant new arts quarter of London. Proposed new structures are inserted into the spaces behind the three main existing buildings and underground, preserving the grandeur of the grand central courtyard. A new main entrance is sunk into the courtyard, with an underground library beyond.

ALSOP ARCHITECTS

Alsop Architects is a multidisciplinary international architectural and urban design practice with over 100 staff operating from offices in London and Rotterdam, with further site offices in Canada and Singapore. We believe in a process of design enlisting public involvement and creative debate. Over more than 20 years of professional practice Will Alsop has nurtured an architectural and urban vocabulary based on inclusion, consultation and an imaginative interpretation of the brief. All our work is underpinned by the knowledge that architecture and design have the possibility to enrich lives and empower the communities they help to shape.

Perhaps it is the combination of innovative architecture, creative debate, and the multidisciplinary approach of the practice that has attracted so many Bartlett graduates to Alsop Architects. There are clear similarities between the teaching ethos at the Bartlett and our approach to design. Both encourage the individual to challenge preconceived ideas of space, form, function and use at all scales, and both look to develop solutions that are imaginative, challenging and that enrich the lives of others.

Peckham Library, South London ▶
New build library
Budget: £4.5 million
Completed: 2000
Isabel Brebbia: pod design
Andy McPhee: project architect

Peckham Library is a flagship regeneration project for the Borough of Southwark. The brief called for a building that would redefine the role of the library in the community and engender a sense of ownership and pride in local people.

The result is a unique and stimulating building, with work, archive and meeting spaces of genuine delight. Traditionally a library is conceived as a 'serious' building, but for us seriousness of purpose does not preclude either high style or wit. In section the building is an upside-down 'L', with the main reading room supported on angled columns forming an irregular arcade which encloses a covered extension of the adjacent public square. The reading room is a magical attic space, overlooking London and connecting Peckham to the seats of power and wealth in Westminster, the City and Docklands. Three timber-framed plywood-clad pods inside contain meeting rooms and independent collections. The central pod is lit by a clerestory window shaded by a prominent red rooftop 'beret'.

Peckham Library has no air conditioning, and uses natural light and ventilation, passive cooling and solar shading to reduce energy consumption. The building won the Stirling Prize in November 2000.

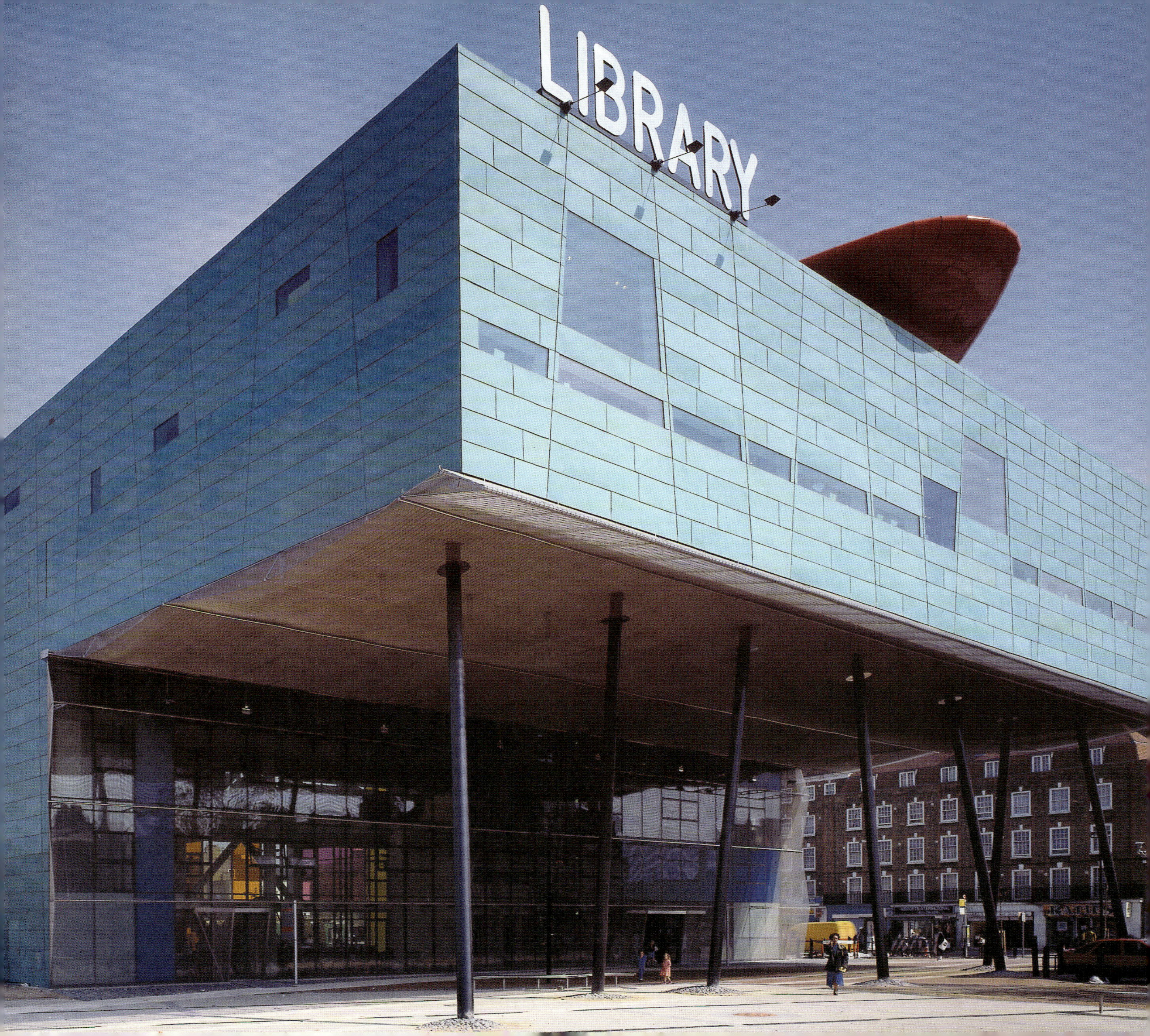
LIBRARY

ALSOP ARCHITECTS

Stonebridge Health and Community Centre, London
New build community building
Budget: £10 million
Completion: 2004
Oliver Blumschein: detail design
Adrian Fowler: detail design
Alan Lai: external envelope, public consultation, design development

The interlocking forms of this mixed-use Health and Community Centre represent successive functional zones which are protected by carapaces of freeform vitreous enamel panels. The panels are part of a rainscreen cladding system that is set off from the envelope of the building to create interesting light and shadow effects by day and night. The subtle diversity of colours on the panels contributes to the effect of a shimmering dappled camouflage of shapes and shadows floating above the muted background colour of the primary weathering surface. Each of the forms is animated by a dramatic cut. These cuts are expressed with coloured and fritted structural glazing, achieving required levels of solar shading and privacy. Behind the cuts for the health centre and community centre entrances, triple height reception spaces are enclosed in intensely coloured lantern volumes.

Stonebridge Nursery, London
New build nursery
Budget: £1 million
Completion: 2002-2003
Alan Lai: design, consultation, detail design

The main concept for this new nursery, designed to very tight budgetary constraints, was to have a large portal frame enclosure sheltering the whole site to provide a covered play-area and circulation space between different internal functions. There will be several differing types of prefabricated portable structures adapted from other uses (traditional yurts, refurbished sea-containers, caravans and mobile-homes are envisaged) under the shed roof. This combination of built and adapted environments will permit a rapid construction programme and is a flexible and idiosyncratic response to the demands imposed by the daily activities of very young children, at a relatively low cost. A sculptural metalwork screen around the perimeter of the portal frame provides security and solar shading to the enclosure.

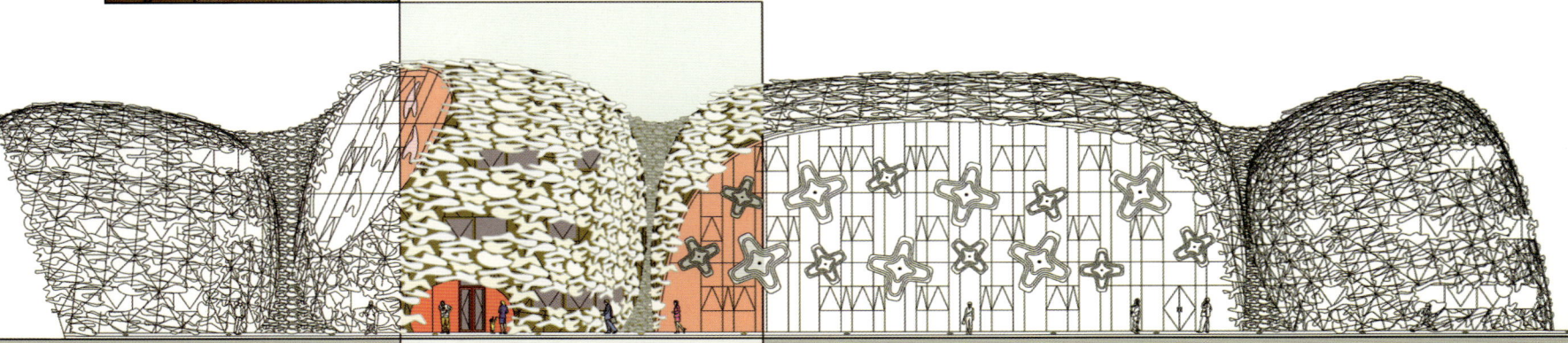

HEALTH CENTRE ENTRANCE

14 ALSOP ARCHITECTS

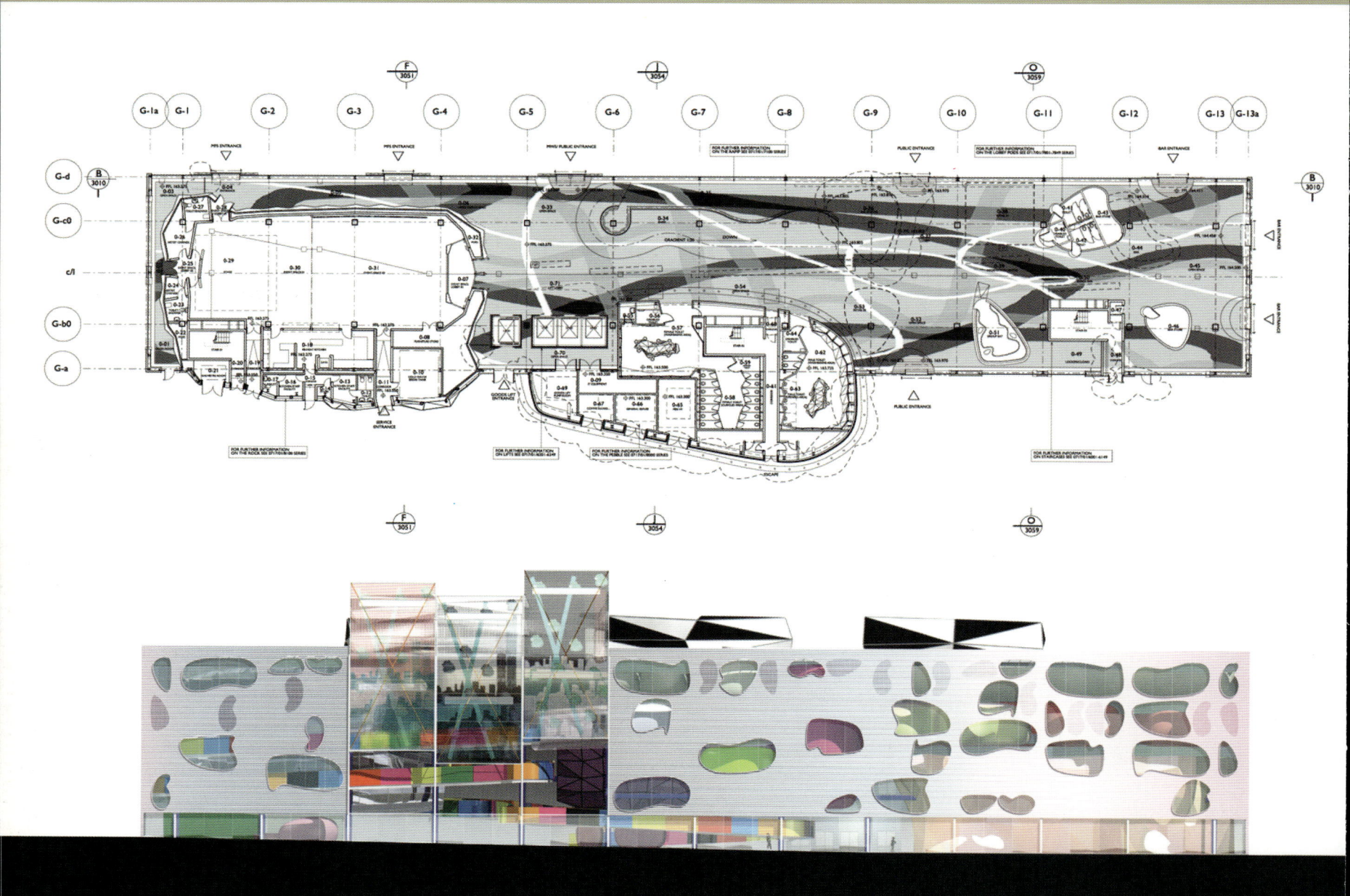

This project is born from the conviction, shared by our client, Jubilee Arts, that architecture and the arts can be a catalyst for regeneration and renewal amongst the alienating and mediocre architecture and public space that post-war development has inflicted upon the Birmingham conurbation of West Bromwich. A dynamic consultation process has already engendered a sense of ownership and involvement in the local community. The building is designed as a box surrounded at ground level by a pink glass skirt, drawing the public in and reclaiming the ground plane. Three polycarbonate doors that open up in fine weather run the full height of the building and mark the entrance. Beyond the skirt two large zinc-clad sculptural elements, the 'Rock' and the 'Sock', and a third cushioned element, create an extraordinary spatial and visual experience. The experience of visiting is enlivened by dramatic interventions, with interior spaces linked by a snaking ramp topped by a series of hung 'Lily Pads'.

◀ **c/PLEX, West Bromwich**
New arts building
Budget: £20.7 million
Completion: 2005
Laura Guenzi: structural coordination, interiors
Ed Norman: gallery ramp design
Spiros Pappas: planning submission, presentation images
Barry Simpson: lily pads
Max Titchmarsh: façades/envelope

OCAD, Toronto, Canada (In collaboration with Robbie, Young and Wright Architects) ▶
Extension to existing college
Budget: C$41 million
Completion: September 2004
Isabel Brebbia: project architect/lead designer
Jonathan Leah: director in charge
Greg Woods: project architect for RYWA

In a series of workshops with staff and students to develop early concepts for the design of the extension to the Ontario College of Art and Design (OCAD) in Toronto, conventional ideas of teaching, learning and architecture were questioned as we sought to re-define the college. The resulting ideas are embodied in the final scheme for the new Faculty of Design, housed in a vividly patterned translucent rectangle, or 'table top', raised eight storeys above the ground. Existing brick structures beneath, the park to the west and McCaul Street to the east are brought together by the design. The park will become the home to contemporary sculpture and school events. In addition to teaching and administrative functions the project incorporates gallery spaces, design and research centres, lounge and meeting areas, and design crit spaces. The new building will mesh with the revived urban fabric, contributing distinctive public areas, internal and external, to this quarter of the city.

16 ARCA

The way I work now has been shaped in three ways by the Bartlett:

First, there was the late Steven Groák, who shared his enthusiasm for Aalto and the DIN system of paper sizing. Second, there was the design studio, where I tried to obey rules producing rigorously engineered solutions (carefully watched by Derek Sugden) whilst studying the rich, evocative work of Scarpa and Miralles. Third, with the Space Syntax Unit, I found a way of visualising and understanding what I recognised intuitively as effects of spatial organisation. When I started Arca, I wanted to develop these ideas into an architecture responsive to people and how they interact with their physical environment. Key to this is the use of raw materials whose surface texture marks the passage of time and change.

John Lee

Mancunian Way Footbridge, Manchester
New bridge
Budget: £1.3million
Completed: July 2002
John Lee: project architect

Less than twelve months after founding Arca we won the design competition for this new bridge, which allows safe access across the Mancunian Way motorway to Hulme Park from Moss Side, and forms an important link in the city-wide cycle route network. The bridge is horseshoe-shaped in plan, with a seemingly unsupported deck. The steel and timber superstructure has an asymmetric tapering structural cross section that rests on four points – two inclined concrete piers, and concrete ramps leading down to ground level. The deep truss, clad in Cumaru (an ethically sourced Brazilian hardwood), offers shelter and enclosure to users – a 'third space' between the park and the city centre. The sensory properties of the timber give pedestrians a tactile, responsive experience in crossing the motorway.

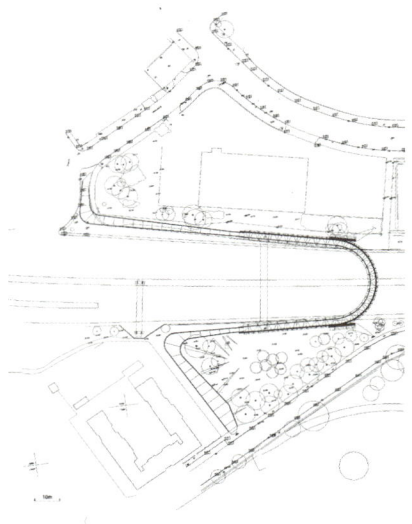

ARCHIDESIGN

During the darker years of World War Two whilst at school in London (1940-41), I somehow or other decided I wanted to be an architect. This profession was unfamiliar at the time to the public, and even to my family! I was the first pupil from my school who had ever wanted to do such a strange thing. But encouraged by my art teacher and the headmaster, by dint of much work I managed to obtain a scholarship to the Bartlett, already evacuated from Gower Street to St Catherine's at Cambridge University.

In Cambridge the school was housed in Scroope Terrace in four linked town houses. In those years we learnt how to draw, stretch Whatman paper on our boards, render classical orders with graded washes in ground Indian ink, copy the Roman alphabet, and even to design.

Returning in 1947 from being a soldier, I found the school back in Gower Street, where I picked up the threads and with my fellow ex-soldiers and sailors qualified in 1950. As there were few jobs available, I came to France for a six-month stay, and am still here and practising today!

Neil Hutchison

Dominican Monastery, Lille, France (with Pierre Pinsard) ◄
New build monastery
Completed: 1953-65
Neil Hutchison: architect

We commenced the design of this monastery at the time Le Corbusier was designing La Tourette, and naturally were intrigued to find out what his solution was going to be for the same religious order. It transpired that we had completely different ideas on how a 20th century monastery should work. However, my French partner, Pierre Pinsard, also had different ideas to me about 20th century architecture: fresh from the Bartlett, I tried to influence his thinking about 'form follows function' and 'brutalism', of which he had never heard!

The programme included a chapel, cells for Friars and Novices, hostelry and refectory, all built on a shoestring budget – note that it took about twelve years to complete! Nevertheless, the buildings are going to be listed very shortly, which is very satisfying: at least something I have done will not be demolished.

Maison Seynave, Beauvallon, Var, France (with Consulting Engineer Jean Prouvé) ▼
New build house
Completed: 1961
Neil Hutchison: architect

This house was designed using the Prouvé system of prefabricated housing. I had been working for Prouvé on this extremely difficult subject several years earlier, and having become an independent architect was asked by him to design this house and two or three others. Beauvallon had become in need of repairs very recently, until a Prouvé enthusiast bought the house and set about refurbishment. The local Prouvé society has succeeded in getting the house listed as a rare example of his techniques in the department of the Var.

18 ART2ARCHITECTURE

Lighting artist Peter Fink formed art2architecture in 1997 with architect Igor Marko to explore collaborative and interdisciplinary ways of working. Nerma Cridge joined in 2000 and is the only other permanent member. We work on a range of projects including architectural and multimedia design as well as lighting.

Peter has been teaching the diploma technical dissertation group 'Light' at the Bartlett for four years. The group approaches lighting as a driving force in design. Students' research includes such defined subjects as twilight, moonlight or aspects of colour, as well as ephemeral and intangible subjects such as the angelic lights of historical sites in Jerusalem. There is a two-way exchange of ideas, with students and art2architecture finding inspiration in each other's projects.

Lightlines, Wolverhampton ▸
Permanent light installation
Completed: December 2001
Peter Fink: lead artist, project manager
Nerma Cridge: designer

Lightlines, a project won in an open competition, transforms the repetitive 1960s Wolverhampton University Faculty of Art and Design building by animating the main façade, visible from a great distance as one approaches Wolverhampton, with a dramatically changing flow of coloured light. Initially we programmed the light sequence in a continuous ten-minute loop, but in the future it can be reprogrammed and appropriated by the students and staff. Lightlines is the largest cold cathode art/architectural lighting installation in the UK to date, with 98 individually controlled three-metre long cold cathode tubes mounted between the window reveals.

Mersey Wave Gateway, Liverpool ◂
Landscape and lighting design
Completion: September 2003
Peter Fink: lead artist, project manager
Nerma Cridge: designer

Mersey Wave Gateway, marking and leading the way to John Lennon Airport, resembles two tidal waves of the Mersey. Constructed in a progression of twelve thirty-metre high fins, with its monumental scale it is designed to have a distinct presence when seen from cars driving to and from the airport, without interfering with the flow of traffic. At night, waves of blue light slowly moving on the surface of the fins further evoke the experience of a tidal river for oncoming traffic.

Paddington Central Gateway, London ▸
Urban feature
Completion: March 2004
Peter Fink: artist
Nerma Cridge: designer

We won this project in an invited competition. Our proposal ameliorates the oppressive impact of the elevated road over the canal at Paddington by transforming its undercroft – the most critical aspect of the site. Reflective stainless steel sheets inserted into the existing space encourage movement and connectivity. The planar geometry exaggerates and distorts the perception of perspectival depth, creating an intriguing pedestrian-friendly environment. At night, lighting transforms the space while the vertical feature acts as a beacon for the Paddington station development.

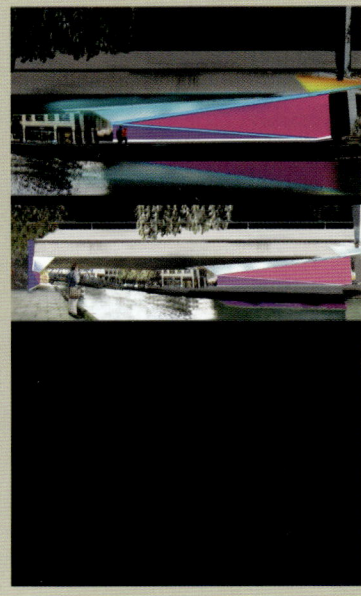

ASHTON PORTER STUDIO

We both graduated with distinction from the Bartlett in 1994. We were jointly awarded both the Bannister Fletcher Medal and the Royal Institute of British Architects Silver Medal. After working for Christine Hawley Architects, in 1999 we set up in partnership and have since completed a number of residential and commercial commissions and competitions. In addition we have taught at various schools of architecture and design including the Bartlett, where we are currently tutors in the BSc and Masters programmes. Our Stockport Town Centre, Grand Egyptian Museum and Osaka Masterplan projects were all selected for the 2003 Royal Academy Summer exhibition.

Abigail Ashton and Andrew Porter

Mongrel, Clerkenwell, London
Office refurbishment
Budget: £600,000
Completed: 2001
Abigail Ashton: designer
Rachel Cruise: assistant
Tim Furzer: assistant
Andrew Porter: designer

Flexible office space for 60 to work in various configurations in a single floor of a large industrial building: The 'engine room' for PC-based teamwork is dominated by a series of workstations with six-metre clear spans, supported only by steel plates at either end, and networked to a single bulkhead wall. The wall unifies the space and carries air conditioning, networking and power. Workers' personal effects are retained in custom-designed numbered orange trolleys that are docked into the wall when not in use. Windows above eye level give good natural lighting but restrict views, so we brought views in with small aircraft LCD screens connected to surveillance cameras looking outside. The screens are protected by custom-made inflatable jackets and are placed in the reception and meeting spaces so workers can meet and relax and watch the street life below. The main meeting space can be divided off from the reception by a large sliding wall.

20 ASHTON PORTER STUDIO

Formation, Clerkenwell, London ▶
Office refurbishment
Budget: £60,000
Completed: 1999
Abigail Ashton: designer
Phil Ayers: furniture maker, responsive installation
Chris Leung: programming, responsive installation
Andrew Porter: designer

The boundaries of this small graphic design studio, housed in an old Victorian meat smokehouse, are extended by reflected views of an exterior courtyard and the meeting room/entrance below. Two further interactive mirrors, guided by a complex series of custom-made multi-directional motors and arms, move in response to people breaking a series of invisible beams on the stair, following them like a pair of eyes. When there is no activity the mirrors continue their game, occasionally mischievously flickering to remind fellow occupants of their presence.

Grand Egyptian Museum Giza, Cairo ▶
Competition entry: shortlisted for publication
Budget: $350 million
August 2002
Abigail Ashton, Tim Furzer, Tom Holberton, Andrew Porter: design team

Our proposal is defined by two landscapes, one virtual and one solar. Virtual visitors can tour the empty galleries at night by CCTV. By day these nocturnal virtual visits are played back on huge screens at the entrance of each gallery zone. The solar landscape is created by a series of heliostats that reflect shafts of sunlight into the Grand Foyer and out to an external light park. Two restaurants move slowly along the inside of the façade in a daily cycle, intermittently interrupting the shafts of sunlight and reflecting them into the foyer, momentarily transforming the space.

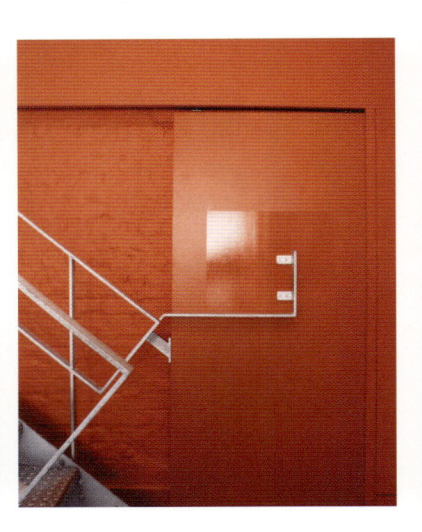

ATELIER KO / ARCHITECTS

Born in Tokyo, I came to London to study on the MArch in 1995. I set up ATELEIR KO with Florence Gay in 1998. We have since won a number of competitions and awards and have designed private houses both in Japan and England. I am excited by the process of finding the 'simplest' spatial composition or construction method to tackle a design problem and produce a coherent solution. Studying with Peter Cook I also learned that by introducing some humour architecture can become more than just building.

Akira Koyama

Takahata House, Yamagata Prefecture, Japan
New build house and music school
Budget: 30 million yen
Completed: April 2002
Florence Gay: lighting consultant
Akira Koyama: architect

To preserve privacy from future neighbours, the double-height living space at the centre of this northern Japanese house is screened by surrounding rooms. High level windows bring in light and maintain a sense of openness, and there are panoramic views of the surrounding mountains from the loft. All other rooms open directly off the central space, avoiding space-wasting corridors. A raised tatami room serves as a traditional reception or guest room and can be opened up to the living space, acting as a bench with drawers hidden below, or isolated from it by sliding doors. One of the clients runs a music school from home and a large practice room can also be opened to the central space, becoming a stage for concerts while the latter becomes an auditorium.

Snowfalls in this prefecture often exceed one metre; the house is raised to preserve access in winter and the flat roofs are easily accessible for safely removing excess snow. The house is clad in low maintenance, coloured, galvanised steel sheets.

This was my first private project completed in Japan. The entire fee was sucked up by airfares…

22 AZHAR ARCHITECTURE

I started my Degree at the 'old' Bartlett in the late 1980s with a sensible, broad-based preparation for practice in the built environment, and ended my Diploma in the 'new' Bartlett exploring the senses and the possibilities of speculation. Both approaches were inherently multi-disciplinary. Architecture is about curiosity and exploration, but also about social, economic and environmental responsibility, and combining function and beauty. On reflection there are paradoxical issues that don't change – the need to be both realistic and speculative, practical and inventive – only the context of practice changes. My time at the Bartlett reflected this paradox. One has to learn not only to resolve contradictions but also to embrace them.

Azhar

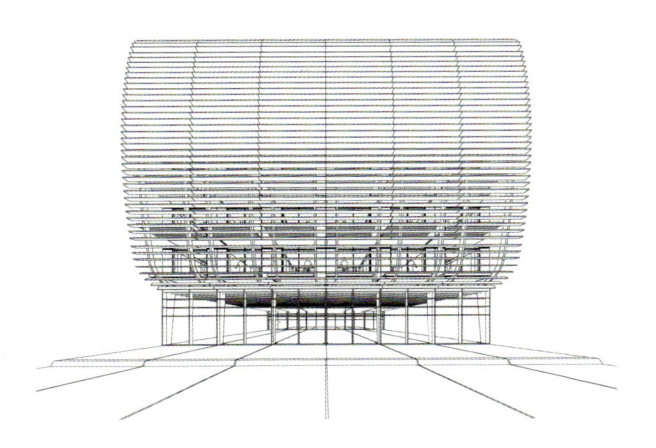

Skin – keyworker modular housing, Stratford, London ▲
Proposed affordable housing
Budget: £4 million
Unbuilt
Azhar: project architect

The central concept in this design for modular housing for keyworkers (teachers, bus drivers etc.) in a tough urban site is that apartments are minimally sized and complemented by maximising public space and amenities, including a café bar, swimming pool, gym and roof garden. The building is wrapped in a 'skin' consisting of a series of louvres made from compressed bamboo, acting as a solar and acoustic buffer. Photovoltaic cells are attached to the louvres taking advantage of the southern orientation.

Modular Offices Roof Extension, Holborn, London ▶
Proposed offices
Project value £600,000
Unbuilt
Azhar: project architect

Eight trapezoidal modules are lifted onto the roof of an existing flat-roofed 1950s industrial building, layering the city with new forms. Their shape is determined by 'rights to light' and solar orientation. The roof is composed of a series of elements that are simultaneously roof lights, solar thermal panels and photovoltaic cells. Silk-screened photovoltaic louvres are also hung from the modules to cloak the existing building.

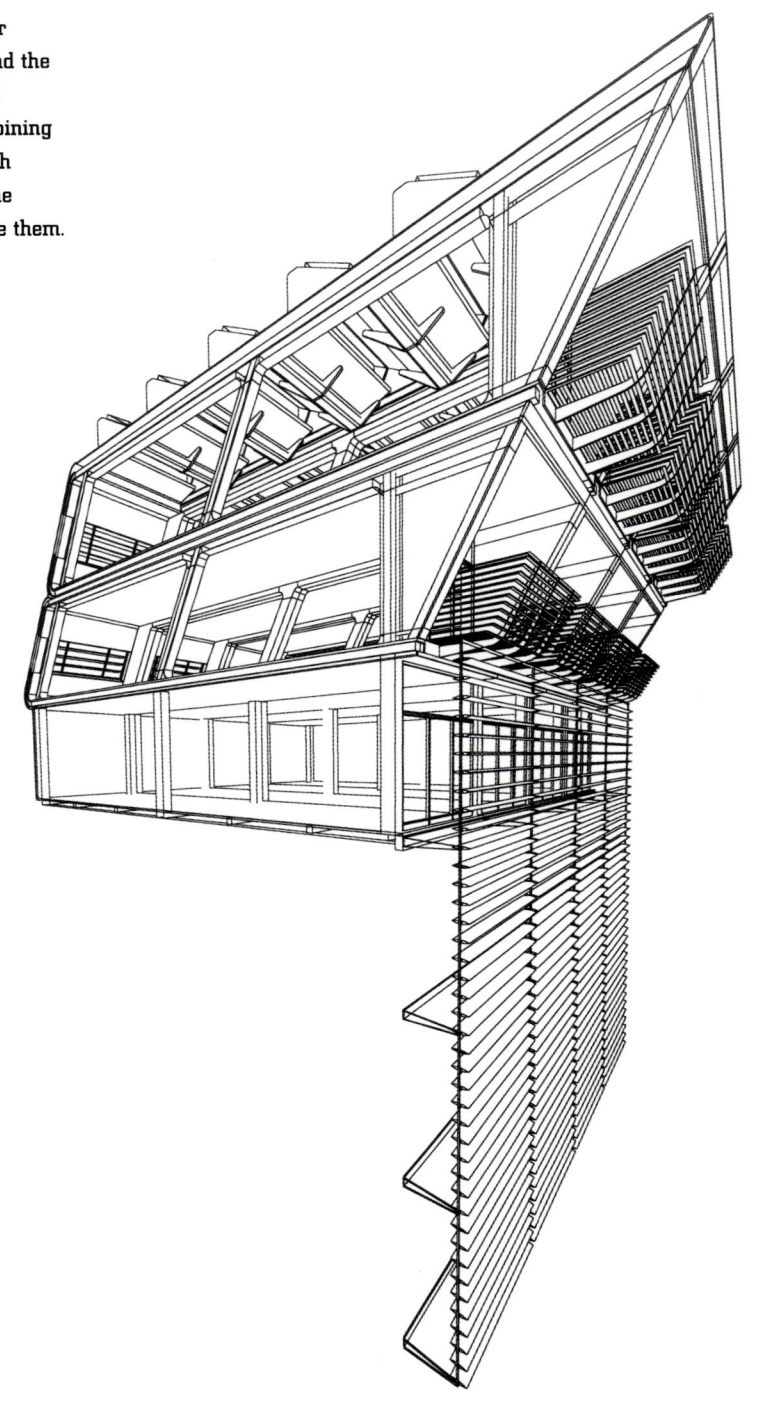

BLOCK ARCHITECTURE

The connection between the abstraction of the Bartlett and the vicissitudes of practice may at first seem pretty remote. However, throughout our time in the school we were encouraged (or provoked) to pursue research and creation with an individuality and single-mindedness that has always been intrinsic to our design approach as practising architects.

At the Bartlett we spent a large percentage of our time in the workshop covered in filings/shavings/paint/resin/wax/plaster/wiring or any combination thereof. Our experience was strongly rooted in materiality and making as a conduit of expression for the development of spatial and theoretical ideas, exploring the physical and metaphysical in equal measure, and this is something that we have tried to keep with us in practice. Throughout our work we try to generate responses which we hope offer an antidote to our increasingly packaged environment.

Zoe Smith and Graeme Williamson

Tree House Apartment, Hoxton, London
Private apartment
Budget: £100,000
Completed: December 2000
Zoe Smith and Graeme Williamson: architects/designers

This apartment is on the top floor of a building overlooking treetops and the City of London. The space has a cantilevered bed platform made from timber frames and slatted wood. The treehouse was an interesting reference for us in the design, for its association with such common experiences as early creativity, independence, escapism, solitude, a first kiss or illicit liaison.

Grand Central Bar, Shoreditch, London
Bar/restaurant
Budget: £200,000
Completed: June 2001
Zoe Smith and Graeme Williamson: architects/designers

Grand Central bar uses light, movement and electricity as physical building elements to create an environment based on city flux. To visualise this, we drew from long exposure photographs of traffic flow. Through these studies we constructed 'lightstream' walls to create the impression of passing car head- and tail-lights. A lighting rig reminiscent of a tube map or circuit diagram runs through the space.

24 BLOCK ARCHITECTURE

Museum of Modern Art, Oxford
Refurbishment
Budget: £300,000
Completed: November 2002
Zoe Smith and Graeme Williamson: architects/designers

Our redesign of the Museum of Modern Art, Oxford, housed in a former brewery, was inspired by our interest in how social spaces work and are used. A previously dark and compartmentalised space is opened up to form a single light and open 'platform' level. This central hub of activity is capable of hosting a number of different functions – where the social and cultural can interact. A new stair slot running the full length of one side of the building connects all three floors in one strong element, improving physical and visual accessibility. A utilitarian palette of light grey concrete, grey powder-coated steel for balustrades, natural green glass and dimmable strip lighting above gives the sense of a depot or delivery bay, further augmented by the positioning of two large 'packing crates', forming information and servery counters, to the rear.

BLUSTIN HEATH DESIGN

Not wishing to give up the range of exploration that the Bartlett had allowed, on graduating Oliver and I established our Bacon Street studio as a hub of mixed talent where a variety of disciplines operate independently but come together to discuss ideas and joint projects — from installations to roof-top cinema events and parties. Questions posed from studying in Diploma are still of interest within my work. There is often a strong emphasis on the activity>movement>reaction of individuals as they climb and swing through their environment, controlling and changing it.

Nikki Blustin

I just had too much fun at the Bartlett, making films, creating kinetic instruments and building multi-sensory installations, to give it all up and sit in front of a computer screen afterwards. So maybe it's appropriate that much of my work (and yes I do still call it work!) is media-based. Rarely are two days the same, and keeping a sense of fun and energy about what we do is ultimately as important as ever in achieving creative satisfaction from our working lives.

Oliver Heath

Warehouse Conversion, London
Domestic interior design and build
Budget: £2,000
Completed: 1998
Nikki Blustin: partner

A disused warehouse converted into a flexible and fun live/work space on a minimal budget transforms between day and night whilst retaining a rich sense of urban luxury. Frosted sleeping pods allow daylight to filter through, and glow by night; a sleeping platform cradled overhead affords views across London; the dining table can be winched up to the ceiling to make space for parties; and the lounge comes complete with luxurious velvet-covered mobile chaise longue, pull-up bar and swing.

BBC Homefront, BBC Changing Rooms, From House to Home – Channel 4
Television presenting
Budget varies from £500 to £10,000
1998-ongoing
Oliver Heath: television designer, celebrity and all round entertainer; imparts domestic design advice

Since I won the 1998 Young Designer of the Year Competition on BBC Homefront I have completed many Homefront and Changing Rooms shows for the BBC, and featured as a designer/presenter in From House to Home on Channel 4. When I started I felt it was important that architects infiltrate the world of media design and that some thought should be given to issues such as the environment, technology, materials, communication and the family unit, albeit with a liberal dose of entertainment and gaudy paint colours. I was intrigued to find out whether the restrictions of a £500 budget and a two-day deadline could produce interesting results and new ideas.

26 IAIN BORDEN

My first encounter with the Bartlett came in 1985, when I applied to do the Master's Degree in the History of Modern Architecture, then taught by Adrian Forty and Mark Swenarton. Summoned to an interview, I asked if it was true, as I had heard, that the course was 'political', for I desperately wanted to know more about architecture beyond connoisseurship concerns with attribution, style and chronology. I cannot recall their immediate reply, but I can most certainly remember the course that they subsequently delivered up, and which did far more than answer my question. 'HMA', as it was normally called, took me on a roller-coaster ride through the world of buildings, cities, texts, authors, designers, ideas and interpretations. It introduced me to Marx and Hegel, Loos and Venturi, Frampton and Benjamin. It asked me to confront structural brickwork and historical materialism, as well as plan, space and gender, or façade, aesthetics and ideology... As a result, HMA more or less wholly transformed my entire outlook not just on architecture but on cities, life, the universe and everything. It was a year of iconoclastic radicalisation, twelve months in which the world turned upside-down.

And since then things have never been quite the same. My thoughts and writings over the past couple of decades have been on all manner of things architectural, from books on office practice, urbanism, critical theory, the Situationists and skateboarding; to articles on Renaissance perspective, social housing, architectural photography and the films of Jacques Tati; to exhibitions on utopia, photography and urban life... and in all of this I have tried to focus on the incredible range of ways by which architecture enters into the everyday lives of urban dwellers, whether as place of home and work, as building and urban space, as site of stimulation and inspiration, or as catalyst for ideas, actions and desires.

Increasingly I now find myself with less time to write, but more involved with other people outside of academia. So along with my outstandingly challenging yet supportive colleagues, I now also work with art galleries, professional bodies, government committees, and municipal authorities. Yet while the products may be broader – reports, decisions, events and policies as well as publications, lectures and exhibitions – in many ways my motivation remains the same: a belief that architecture has the potential to truly please and puzzle, service and stimulate, comfort and challenge.

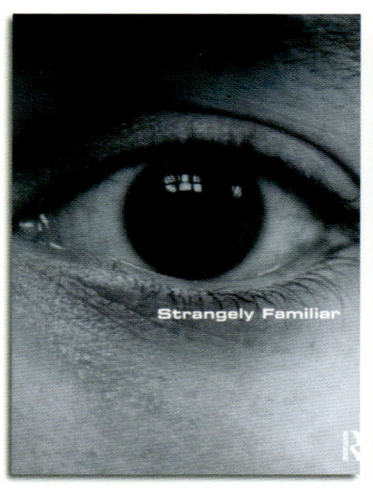

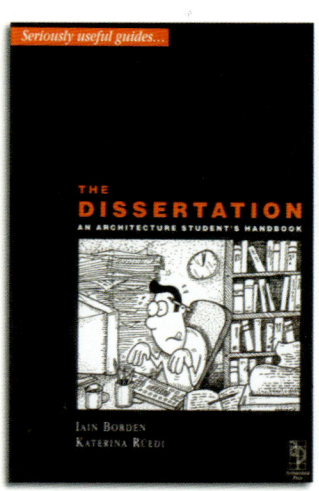

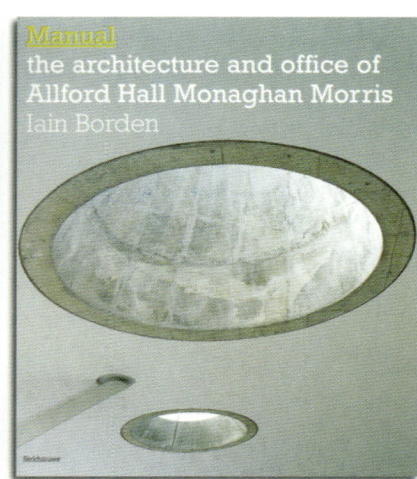

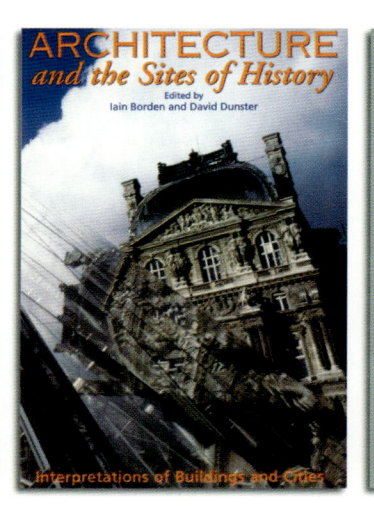

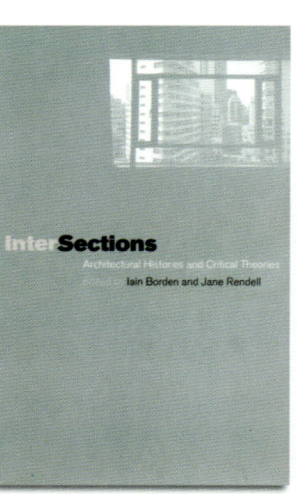

Book covers

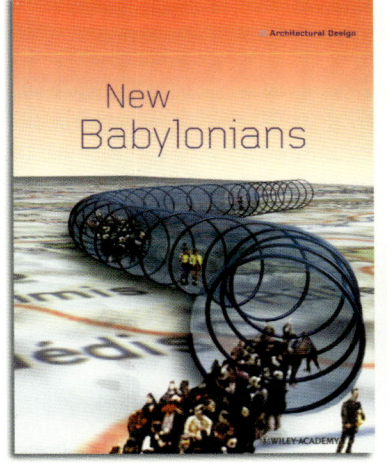

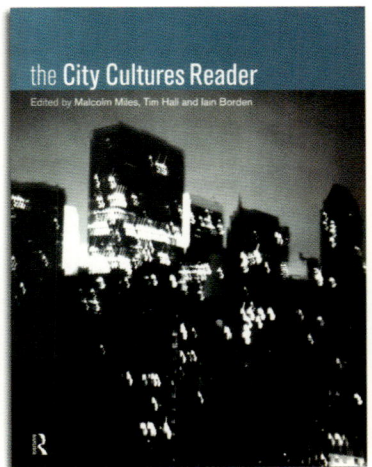

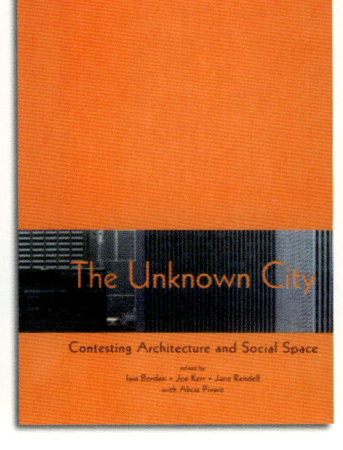

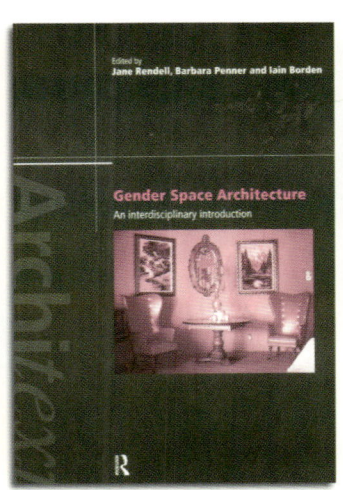

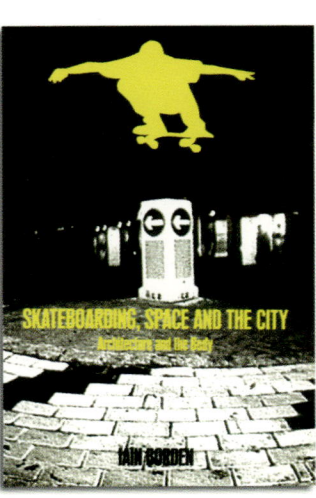

- *New Babylonians* (Architectural Design)
- *the City Cultures Reader* — Edited by Malcolm Miles, Tim Hall and Iain Borden
- *The Unknown City: Contesting Architecture and Social Space* — edited by Iain Borden, Joe Kerr, Jane Rendell with Alicia Pivaro
- *Gender Space Architecture: An interdisciplinary introduction* — Edited by Jane Rendell, Barbara Penner and Iain Borden
- *Skateboarding, Space and the City: Architecture and the Body* — Iain Borden

28 BRANSON COATES

Many of our ideas on architecture have their roots in contemporary lifestyle. Our work is as much about the communications age (nightclubs, theme parks, the internet) as it is about historic continuity (the avenue, the axis, classical types). The Bartlett shares many of these interests. It follows, both in theory and practice, that we should have an affinity with Bartlett students — many have passed through our doors and contributed greatly during their stay. Guy Dickinson in particular has been involved in several key projects.

Nigel Coates and Doug Branson

National Centre for Popular Music, Sheffield, England
New build public/arts building
Budget: £8.5 million
Completed: May 1999
Guy Dickinson: lead assistant (main building), project architect (ground floor fit-out)

The sound bite description is 'four steel drums held together by a glass cross'. The arms of the cross mark the connection to the surrounding Cultural Industries Quarter, two forming public entrances. The ground floor concourse opens to the main public facilities and gives access to exhibition spaces above. Though it's a shame that the NCPM never really fulfilled its ambition as a popular music venue, we hope that in its new role, as a Students Union for Sheffield Hallam University, it will succeed.

MICHAEL BROWN

After completing my MSc in the History of Modern Architecture at the Bartlett I returned to Adelaide to work for the City Council. I completed a couple of architectural commissions, the first of which was the MacGregor House, but unfortunately there is little demand for this type of building and I have remained a 'council bureaucrat' for seven years. A Masters Degree in a thinking discipline is very good training for a bureaucrat, though I still hanker to become an architect.

Michael Brown

Macgregor House, Brownhill Creek (a small rural area very near Adelaide, Australia)
New build house
Budget: A$200,000
Completed: 1994
Michael Brown: architect

This house is built in an idyllic site adjacent to a creek lined with mature exotic deciduous trees. Rooms to the north of a monolithic rammed earth wall open out to the vista and towards the (southern hemisphere) sun, living spaces have lift-up doors for outdoor entertaining in mild weather. Ancillary spaces (study/kitchen/deck/bathroom), accessed through apertures in the wall, cantilever out over the creek between the trees to the south. A small tatami bedroom for the owner has its own private views out, and access to a grassed deck over the garage.

JASON BRUGES STUDIO

29

My main interest is in using ambient intelligence to create interactive art, design and architecture. Past projects have included sculptures and installations, most involving dynamic light projection in response to stimuli detected by sensors, exploring people's relationships with their environment, and stimulating interaction and dialogue. My most recent work also seeks to encourage orientation.

The Bartlett very much taught me to think laterally, to look outside preconceived routes to answer problems and realise concepts. In particular this has led me to produce technological prototypes and new composite materials as a result of artistic investigations.

Jason Bruges

CowParade Interactive Cow, London ▲
SMS art project (unrealised)
2002
Jason Bruges: artist/creative director (concept, feasibility studies, technology integration)

CowParade introduced a herd of fibreglass cows to central London, each decorated by a different artist. In collaboration with Simon Darling (entrepreneur and viral marketing specialist) and Simon Daniel (artist, management consultant and inventor of the Palm fold-out keyboard) we proposed an interactive cow. The hide was to be created from a two-way curved matrix of LEDs that would display text messages from the public, or change colour in response to messages. The cow would act a barometer for the public mood, and give feedback to the city. It would take text messaging beyond one-to-one interaction into a shared dialogue between many respondents.

SmartSlab™ ▲
Interactive building product
Jason Bruges: interaction designer (consultancy, feasibility studies, technology integration)

SmartSlab™ is a digital display system with 60-centimetre-square tiles that can be combined to create massive screens. Designed and developed by Box Consultants, the tiles are made from aerospace composite materials, and are strong and slim enough for use on interior or exterior walls, ceilings or floors. I am working with Box and QinetiQ (formerly the MOD technology arm) to make the system interactive. Some amazing sensor arrays will be embedded within the tiles, to enable the system to sense if people are present, and even if they are looking at the screen.

We are looking at applying the tiles to the ceiling of Foster and Partners' new Imperial College building. With 'motion tracking' sensors to detect the movement of people below, the ceiling could be security monitoring device and electronic artwork combined into one.

30 CAMPKIN, PENNER AND RENDELL

Ben Campkin, Barbara Penner and Jane Rendell are all graduates of the Bartlett's Masters in Architectural History/History of Modern Architecture, and all currently teach History and Theory within the School. Ben came to this project after writing a dissertation 'Degeneration and Regeneration in King's Cross', the subject of which — concepts of dirt and cleanliness in relation to architecture and regeneration — has since been developed into one of the thematic Year 3 history and theory dissertation groups, 'Dirt and the City'. Barbara and Jane, previous collaborators on the book *Gender Space Architecture* (Routledge, 2000), came to the project with their own research interests in mind. Barbara's work on literature, everyday spaces, space and subjectivity are all evident in 'The Pleasure of Treasure'; as are Jane's concerns with writing as a critical spatial practice, and with public art and site specific writing.

The Pleasure of Treasure and *King's Cross Journey*, King's Cross, London (with Artangel)
Art/architectural and urban history/education projects
August 2002-ongoing
Ben Campkin, Barbara Penner and Jane Rendell: collaborators

These two projects, 'The Pleasure of Treasure' and 'King's Cross Journey', were developed on the doorstep of the Bartlett in King's Cross and commissioned in response to artist Richard Wentworth and Artangel's project, 'An Area of Outstanding Unnatural Beauty' (2002). Both projects elaborate on Wentworth's interest in how we experience, view, map and animate the city, and in the simultaneity and incongruities of these processes.

'An Area of Outstanding Unnatural Beauty' consisted of a site-specific installation in a vacant plumbing warehouse, General Plumbing Supplies in York Way. This installation was the point of departure for a series of walks, talks, games and other events that brought together a broad cross-section of visitors, from long-time residents of the area (like Wentworth) to newcomers. It encouraged all visitors to think about the history, identity and mapping of King's Cross, an area undergoing rapid physical and social transformation due to the Channel Tunnel Rail Link development and associated urban regeneration schemes.

In devising 'The Pleasure of Treasure', Penner and Rendell collaborated with Kathy Battista from Artangel Interaction, urban geographer Steve Pile of The Open University, and sound artist Brandon LaBelle from the London Consortium. After much discussion on the topics of mapping and regeneration in urban neighbourhoods, the group decided to produce a treasure hunt — an interactive map that would avoid being didactic and could be followed by people of all ages and abilities. The map was designed with graphic designer Ian Vickers: one side is based on a contemporary ordinance survey map, with clues that form the treasure hunt and questions to be answered; the other side is comprised of an 1868 parish map, with quotations from authors who have written about King's Cross, including Charles Dickens, Thomas Hardy, Salman Rushdie, Mary Wollstonecraft and contemporary poet Aidan Andrew Dun.

On the 25th of October 2002, the map was launched in a public event at General Plumbing Supplies. The participants described their sources of inspiration, from the Regency rambler to Edgar Allen Poe's detective fiction, and LaBelle did a short performance piece. The map was printed in an edition of 5,000 copies, which were available free to all visitors to the Wentworth project, as well as at The British Library and the Camden Local Studies Library. One of the clues on the map asked participants to bring back an 'object of unnatural beauty' with their maps. The objects and maps were later displayed, with prizes given to the most unnaturally beautiful.

In the second project, 'King's Cross Journey', Campkin, together with artist Nahoko Kudo of the Royal College of Art, led a series of workshops with blind and visually impaired participants, exploring the history and architecture of King's Cross, and making Wentworth's work more accessible to them. A series of Braille maps and raised drawings of Wentworth's photographs were displayed, prompting visitors to think about the theme of vision and the city. This subject was discussed in a public launch event for the project.

In the workshops participants developed their own photographic project and sound installation, creating narratives based on their own experiences of the area. The final photographic project forms part of an ongoing exhibition entitled 'Pausing for Thought' at the headquarters of the Royal National Institute for the Blind, recently relocated to King's Cross. In the exhibition, the photographs are paired with raised drawings (see far right), mimicking their composition so that those without sight can perceive them. These visual and tactile images work together with a video and sound installation by Kudo where fragments of text and voices fade in and then dissolve away again, mapping the area through a number of subtle personal landmarks, and individual memories of sensations and movement. These journeys make it clear that King's Cross exists as a tactile environment, characterised by movement, noise, texture. The work suggests both subjective and shared experiences of the urban environment, and the role of architecture in framing this experience, causing us to pause for thought at a timely juncture in the history of the area.

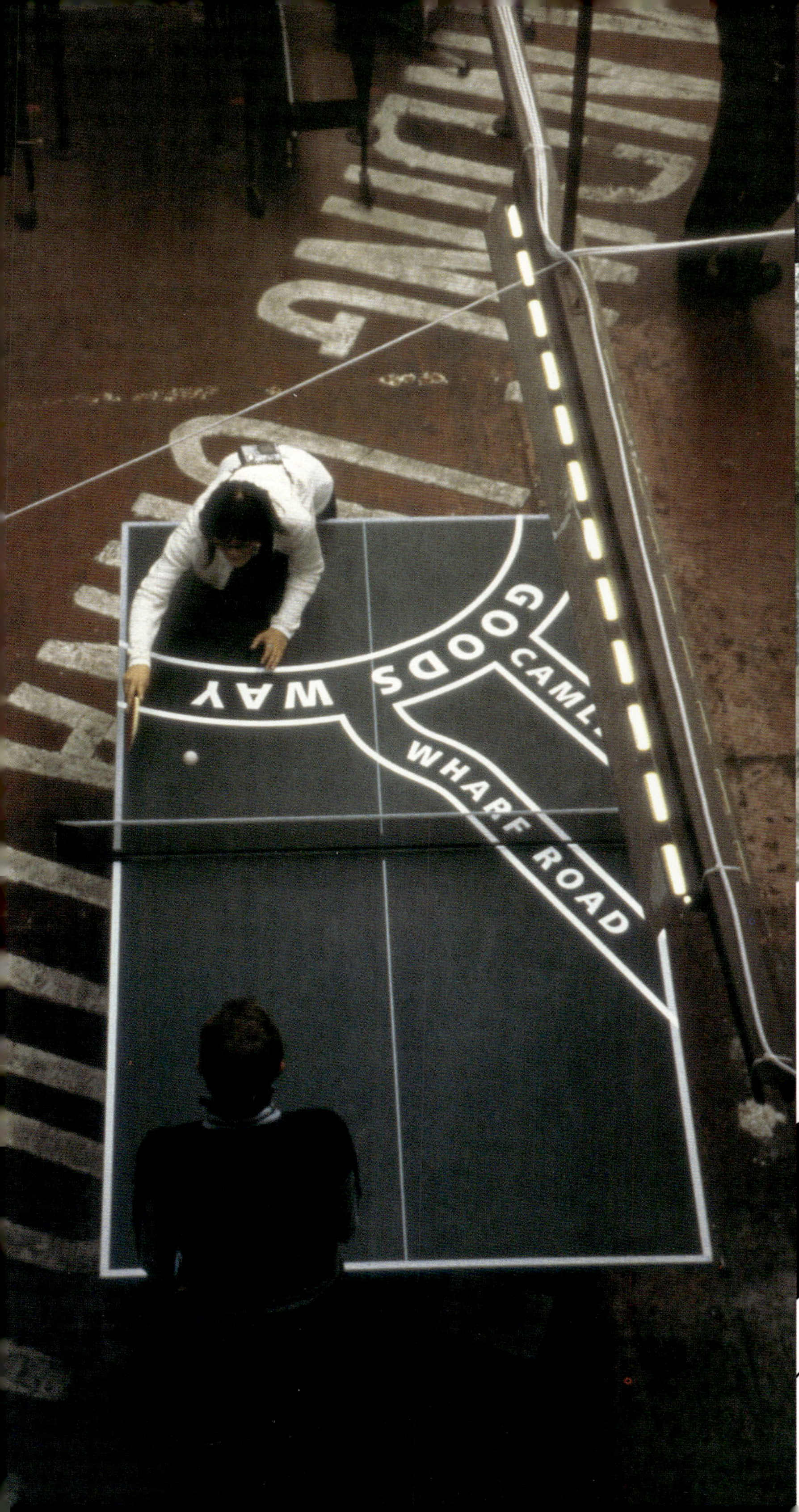
GOODS WAY
WHARF ROAD
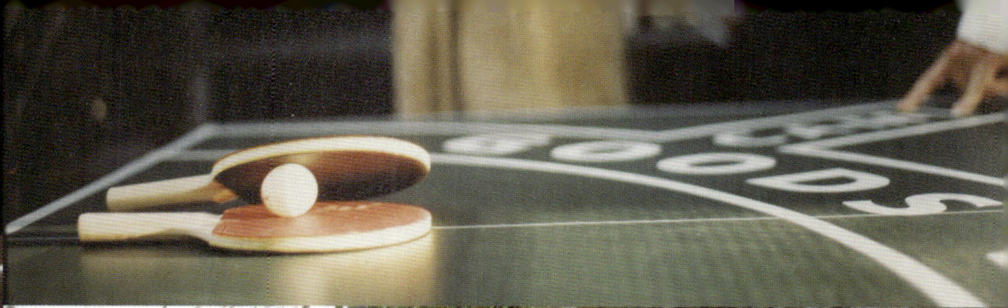
GOODS
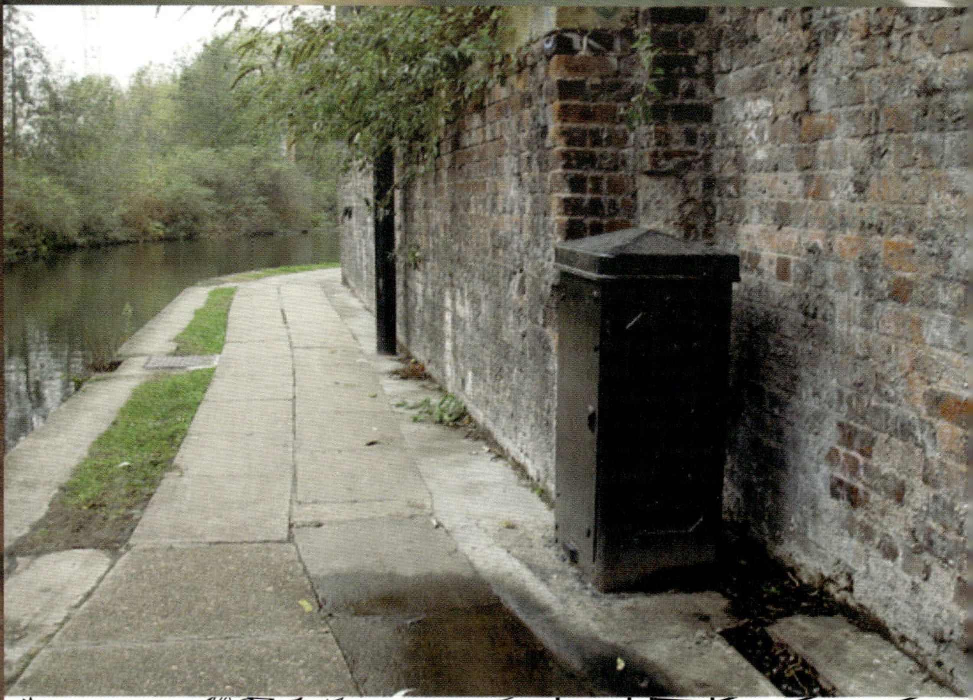
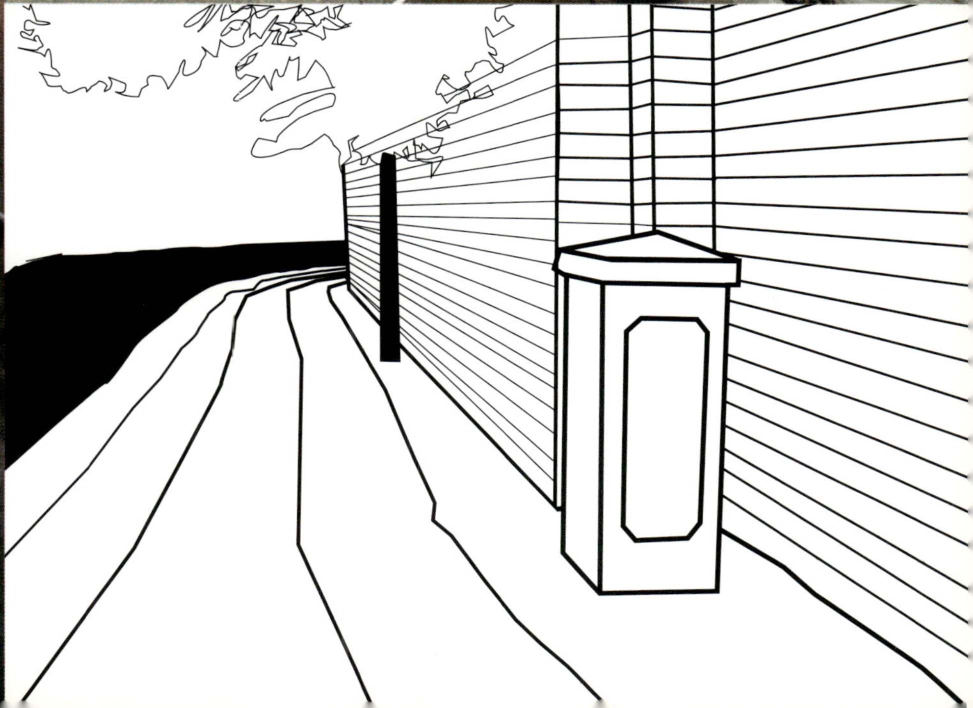

32 CHANCE DE SILVA ARCHITECTS

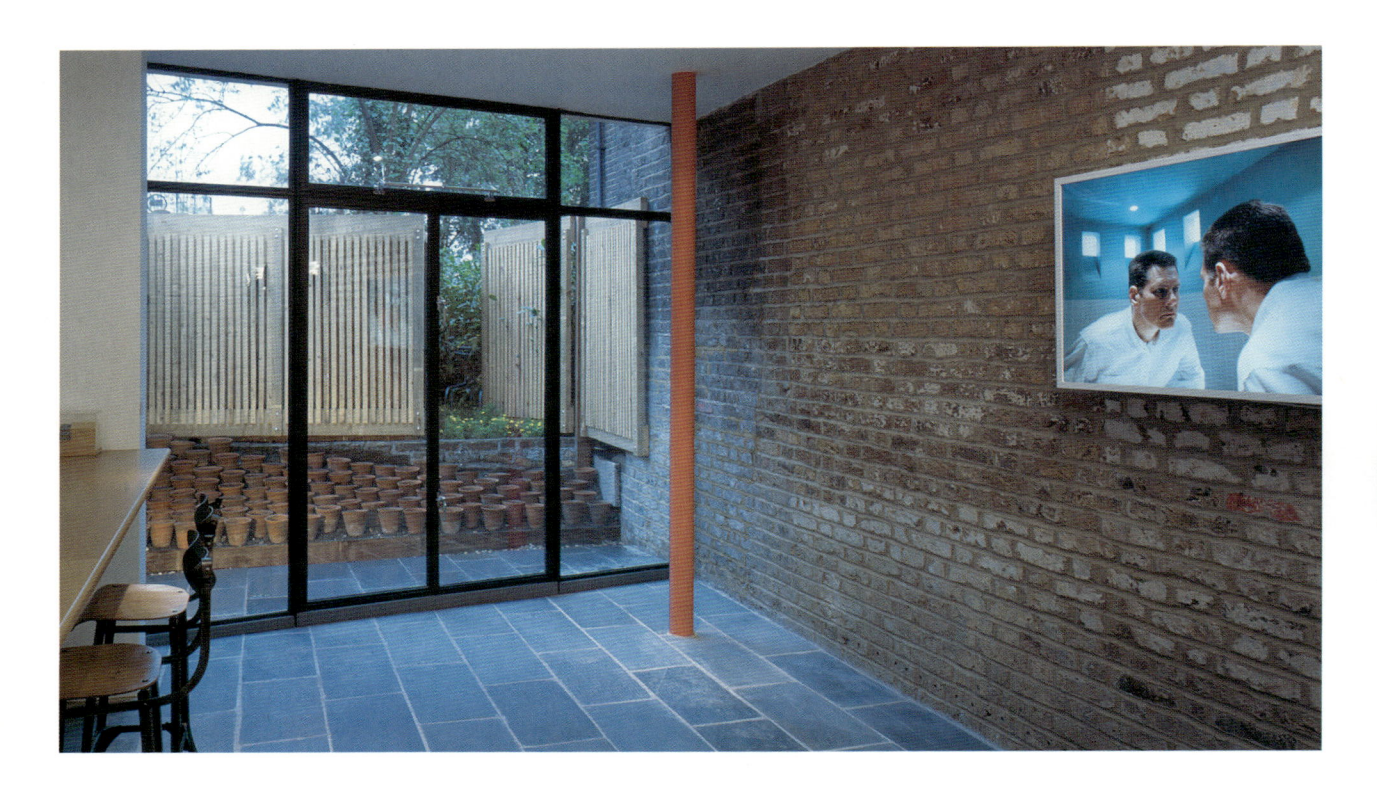

We like to explore new possibilities in architecture with artists, designers, musicians, community groups or performers. For example, artist Matt Hale's work became an integral part of our project Venus. We seek projects allowing investigation and experimentation into new materials, or using materials in new ways. Our work is not just about space, or the qualities of materials, but about what they evoke or express.

Of our tutors at the Bartlett, we particularly appreciated Robin Webster and Bob Allies for their encouraging, undogmatic approach.

Stephen Chance and Wendy de Silva

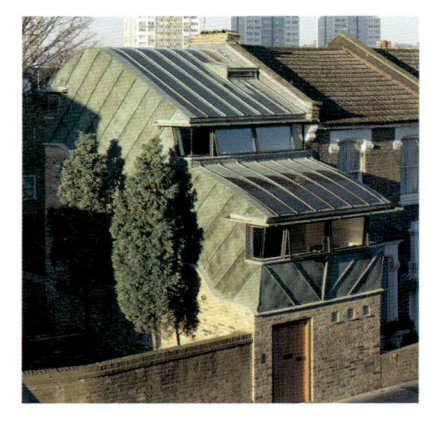

Venus, Highbury, North London ▲
Studio/house/gallery
Budget: £102,000
Completed: May 1998
Chance de Silva: site acquisition, fundraising, design and implementation

We had visited modern buildings in Japan influenced by the *machiya*, traditional Kyoto city-houses. Venus addresses the street in a similar way, very private and defensive at lower level but opening up at higher levels to let in light and permit views out. A timber frame structure clad in post-patinated copper sits on a base of recycled bricks. On completion Venus was used as a gallery, it is currently our live-work space and we plan to stage further exhibitions in it in the future.

Two artists contributed to the project. Matt Hale created a 'stained' window of glass tubes filled with coloured domestic fluids such as shampoo and detergent, and Frank Watson installed his 'Interior World' light boxes.

Cargo Fleet, London N5 ▼
New build studio-houses
Budget: £217,000
Completion: July 2003
Chance de Silva: site acquisition, fundraising, design and implementation

Cargo Fleet, two new studio-houses linked by a ramp, takes its name from a demolished station on the railway line by which it is built. The project explores ideas of memory and ephemerality, and is clad in rusted steel, a material evocative of the passing of time. Industrial forms and imagery — a projecting 'shed', gables clad in rusty steel, gantry balustrades, 'signal box' corner windows, industrial glass — were initially collaged very directly from the steelworks landscape to inform the design, before being reprocessed to express something new at an approppriate scale for a small domestic project.

DAVID CHIPPERFIELD ARCHITECTS

David Chipperfield Architects, founded in 1984, is internationally renowned for its architectural, masterplanning, interior, product and furniture design, and has completed a range of museums, galleries, private houses, hotels, offices and retail facilities. Based in London and Berlin, the practice is multilingual and multicultural, balancing youth and experience. We employ over 90 staff from 16 countries, speaking 22 languages; they are our greatest resource and their diversity is crucial to our design vision. Judith Brown joined David Chipperfield Architects in March 2000, and has mainly worked on two large-scale projects in Italy – the Law Courts in Salerno and the extension to the San Michele cemetery in Venice. As one of the few people in the office with experience on UK projects, she is currently running the refurbishment for David Chipperfield's own flat in London.

San Michele Cemetery, Venice, Italy
Redevelopment of, and additions to historic cemetry
Stage one budget: £14million
Stage two budget: £28million
Stage one: 2006
Stage two: 2010
Judith Brown: project architect

In 1998 we won the competition to redesign the historic cemetry island of San Michele in the Venetian lagoon which has been in continuous development for over four hundred years.

The romantic image of the island from the lagoon is in stark contrast to the somewhat dour municipal character of its interior. Our proposal seeks to redefine some of its former tectonic and physical qualities.

The project comprises two phases: in the first a series of new courtyards, a crematorium, and a chapel will be built on the existing island. In contrast to the existing uniform rows of tombs an organisational structure has been developed which groups buildings together to form a greater sense of settlement and enclosure. Informed by the principles of *scorci* (views), *giardini* (gardens), and *corti* (courtyards), this spatial organisation creates a more varied and yet clearly defined San Michele landscape.

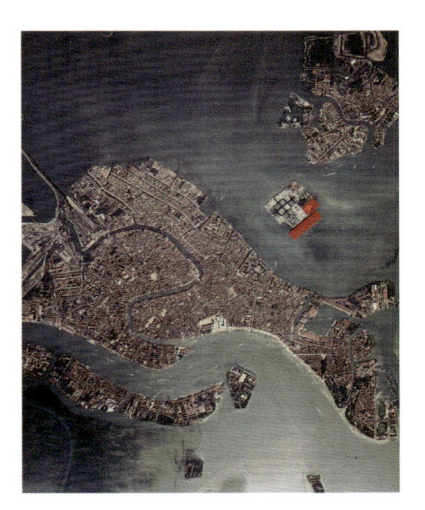

The larger second phase of the project is for the construction of a new island adjacent to the existing one but separated from it by a 15 metre-wide channel. The new island will feature four tomb buildings designed as simple, sculpted blocks, together with a series of gardens at water level. The new island will be higher than the existing cemetery, and is intended to create a more open, accessible monument with a greater sense of place.

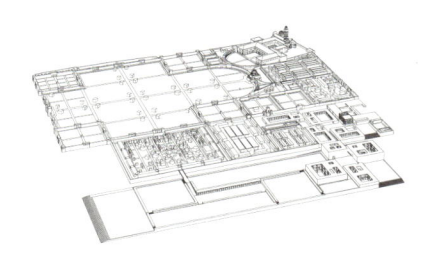

34 COOK AND FOURNIER – SPACELAB

Spacelab was created within the Bartlett for the specific purpose of taking part in the international competition for the new art museum in Graz. The Kunsthaus was the result of three successive competitions. We did not take part in the first competition, which was held almost 20 years ago, but we entered the second, supported by a team of recent graduates including David Ardill, with a project we called 'the tongue', a device creeping out of the side of the 'mountain' that stands in the middle of Graz. The site, dug out of the rock, was far too constricted. The jury ignored our scheme, but not some leading cultural personalities in the city, notably Peter Weibel, a key figure in electronic art, now Director of the ZKM in Karlsruhe: they thought that it should be built. But we were very 'British' and acknowledged that the jury had the right of refusal.

As it turned out, the winning entry was never built and a third open competition was held, on a much better site and with a jury presided over by Volker Giencke and including Odile Decq, Kjetil Traedel-Thorsen (of Snøhetta) and Kaspar König. Zaha Hadid, Coop Himmelblau, Itsuko Hasegawa and Hans Hollein, amongst many other participants, had also been invited to compete.

A strict regime of two hours every day in Colin's corner office with the basic team (Niels Jonkhans as the boatswain of the ship, Mathis Osterhage experimenting with models, Marcos Cruz with latex skins, Jamie Norden with layers and an end game with some brilliant visuals by Nicola Haines) passed through a turbulent gestation period until we chose to focus on the 'pin and skin' concept, one of just wrapping the site and moving across on the diagonal from the obvious entry point.

Inevitably, after the competition win came the politics: delays to find money, to wait for various election results, to cajole us into a local tie-up. Gradually the office operation moved over to Graz.

Peter Cook and Colin Fournier

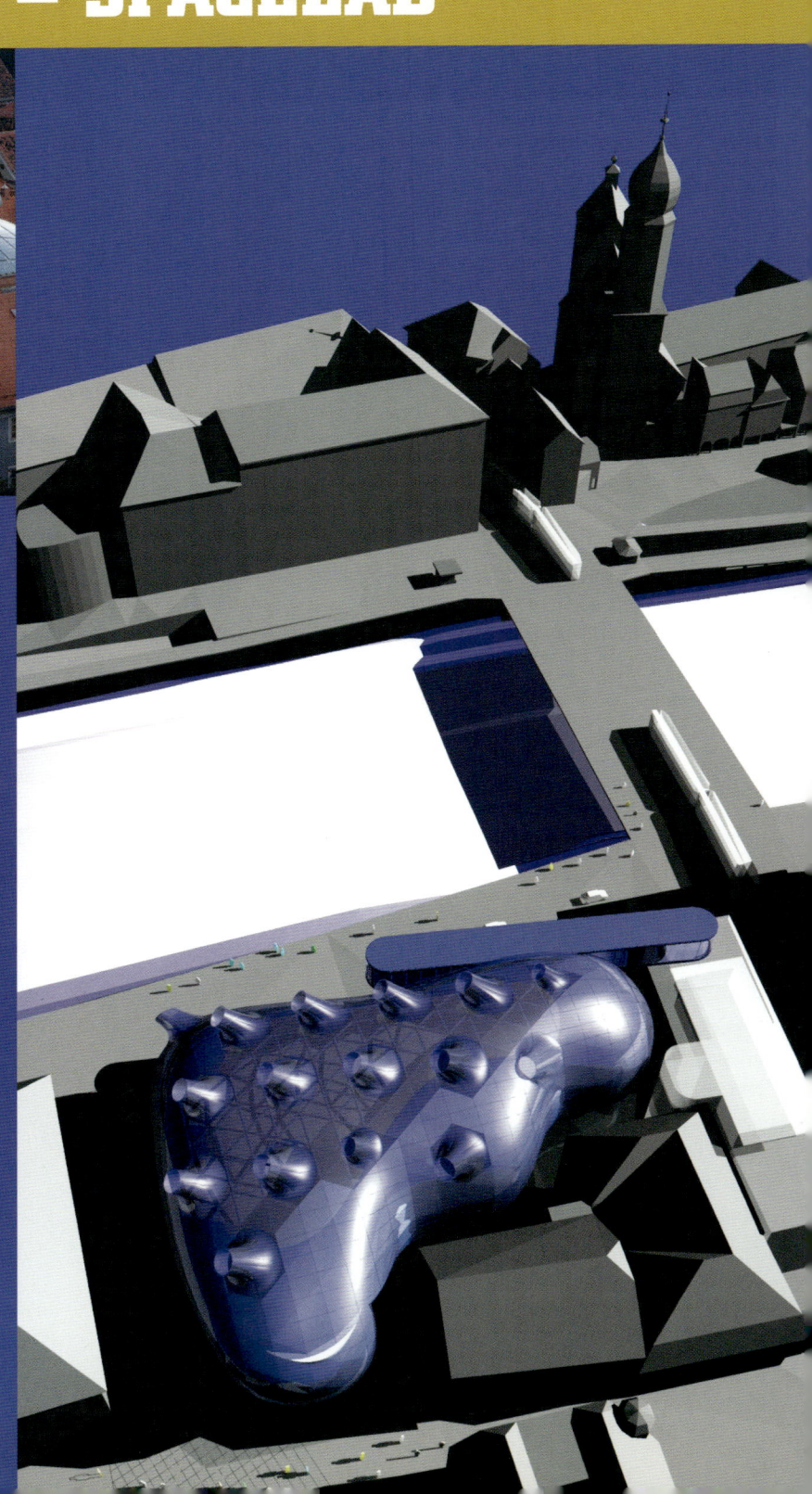

Kunsthaus Graz, Steiermark, Austria
New build gallery
Budget: £34 million
Completion: September 2003
Spacelab: designers

The Kunsthaus was conceived as a 'skin' and a 'pin'. The skin: a smooth double-curved surface animated by an electronically programmable array of light pixels that will allow it to display information and constantly change its outer appearance. The pin: a slim one-way travelator that runs up out of the daylit underbelly into the mysterious darkness of the lower (multimedia) gallery and then zips back up into the brightness of the top gallery.

A place of simple and direct parts (two open, flexible decks that can be reconfigured at will by different exhibition curators, raised above ground and wrapped in a single enclosure) but of considerable theatricality and naughtiness in form and substance.

Amazingly, we were able, in the built result, to hold on to most of the key features of the original scheme. After all, Graz is a charming and absorptive city that can encompass the baroque, the quaint, the banal, the pompous, even the zigzags of the 'Grazer Schule', and now has to handle the landed porcupine. Ironically, the one piece of 'old Graz' that we had to retain, a cast iron building of the mid 19th century, now adopted as an integral part of the new museum, was actually prefabricated in Sheffield: so much for genius loci.

Peter Cook and Colin Fournier

The 'Friendly Alien', as we call the Kunsthaus Graz, is a simple project: two main exhibition decks, wrapped in a double-curved skin and sitting on columns above a transparent ground floor housing such public functions as the foyer and café/bar. To achieve such clarity and simplicity in the competition stages we re-examined our ideas over and over again.

During the design development the same steps had to be taken again, but this time on a different level: since the project is technically extremely challenging, especially given the short time span in which it has to be built, both its form and technical specification have required lots of prototype-thinking. In order to find the best way of architecturally translating the competition ideas, they had to be exposed to continuous reappraisal: asking what the 'skin and pin' idea is all about? And how can we achieve it?

Having been project architect for the competition I moved with my colleague and wife Anja Leonhäuser to Graz to take on the challenge of realising the building. Our team has now grown to 18 people.

Niels Jonkhans

36 COOK AND FOURNIER – SPACELAB

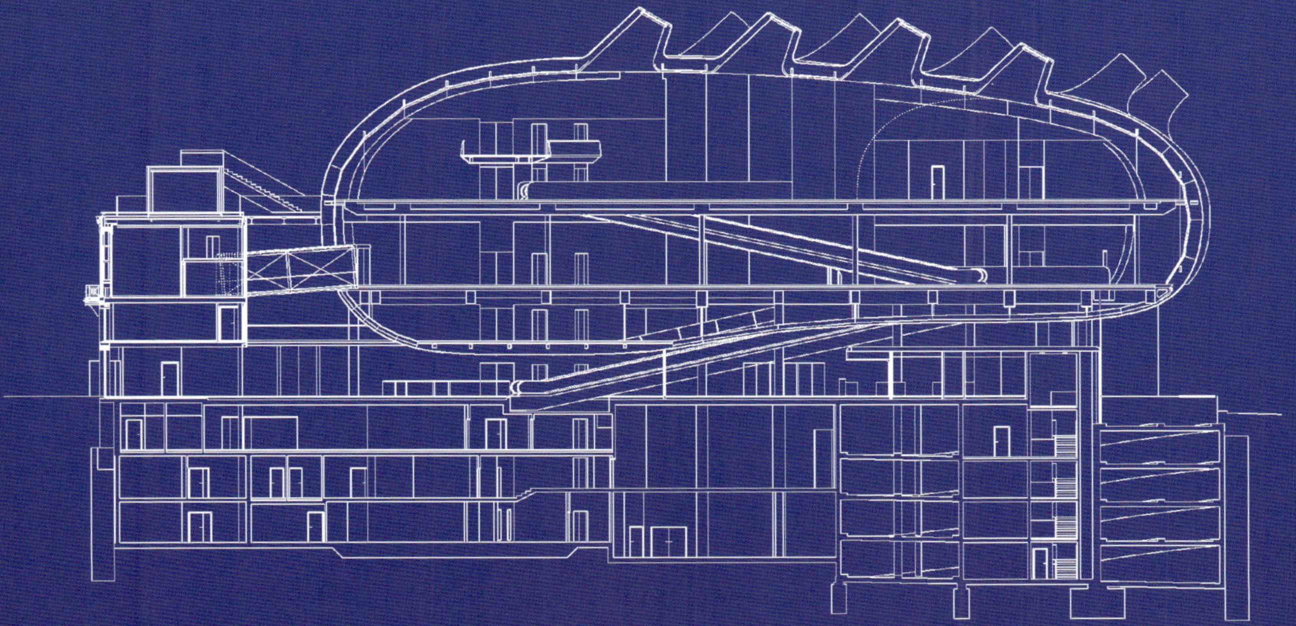

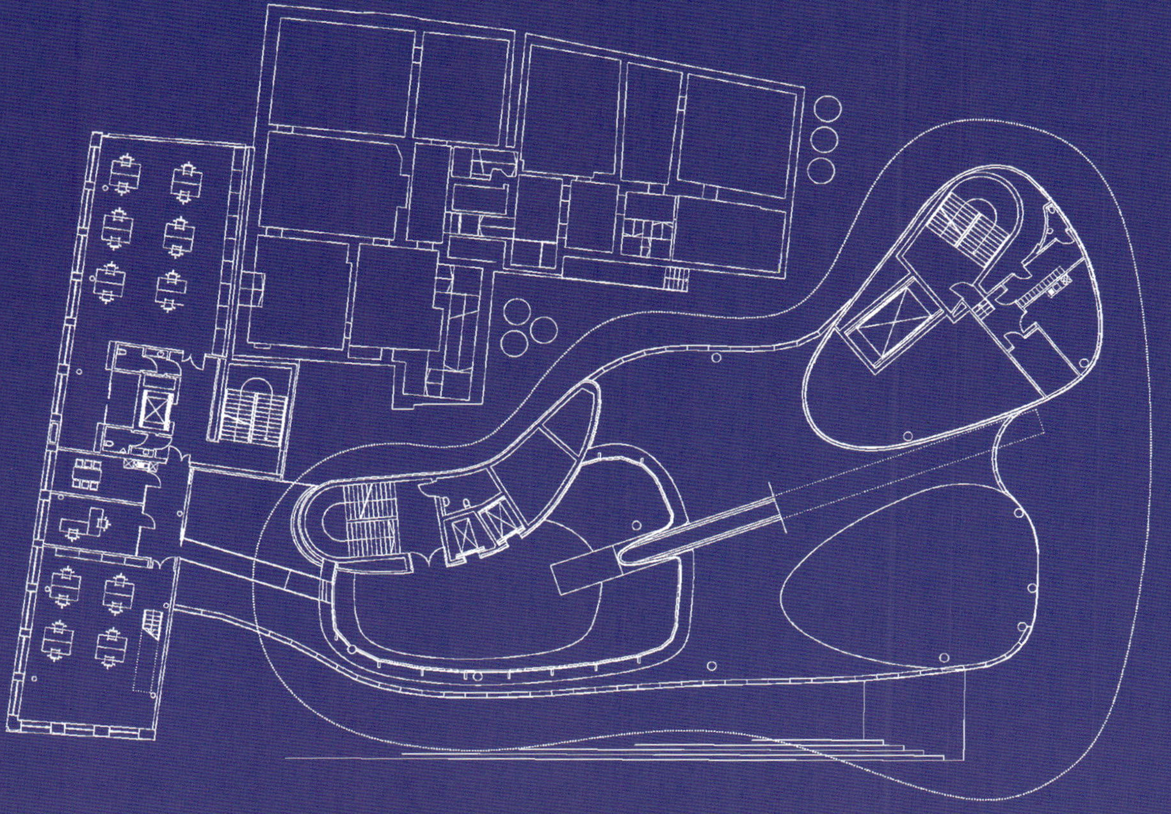

38 COOK AND FOURNIER – SPACELAB

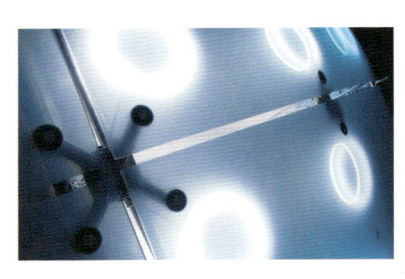

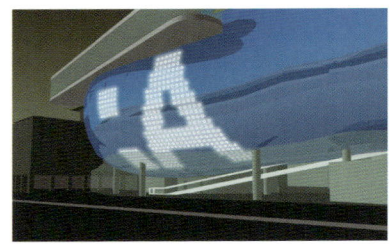

BIX is a light and media installation – we call it a 'Communicative Display Skin' – for the Kunsthaus Graz. BIX is an extra layer of approximately 1,100 circular computer-controlled fluorescent light tubes which is mounted behind the outer acrylic glass skin covering most of the main eastern façade. By individually switching and dimming the fluorescent tubes, a 45-metre wide and 20-metre high low-resolution greyscale display field forms, which follows the double-curved façade structure. Simple messages, icons and animations and also low-resolution video sequences can be sent out into the city of Graz, becoming a unique artistic message format for the new Kunsthaus.

The BIX concept was developed by realities:united in early 2001 as part of the thorough integration of media technology into the architecture of the Kunsthaus. A first prototype of the BIX installation was shown at the eighth international architecture exhibition La Biennale di Venezia as part of the Austrian contribution 'Kunsthaus Graz'.

Jan Edler, realities:united

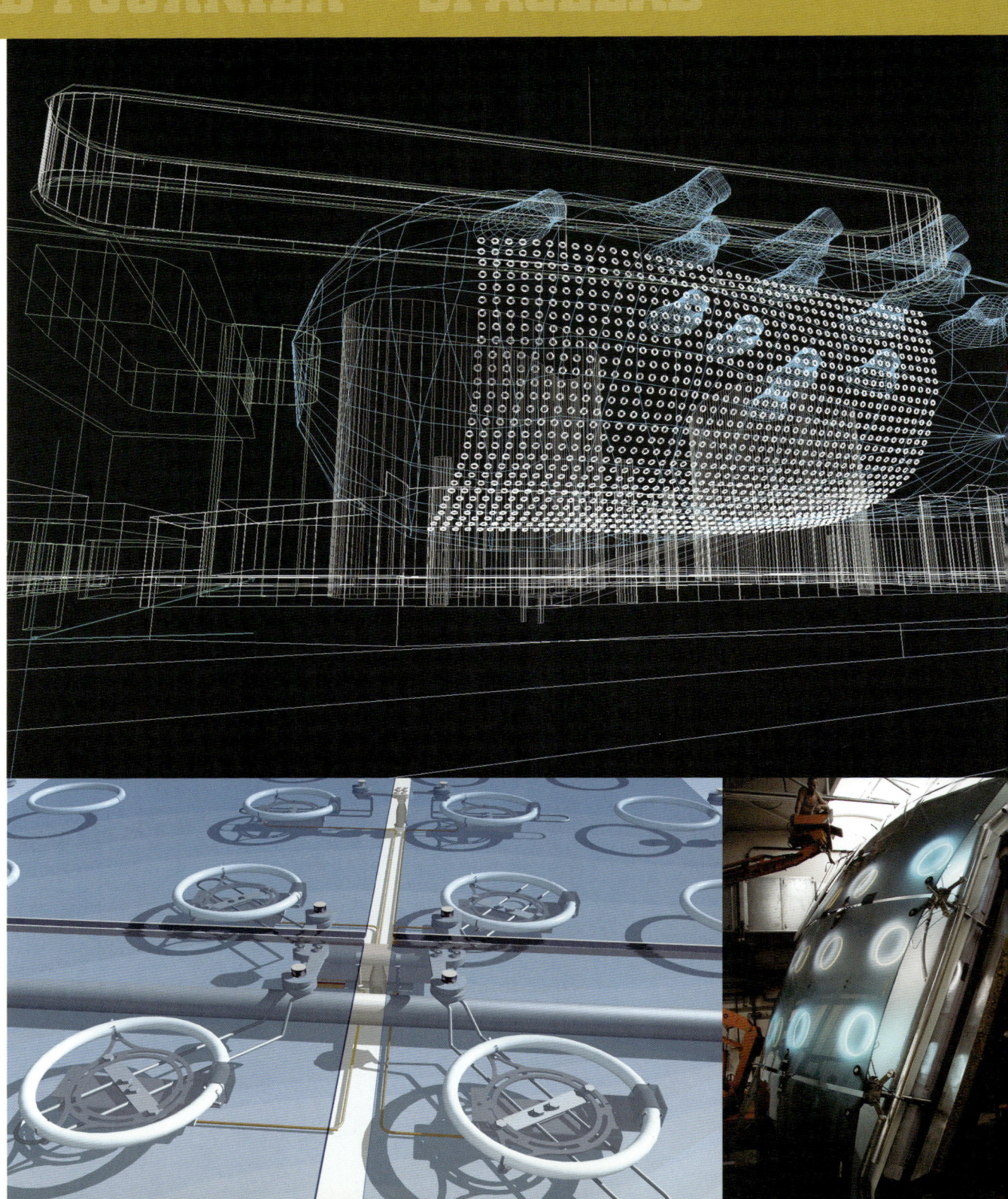

COOK WITH PÉREZ ARROYO + HURTADO 39

In the nine or ten years that Salvador Pérez Arroyo has been coming to the Bartlett as a visiting professor and unit tutor, I have come to regard him as one of my closest friends and confidants. He has a wonderful range of expertise: politics, culture, art, technics; and a brilliant library. The architecture of Salvador and his wife and partner Eva Hurtado is always explorative. Eva and my wife Yael Reisner have also become close friends: sharing many aesthetic as well as intellectual views. Both Yael and Eva have, as architects, territories of sensitivity and finesse that we blokes might easily miss.

Peter Cook

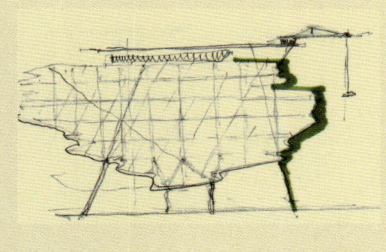

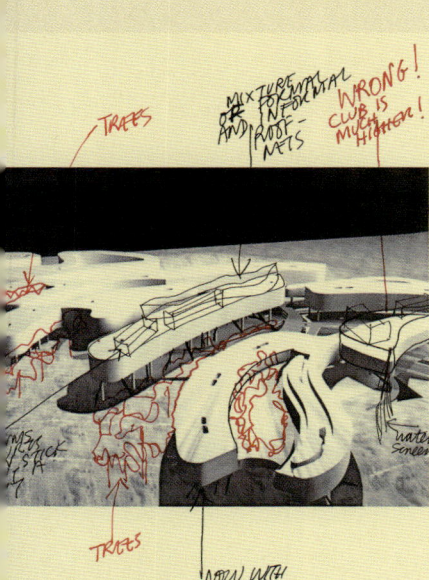

Punctum Millennium Pinto New Town Masterplan, South Madrid, Spain
Proposed masterplan
Ongoing
Peter Cook, Eva Hurtado and Salvador Pérez Arroyo: architects

When it was suggested by the Mayor of Pinto (a small town in a kind of 'Woking-to-London' relationship to Madrid), that a known foreign architect should join Salvador and Eva in making a masterplan for the addition of 25,000 people, offices, hotels, a college and so-on, the Graz project had just recently been in the Spanish newspapers. With Salvador and Eva in El Escorial – delightfully cooler than downtown Madrid – and myself in Swiss Cottage, we have been making models, scribbles, Academy paintings, more models.

The site is flat and featureless: so we invent a 'landscape': a two-kilometre long ridge concealing three levels of parking runs down one long side, culminating in an 'acropolis' of offices, hotels and showrooms. There is a golf course nearby and then housing. 'Edge' strips have apartments and several types of 'cluster' housing and a wide range of villa types. There is a 'boardwalk' running around the acropolis that provides for cute or ramshackle bars, kiosks and hang-outs. Swimming pools cascade down the slopes, tennis and golfing nets crown the commercial buildings. A giant waterfall acts as a movie screen...

The 'acropolis' has been but one of a whole series of exercises that I hope will lead to a real building.

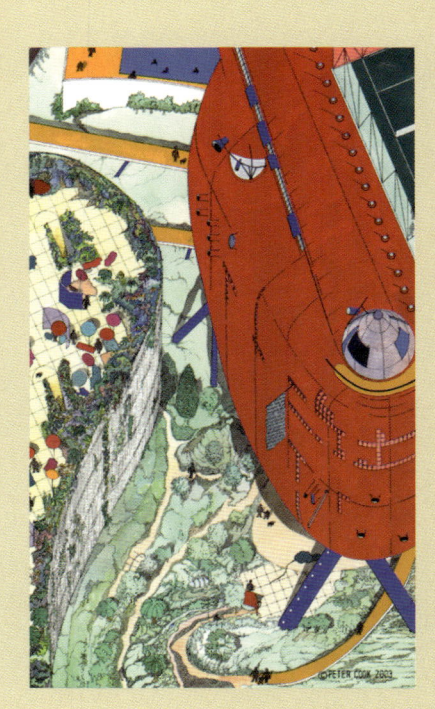

40 ODILE DECQ-BENOÎT CORNETTE

Our work is about dynamism, complexity and tension, responding to the conditions of the early 21st century. This is evident in all our projects, including the Banque Populaire de l'Ouest in Rennes and a motorway control centre slung underneath an elevated section of the A14 road west of Paris, for which we are best known. My association with the Bartlett has included teaching, external examining and lecturing. I have also taught in Montreal and Grenoble, and am Professor and Head of School at the Ecole Speciale d'Architecture in Paris.

MACRO: Museo d'Arte Contemporaneo di Roma, via Nizza, Rome (with Burkhard Morass)

New gallery
Budget: £15 million
Completion: 2005
Odile Decq: architect

The commission for this new gallery was won in an international open competition organised by the city of Rome. Inserted into a complex context and confronted with a rich historical inheritance, our new museum responds to the existing static condition of the site with dynamism and movement in the foyers and public spaces. In architectural works the section reveals the invisible. In our design the section is exposed through the translation from horizontal to vertical, from inside to outside, from foyer to roof-landscape-garden. We establish a system of transition in which the new contaminates everything around, and every part, old and new, becomes beautiful through its individual articulation within the whole. In contrast, the exhibition rooms are simple spaces given over to the artists, offering multiple ways to exhibit their work: hung, suspended, floating, on/in the floor...

The roof surface above is an abstract continuation of the works below, an art garden both for visitors and for the city. Textures underfoot have a range of material qualities: rough, smooth, soft, deep, dense, bright, matt... A central pool of running water refreshes the air. Sand, gravel, smooth limestone, grasses and the bright surface of the water make the landscape terrace a place of calm, freshness and sensuality.

42 DILLER + SCOFIDIO

Diller + Scofidio and the Bartlett taught me that in order to survive one has to be independent, highly motivated, opportunistic, competitive, ambitious, confident, and self-critical. At both places, I realised that I could practise architecture without necessarily being involved in the production of buildings. I continue in this practise of architecture in partnership with Shumon Basar. We have completed an interior at Topshop and an art installation at the Laban Centre. I am also the local curator for a global urban research project entitled 'Shrinking Cities'. It is such different scales and strategies of intervention that we are interested in.

Joshua Bolchover

blur: the making of nothing
Book
US$30.00 per copy
Published: 2002

Joshua Bolchover: project leader, content research, concept development, designer

The book *blur: the making of nothing* follows the development of a temporary experimental media pavilion designed for the Swiss Expo 02 from its initial conception in June 1998 until its final completion and opening in May 2002. The project of the book is to reveal the complexity of the architectural process in order to realise what essentially is nothing: a floating mist cloud hovering over the Lac de Neuchatel in Yverdon-les-Bains. This process incorporated design team in-fighting, political wranglings on a national scale, financial crises, as well as abandoned schemes and ideas, the technical development of the structural system and the sophisticated deployment of 31,000 nozzles in order to create 'fog'. The book is organised as a dynamic, chronological system and is conceived as a collection of artefacts, a mounting body of evidence and correspondence arbitrating between the creative idea and the difficulty of its manifestation.

002-003    022-023    046-047    114-115

124-125    154-155    172-173 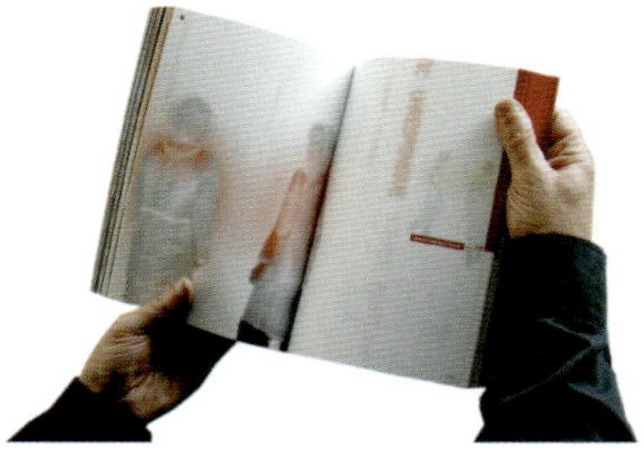   224-225

240-244    268-269    284-285    328-329

TOM DYCKHOFF

What have I done? Tricky one, that. If you're an accountant, an academic or an architect, you've at least got a vaguely defined career path. I don't. In fact I don't really know what I do. Nothing the world couldn't do without, for sure. So far life's meandered like this: geography at Oxford, architectural history at the Bartlett, writing for Prince Charles's mag, *Perspectives* (stop sniggering), a spot of teaching, a bit of curating at the RIBA, a brief, peculiar spell in publishing, a lot of writing about lofts and the latest in coffee tables at *The Guardian*, and now architecture critic at *The Times*. See, all over the place. All I know is that I like what I do. And I know what I like. And I want others to like what I like too. General enthusiasm and map reading are my only skills. I just had to figure out how to get paid for them.

That's what I've done. But what do I still want to do? Something useful, for a start. I'd like to write a book, when I have something to say. I'd like to visit the Dogon villages in Mali, and Bramante's Tempietto in Rome. I'd like to figure out why the British only think of design in terms of how much money it can make/save them, not how happy it can make them feel. I'd like to interview Peter Zumthor and Philip Johnson. I'd like to root out exactly how property developers make their money. I'd like to do a PhD, when I'm older and wiser. And having been weaned on Marxism and converted to Sam Mockbee, I want to save the world. But most of all, I want to be an architect. I know, I'm going about it a particularly long and stupid way. I blame bad career advice, gas bills to pay and an easily distracted mind. But I'll (possibly) get there in the end.

Wittgenstein's curtains
Magazine article
From Weekend magazine, *The Guardian*, 12 January 2002
Tom Dyckhoff: architectural journalist

In this piece I try to slip the serious matter of architecture and a serious exhibition at the serious British Museum into a weekly column on fluffy lifestyle things like cushions and coffee tables in *The Guardian*'s Saturday colour supplement. Sometimes you have to be crafty to sell architecture to commissioning editors in newspapers and magazines. It's a bit like selling your wares in an incredibly busy market where passers by are far too busy with far more important things and don't even think what you're selling is in the least bit interesting unless it has something to do with Posh 'n' Becks or selling advertising space. But sometimes you happen upon a friendly/gullible/genuinely interested face:

It's not often I get the chance to mention logical positivism and curtain fabric in the same sentence, but, what the hell, the time has come. Ludwig Wittgenstein, besides being a man with a lot to say about structures of language, also fancied himself as an architect in his spare time. In fact, for a spot of light relief, he built his sister a house in Vienna from 1926-28, for which he knocked up some nifty metal curtains (not as cosy as chintz or dralon, true, but awfully good for security). Wittgenstein's curtains are things of beauty. He devised an intricate pulley system to haul all 150kg as if it were as light as gauze, one of the revelations in a nice little show now on at the Royal Academy. Philosophers, you think, should have loftier things on their mind than soft furnishings. But not old Ludwig. When he wasn't worrying his copious brains over the fact that language and thought structures could only indicate, but not represent, their correspondence to reality (keep up), he was wracked with anxiety about paint swatches. In the end he went for a warm yellowy-red with grey-green doors (hurry, hurry to B&Q before the rush starts). The house is, as you might expect, a rather austere, mittel-European affair, all polished stone floors and tidy cupboards. But, like his seminal Tractatus Logico-Philosophicus, with which I'm sure you're all familiar, its simplicity hides a cunning complexity. Being a logical sort of chap, Wittgenstein was a stickler for precision, and, I imagine, a bloody nightmare for the builders. He took a year to design the door handles. He took another year to design the radiators, rather lovely radiators, it must be said. But nothing was ever quite as good as it was in his head. He was so sensitive that he had the hall ceiling raised by 30 millimetres just as the builders were tidying up. There's no record of their reaction, but I'm sure there was a lot of mittel-European tutting. Wittgenstein didn't build again. And became easily depressed.

44 EMULSION

I studied Diploma at the Bartlett, qualifying in 1998, when I also founded my practice. Unit 12 still remains close to my heart – it was there that my obsessions with texture, surface and notation were nurtured. My interest in the contradictions that are necessary to create architecture evolved into Emulsion – an emulsion is a mixture of elements shaken together, which will settle back into their separate parts. I enjoy combining people, design, skills and components to make the tactile spaces of Emulsion Architecture.

Yen-Yen Teh

Mathengine Stands, CEDEC99 and GDC2000 Developers' Conferences
New build exhibition stands
Completed: 1999/2000
Yen-Yen Teh: architect

These exhibition stands for Mathengine have no tangible product on display. The client is a middleware developer in computer gaming physics, and each stand was inspired instead by their current research. At the CEDEC99 conference in Tokyo, Japan, presentations were given on movement dynamics, fluidity and modular programming. Our design response was to create a tactile curved rubber surface alluding to movement, its futuristic whiteness suggestive of possibilities open to product users. Individual strip modules slot together to house such functions as audio-visual presentations and demo-stations.

At the GDC2000 exhibition, in San Jose, USA, the focus was on work in progress and one-to-one consultations. Our solution was an imposing temporary enclosure constructed from steel scaffolding, containing desk spaces and demo-stations, providing privacy while allowing glimpses of the interior.

EVENT

Event Communications is a multi-disciplinary exhibition design company – we work on permanent and temporary installations, museum design, software production and films. We often work collaboratively with architects, designers and artists to integrate enclosure and content, before developing projects in detail. Projects include three inflatable mobile exhibition pods that are currently on the road travelling round Wales, animations projecting a company's identity onto the front of their corporate headquarters, a park in France in which alien plants and materials are surreally displaced, and new media archiving systems opening new ways of accessing museum collections.

I am a project designer – taking projects right through from concept design through managing site works to completion.

Gavin Robotham

Magna exhibition, Rotherham, Yorkshire ◄
Permanent exhibition installation
Budget: £12 million
Completed: April 2001
Gavin Robotham: project designer

The enormous Templeborough Melting Shop at Rotherham, 350-metres long and seven-storeys high, was once the largest steel-making plant in Europe, but closed in the early 1990s. It is now occupied by Magna, a discovery centre for science and industry. Four pavilions, conceived by Event and designed by Wilkinson Eyre, are located within the vast cathedral-like shed, each one devoted to learning about one of the four elements that combine to form steel: earth, water, air and fire. Visitors experience the elements in their many forms, exploring the ways in which mankind has harnessed them and finding out what they contribute to the story of steel. A primary objective is to expose children to real-life applications of science and technology, like a giant classroom physics demo.

Imperial War Museum of the North exhibition, Manchester
Permanent exhibition installation:
Completed: 2002
Gavin Robotham: project designer

For the Imperial War Museum of the North, designed by Daniel Libeskind, we created a 'Total Immersion' presentation that integrates historical objects with images, film and sound recordings in a fully immersive visitor experience. This approach sheds new light on the Museum's archive material, bringing it to life and setting the objects on display in their historical context. Colossal images are beamed by 72 projectors onto all interior surfaces of the building and onto the tall 'silo' structures that occupy the permanent gallery, with rapid synchronised changes creating the illusion of movement. Under our creative direction, several production teams produced three separate elements: 'Why War?', 'the Technology of War' and 'Children at War'. An automated delivery system also allows interpreters to select objects from the Museum's collection to show to visitors.

46 EVENT

FEATHERSTONE ASSOCIATES 47

Featherstone Associates' core members are three ex-Bartlett students, Sarah Featherstone, David Appleton and Nicole Weiner. We all came from different years and units but share a common Bartlett desire to challenge architectural conventions. We like to involve a wide pool of people in our design team, drawing from other creative disciplines to produce more resourceful and inventive architecture. We do not take ourselves too seriously, often bringing an element of humour and fun into our work and are concerned with presenting architecture in a more accessible way, to make it inclusive, enabling people to be more involved in shaping their built environment.

Drop House, Northaw, Hertfordshire (by Featherstone Associates, formerly Hudson Featherstone)
New build house
Contract value: £700,000
Completed: 2001
Sarah Featherstone: lead architect with Anthony Hudson
David Appleton: architect in project team

This compact, steel and timber frame, five-bedroom family house is built on a suburban green belt site in Hertfordshire. A large pebble-shaped drop contains wet areas (washing and bathing) and collects rainwater and recycled water. Seen from outside, the drop peeps over the parapet, acting as an orientating device and drawing people in. The interior is sculpted around an inclined wall acting as a light scoop which the main staircase wraps around: the lower part is broad, processional and washed in light, whilst the upper is closed and more intimate. Internal spaces are arranged around the staircase, each room a few steps above or below the next and opening out to different aspects of the surrounding landscape. This fluid plan responds to the demands of a modern family lifestyle while giving a level of intimacy.

48 FEATHERSTONE ASSOCIATES

Voss Street House, Bethnal Green, London
New build house
Contract value: £150,000
Completed: 2001
Sarah Featherstone: lead architect

Built on a 20x4 metre site and comprising a shop on Bethnal Green Road and a new home for Sarah Featherstone, this inward orientated courtyard house can be seen as a prototype for urban terrace plots – we are currently working with developers to incorporate the modular courtyard design into larger sites.

The transparency of the living spaces around the internal courtyard contrasts with the blank street façade, and is only revealed as one peels away from the central spiral stair, which is clad in red leather and artificially lit. This juxtaposition of open and closed spaces has a 'Dr Who-Tardis' effect, making the house appear larger. The play of levels across the courtyard opens the spaces up, with rooms that in a typical terraced house are vertically isolated from one another here drawn together, creating a greater social dynamic.

In October 2002 Voss Street house was featured on Channel 4's 'Not all Houses are Square', which showcased innovative housing in a quest to challenge people's perceptions.

Fordham White Hair and Beauty Salon, Greek Street, Soho, London
(by Featherstone Associates, formerly Hudson Featherstone)
Interior design
Budget: £170,000
Completed: March 2002
Sarah Featherstone: lead architect
Nicole Weiner: project architect

Fordham White are a young hair-stylist duo who approached us to create something fun yet luxurious for their flagship salon in Greek Street. The design unashamedly alludes to local sex shops, creating a sumptuous, sensual environment. To give the salon a street presence its rose-tinted window is punctuated by a floating mirror projecting out across the pavement, a place to catch a glimpse of the before and after hairdo. The front of house is only three metres wide and is a deliberately ambiguous space, dedicated to show and relaxation with a Rococoesque couch adorned in an elaborate Marie Antoinette fabric. It frames the activity beyond where the salon widens out and hair is washed, cut and styled in ten stylists' chairs encircled by rose- and bronze-tinted mirror walls, under a translucent hairy ceiling made from the ubiquitous tassels found in local shop doorways.

FLETCHER PRIEST ARCHITECTS   49

Before I studied with Colin Fournier in Diploma Unit 18 I worked in Tokyo for Itsuko Hasegawa – being immersed in an environment in which all assumptions about urban form and culture are questioned was perfect preparation for study at the Bartlett. Since then, teaching on the MSc Urban Design course has offered me an opportunity to combine experience in practice with a forum for thinking about possible future forms of the city. Developing a dialogue with students from around the world, who bring a huge range of professional and cultural experiences to the course, has helped broaden my thinking beyond the immediate context of London.

I joined Fletcher Priest to take responsibility for their considerable urban design work. In parallel my ongoing MPhil/PhD research investigates the relationship between physical urban form and technological innovation.

Jonathan Kendall

Stratford City, East London (Fletcher Priest Architects are joint masterplanners with Arup Associates and West 8)
Masterplan
Budget: approximately £3 billion
Completion: phase one: 2009, complete scheme: 2015–2020
Jonathan Kendall, associate director and project architect, Fletcher Priest Architects

Stratford City is a masterplan for 73 hectares of brownfield land around the new international railway station currently under construction in Stratford, East London, and is the first stage of the Thames Gateway proposal, fundamentally realigning the balance of London eastwards. The project is huge, a rare and genuine opportunity to make a piece of city. When complete in ten to twenty years it will comprise four urban districts, homes for 11,000 and shops and workplaces for 33,000 more. All of this is made possible by the outstanding confluence of public transport systems at the site, connecting it with London, the UK and mainland Europe.

On a scheme of this scale, no single individual could credibly claim to have 'designed' the project. As with all cities, its form reflects the mediation between a series of forces. One of the most interesting questions has been the degree of detail that is fixed in the initial stages. It is essential to make strategic decisions to realise the future vision, but equally it is necessary to allow for future changing needs and desires.

50 ADRIAN FORTY

I studied history, but came to the Bartlett 30 years ago to learn about architecture. And I'm still learning now. Working in an architecture school has been a wonderful opportunity to observe architecture at close quarters without actually having to join the club and become an architect. My book *Words and Buildings* was written with the benefit of half a lifetime of listening to architects. As a full-time academic, 'practice' means teaching and writing, and a lot of the time it's not really possible to distinguish between the two – ideas from writing flow into teaching, but I get ideas from students and colleagues when teaching that I make use of when I write.

Inside the Whale
Essay
Adrian Forty: author

Things change when we start to talk about them. In a field like architecture, mostly devoted to making stable and more or less permanent objects, these changes aren't always to everyone's liking, and for this reason architects have often been ambivalent about language. On the one hand, words are necessary, and do a wonderful job where other media fail, but on the other hand they move things around and change how we see then, sometimes in sudden and unexpected ways. I'm interested in how people talk about architecture – the sorts of metaphors they use, where those metaphors come from, why some stick and others don't, and why they wear out. For a lot of the 20th century, architects were very suspicious of metaphors; there was a big purge of all the metaphors that had traditionally been used in architecture, and they were replaced by words like 'form', 'space', 'structure' and 'design' that were meant to be purely architectural and not refer to other things. These words became so overworked that, whatever they might once have meant, in time they became almost meaningless. Metaphors are back in favour now, but we need to beware that while metaphors can open our eyes, they can also close them; they may help us to see, but they also prevent us from seeing things for what they are.

'Skin'. It keeps us together, and it gives us away. What a great metaphor for talking about buildings. No wonder people since Alberti have found it irresistible.

But as with all metaphors, this one, while it draws attention to certain things, obscures others. How skin-like really are the coverings of buildings? Certainly there are correspondences, but there are also differences, and it is an effect of the skin metaphor to make thinking about the non-skin-like characteristics of walls and enclosures more difficult. And in particular, the skin metaphor creates some expectations about the enclosing elements of buildings that aren't always justified in reality.

The first of these expectations is of thinness. 'Skin' makes us think of walls as having a membrane-like thinness. But building coverings also have thickness – yet there's no equally compelling metaphor to convey the qualities of thickness. It could be said, though, that the skin analogy is based on a poor knowledge of skins. In fact, skin is made up of three layers, epidermis, dermis and subcutaneous fat, and in certain creatures these layers can add up to something very thick indeed - in a whale, up to 15 inches. Herman Melville, in chapter 68 of *Moby-Dick*, described flensing the whale as an endless peeling back of layers of the same material, blubber, causing him to ask, 'What and where is the skin of the whale?'. And he went on, 'however preposterous it may seem as to talk of any creature's skin as being of that sort of consistence and thickness, yet in point of fact these are no arguments, against such a proposition; because you cannot raise any other dense enveloping layer from the whale's body but that same blubber'. Whales (which, with 'the rare virtue of thick walls, and the rare virtue of interior spaciousness', Melville compared to works of architecture), show that skin is not always thin. Nevertheless, describing a wall as a 'skin' is more likely to encourage us to dwell on its thinness than on its thickness.

The second expectation that calling building coverings a 'skin' sets up is that they should reveal a lot about what happens inside. We think of skin both in a masculine sense as something that exposes the internal muscular structure, and in a feminine sense betraying internal feelings, through blushes. Either way, the skin is a register of what's within. This has become our conventional expectation of buildings' outsides – though this hasn't always been the case, and in previous architectures, like Romanesque, exteriors didn't do this. If we have got into the habit of looking at the outsides of buildings to tell us about their insides, then the 'skin' metaphor has surely played some part in this. We treat buildings rather like 18th century doctors treated their patients – skin colour, texture and marks were the principal means of diagnosis. Only later, with the development of other diagnostic techniques and tools for looking and listening inside the body did the skin condition lose its importance. Thinking about building coverings as skin makes us look for too much on them, so that almost everything we expect of a building becomes condensed onto its outermost layer.

Metaphors can certainly take us to new places, but they can also lead us astray.

52 FOSTER AND PARTNERS

Foster and Partners is an international practice led by Lord Foster, based in London with project offices across the world. The practice has received more than 260 awards and citations for design excellence, and won over 55 national and international design competitions. Our work ranges in scale from Hong Kong's new airport – the largest construction project in the world – to our smallest commission, a range of door furniture. The scope of our work includes masterplans for cities, the design of buildings, communications infrastructure, interior and product design, graphics and exhibitions.

The studio has established an international reputation with buildings such as the new German Parliament in the Reichstag, Berlin; The British Museum Great Court; Headquarters for HSBC in Hong Kong and London; the Commerzbank Headquarters in Frankfurt; the Metro Bilbao; the Carré d'Art Nîmes; Sainsbury Centre for Visual Arts in Norwich; and the Research Centre, Stanford University, California.

Albion Riverside Development, London
New build mixed-use development
Completion: 2003
Alan Chan: coordination on site and design of external cladding envelope

The development of Albion Wharf alongside the Foster studio between the Battersea and Albert bridges reinforces a growing new community on the south bank of the Thames. The mixed-use development promotes a lively urban quarter where people can live, work and enjoy life in the city. The principal building arcs back in an asymmetrical crescent to create a public space alongside the river walk. Eleven storeys high, it respects the heights of its neighbours and frames the river view from the opposite bank.

With primarily glazed façades of varying translucency, the building's appearance changes according to light conditions and from where it is seen. Apartments facing north over the river have sliding doors giving access to balconies with clear glass balustrades, whose horizontal lines reinforce a sense of visual order. The southern façade is expressed as a veil of aluminium rods forming a rainscreen. The roof continues the building's curving form, wrapping over and around in a single sweep.

Wembley Stadium, London
New build sports stadium
Budget: £450 million
Completion: September 2005
Angus Campbell:
project director in charge

Since it was built for the British Empire Exhibition of 1924, Wembley Stadium has become the most important sports venue in Britain, site of the Olympic Games in 1948 and of England's 1966 World Cup Final victory. The key design feature of the new Wembley Stadium is the partly retractable roof. When fully open it will allow sunlight to reach the whole pitch – essential in maintaining world-standard turf. In poor weather, it can be closed within 15 minutes, providing cover for all 90,000 spectators. The roof will be supported by a spectacular 133-metre high arch, an iconic replacement for the old building's landmark twin towers. Illuminated at night it will be visible from across London.

The stadium's geometry and steeply raked seating ensure that everyone has an unobstructed view, and to create an intimate atmosphere during football and rugby games, seats are as close to the pitch as possible. An elevated running track and athletics field can be installed to host track and field competitions. Acoustic studies have been undertaken to ensure that the new stadium recreates the distinctive 'Wembley roar'.

54 FOSTER AND PARTNERS

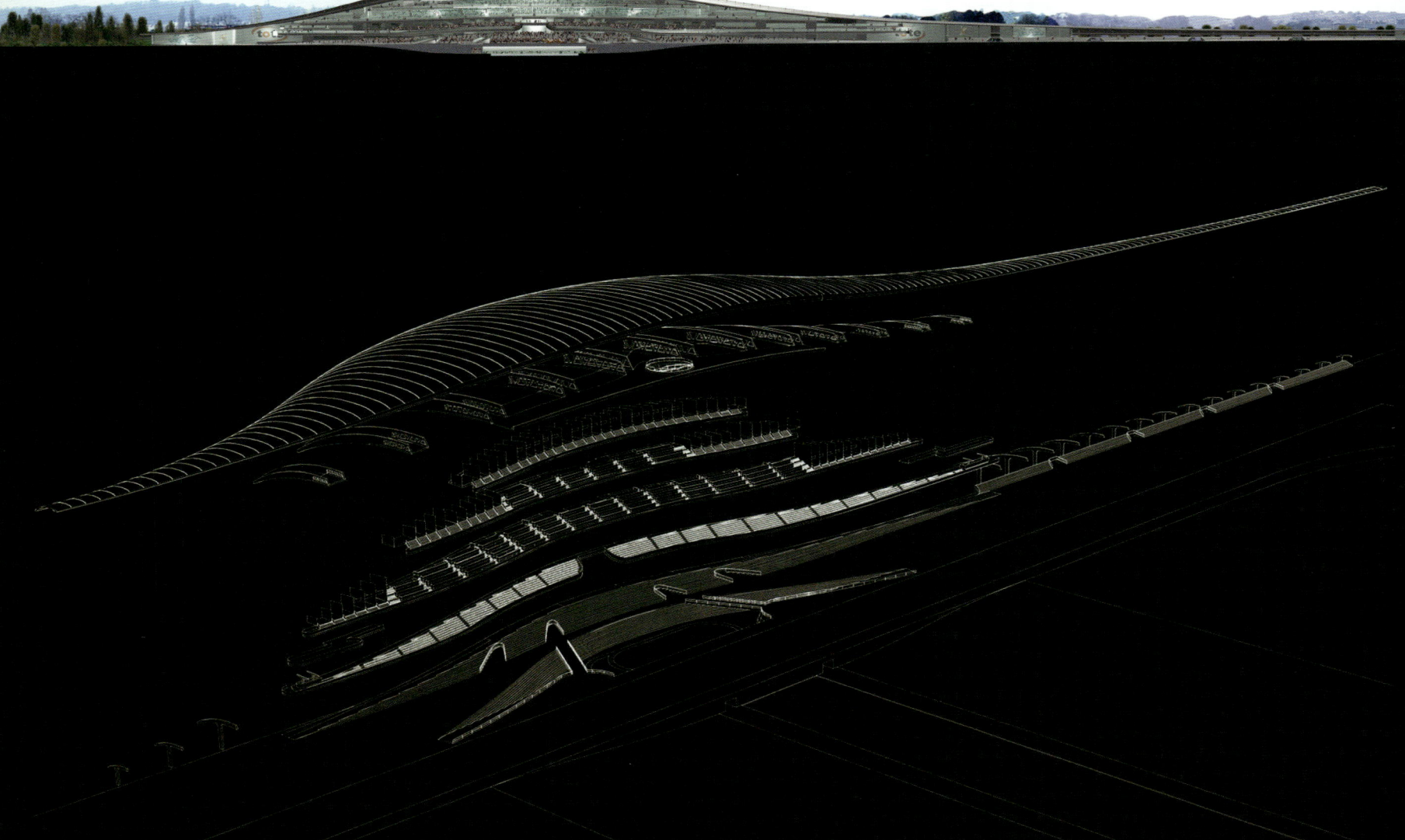

London City Racecourse
New build racecourse
Unbuilt
Michiel Verhaverbeke and Xavier De Kestelier: core design team, visualisation

This would be the first new purpose-built racecourse in England since 1927. The grandstand accommodates half of the 20,000 crowd, with the cantilevered curving metallic roof swelling and tapering along its length, sheltering spectators and the parade ring. The curve of the roof reflects sound into the interior, allowing spectators in the restaurants and bars to share the excitement of the racing experience. The other buildings on the site – stables, a crèche and fitness club – share the roof's curved form. Visitors can watch races from a viewing area within the roof, reached by lifts in the building's structural cores. This space is open to all members of the public, inverting the hierarchy of spectator accommodation found at most racecourses.

New World Trade Center Proposal, Manhattan, New York ▶ ▼
Competition entry (shortlisted)
2002
Jong-Min Kim: architectural assistant

Our twinned towers proposal for the World Trade Center site, one of seven shortlisted designs, is informed by a study into safety in tall buildings we commissioned immediately following September 11. The triangular plan is rotated by 120° every 42 storeys, producing a crystalline form with a diagonal perimeter structure that is immensely strong. Escape staircases running down the edges of the towers enable occupants to travel from one level to another without having to use the central core. The towers 'kiss' at three points, creating escape routes from one to the other, and spaces for public observation platforms, exhibitions and cafés. They break down the tower's scale into village-like clusters, each with its own tree-filled atrium.

Directly underneath, a mass transit hub links the PATH train, subway lines, new airtrains to JFK and Newark Liberty Airports, a bus station and parking. A new park bridges over West Street and extends to the waterfront and Battery Park City. A memorial, built on the footprints of the two destroyed towers, and framed by monumental walls of steel and stone, creates a sanctuary for private remembrance and reflection.

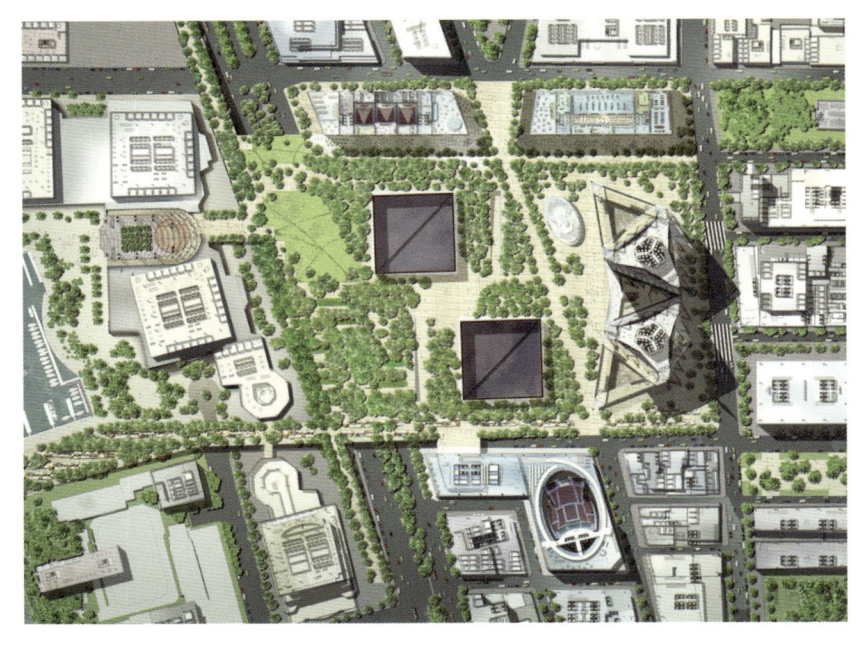

Electronic Arts European Headquarters, Chertsey ▲
New build company headquarters
Completed: 2000
Katy Ghahremani: detailing, site inspection

At Fosters we consistently encourage companies to adopt flexible, non-hierarchical working environments. Electronic Arts, a leading computer game software developer, wholly embraced this philosophy.

Bound to the north by an 18th century lake, the building, which employs a range of new-technology and passive environmental systems, has five three-storey office blocks arranged as 'fingers' projecting into the landscape. The fingers are linked by a sweeping glass wall that forms an environmental buffer and encloses a street-like atrium for primary circulation at ground level, an animated showcase for Electronic Arts' work and the social focus of the campus. The staff takes pride in working as a 'family' with common values. In keeping with this ethos, a huge range of facilities is provided, including games arcades, a gym and sports pitch, a library, bar and 140-seat restaurant. With this wealth of leisure options, staff members have joked that being there is like 'homing from work'.

56 FOSTER AND PARTNERS

Design illustration: City Academy schools and World Trade Center proposal

Narinder Sagoo: visualisation

I work on most projects in the office, often with Norman Foster and the directors, helping to illustrate the thought processes and vision behind designs at all development stages. My drawings are used to present projects to a wide variety of users and audiences, communicating the simplest to the most complex ideas.

I have been involved with a number of City Academy school projects. This drawing (right) was developed with Norman Foster to communicate both the architecture and the conceptual ideas for this new type of school. It was exhibited at The Royal Academy Summer Show in 2002 and won an architectural drawing prize.

In January 2003 my drawings formed the centrepiece of our World Trade Center proposal exhibition in New York. My role was to examine community and neighbourhood needs and represent these graphically. By presenting the project as seen through the eyes of a visitor (above) it was possible to demonstrate the many facets of the scheme to an audience of millions.

My design work has also included a new Elephant House for Copenhagen Zoo. I became the youngest Associate in the Practice in 1999 and a Project Director the following year.

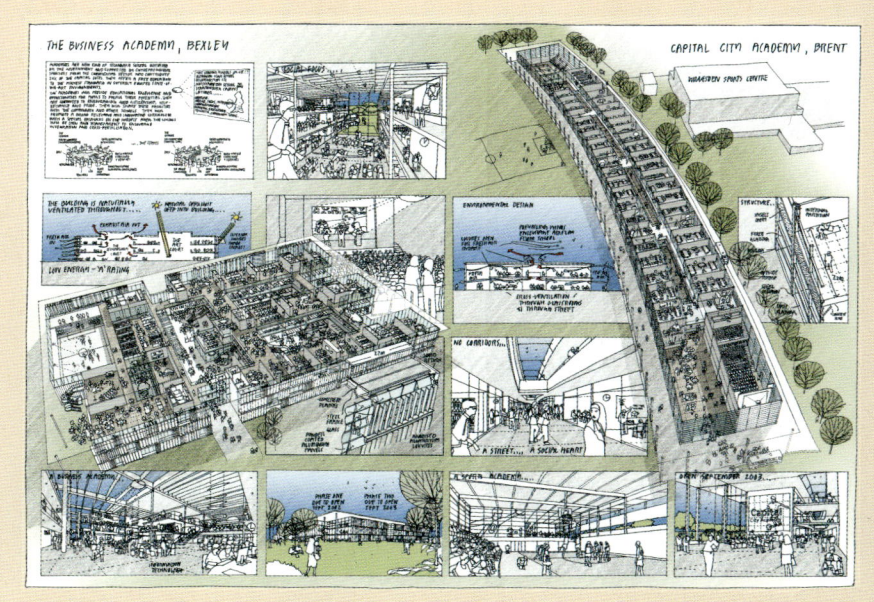

City Hall (Home of the London Mayor and Assembly), Southwark, London
New build government headquarters
Completed: April 2002
Richard Hyams: project director

City Hall houses the assembly chamber for the 25 elected members of the London Assembly and the offices of the Mayor and 500 staff of the Greater London Authority. It is a highly public building, bringing visitors into close proximity with the workings of the democratic process, and set within the 'More London' masterplan on the south bank of the Thames, also by Fosters.

A large sunken outdoor amphitheatre paved in blue limestone leads to a public café at lower ground level, with an elliptical exhibition space directly beyond, below the assembly chamber. Daylight is reflected in by the ceiling's pattern of concentric ellipses of mirror-polished stainless steel. A public ramp coils through all ten storeys to the top of the building, offering views of London and glimpses into the offices of the GLA staff. The ramp leads past the Mayor's Office to a public space at the top of the building known as 'London's Living Room', with an external viewing terrace that can be used for exhibitions or functions for up to 200 guests.

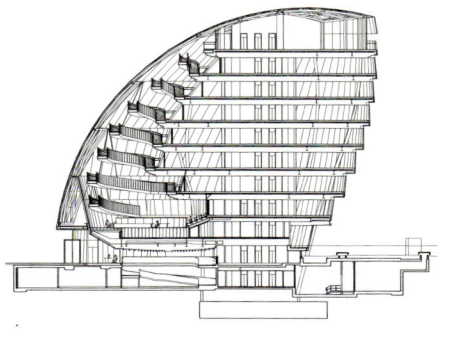

58 FUTURE SYSTEMS

Future Systems' innovative designs are not only visually striking, but are also pieces of highly functional equipment, inspired by both nature and technologies transferred from other industries. We are recognised worldwide for consistently challenging traditional preconceptions of space and demonstrating environmental concern and efficiency. Research is a vital ingredient for the practice and a balance between experimental and real projects is kept in order to remain at the cutting-edge of the field.

Jan Kaplicky and Amanda Levete lead Future Systems from offices in central London. The work of the practice has been widely published and the principals regularly undertake lecture tours internationally.

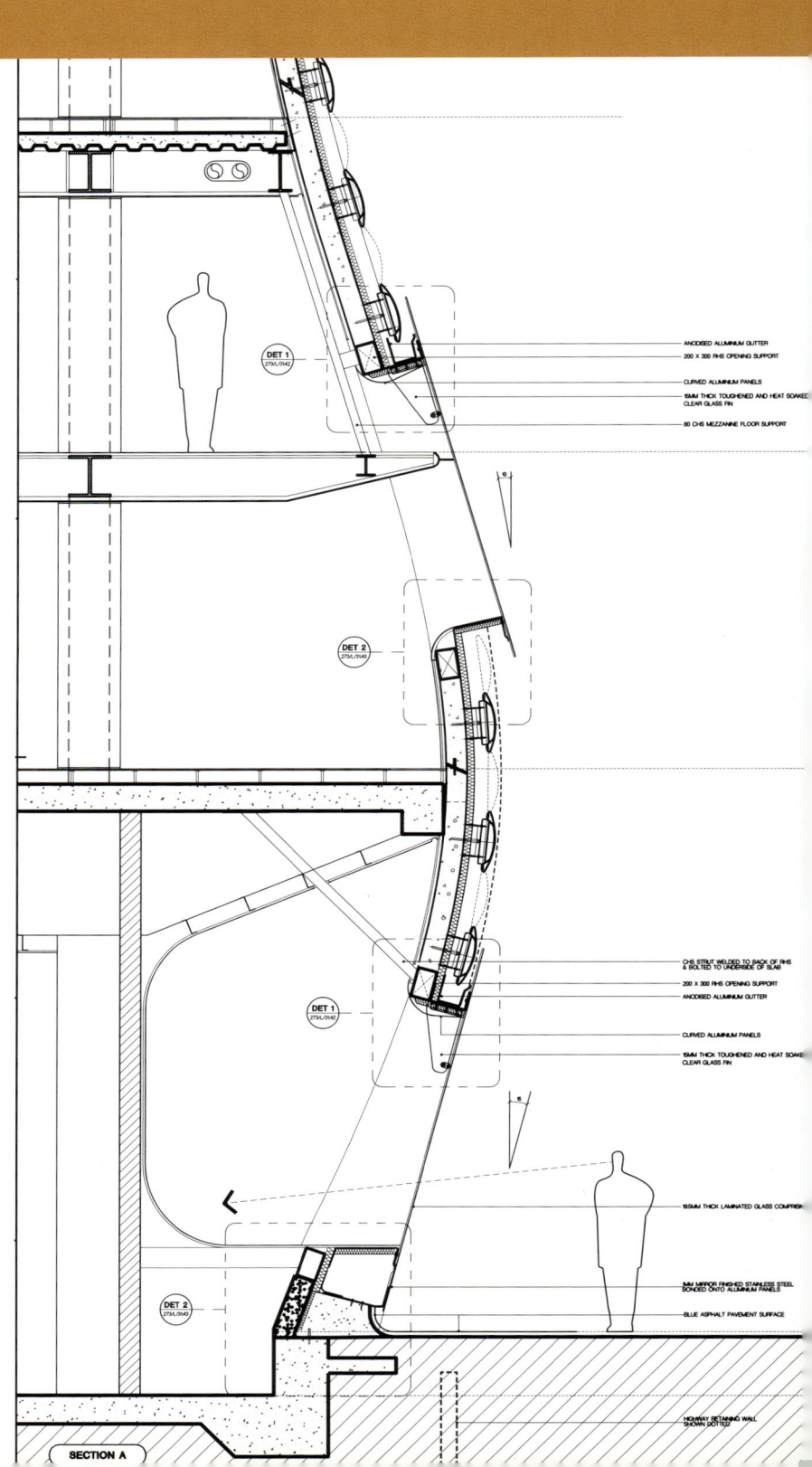

Selfridges, Birmingham
New build department store
Completion: September 2003

Dominic Harris: architectural assistant
Nicky Hawkins: glazing and façade package coordinator
Nicholas Mansour: fit-out architect
Severin Soder: architect

The ambition of this scheme is great. Selfridges required a state of the art department store that would provide an architectural landmark for Birmingham. It is this ambition that drove our design, enabling the building to become a genuine catalyst for urban regeneration.

We have reinterpreted the notion of the department store, not only in its form and appearance, but also in the social function such a building now performs in our society. The form of the building is soft and curvaceous in response to the curve of the site, sweeping around the corner and wrapping over the top to form the roof. The building is aesthetically innovative but also clearly signifies its function as a department store without the need for signage. The fluidity of the exterior is matched inside with an organically shaped atrium stretching across the floor plan. As in an urban canyon, shafts of natural light penetrate through the atrium deep into the building.

60 FUTURE SYSTEMS

Selfridges Foodhall, Manchester
New retail foodhall
Completed: September 2002
Dominic Harris: architectural assistant
Nicky Hawkins: project team leader Nicholas Mansour: assistant architect

The function of a foodhall is an intrinsic part of urban living. At Manchester Central we have reinterpreted the tradition of the foodhall, expressing the idea of the market as a social place, as opposed to one of rapid supermarket consumption.

Inspired by a droplet of water, the sculptural display of fruit and vegetables around the escalators forms the high point in the hall, from which a series of ripples emanate. Eateries, refrigerated counters and display units are all given a soft sculptural form, creating interesting circulation patterns and adjacencies. Finished in a glossy white surface, the display counters are designed to emphasise the inherent colours of the products. Around the perimeter, a sinuous sculpted wall displays a myriad of products in a dramatic form, giving a sense of theatre to the space. A radial array of lights in the ceiling reinforces the free-form social nature of the room.

This is a place to meet, to sample before you buy, to take time out and to enjoy the many colours and aromas of the Foodhall.

Comme des Garçons Tunnel, New York, USA
Shop fit-out
Budget: approximately £70,000
Completed: 1998
Rachel Stevenson: architect

Rei Kawakubo of Comme des Garçons asked Future Systems to design the entrance to her new flagship store in Chelsea, New York. Rather than creating an entirely new façade, we kept the existing 19th century frontage, complete with signage and external fire escapes, and instead grafted a ten-metre long, asymmetrical aluminium tunnel behind the existing arched opening, to transport shoppers between the street and the calm interior.

The tunnel was built in a Cornish shipyard using boat-building techniques. We used a series of rough cardboard models to generate the drawn sections for MDF spacers, around which the aluminium sheet was shaped. The tunnel was constructed in five separate pieces which bolted together to enable it to fit into one shipping container for transport.

A line of red marker lights in the floor guide shoppers in, and are reflected in the raw hand-finished aluminium surface, contributing to a calm but slightly unnerving feel inside the tunnel. A frameless glass door pivots at the narrowest point of the tunnel to form the entrance.

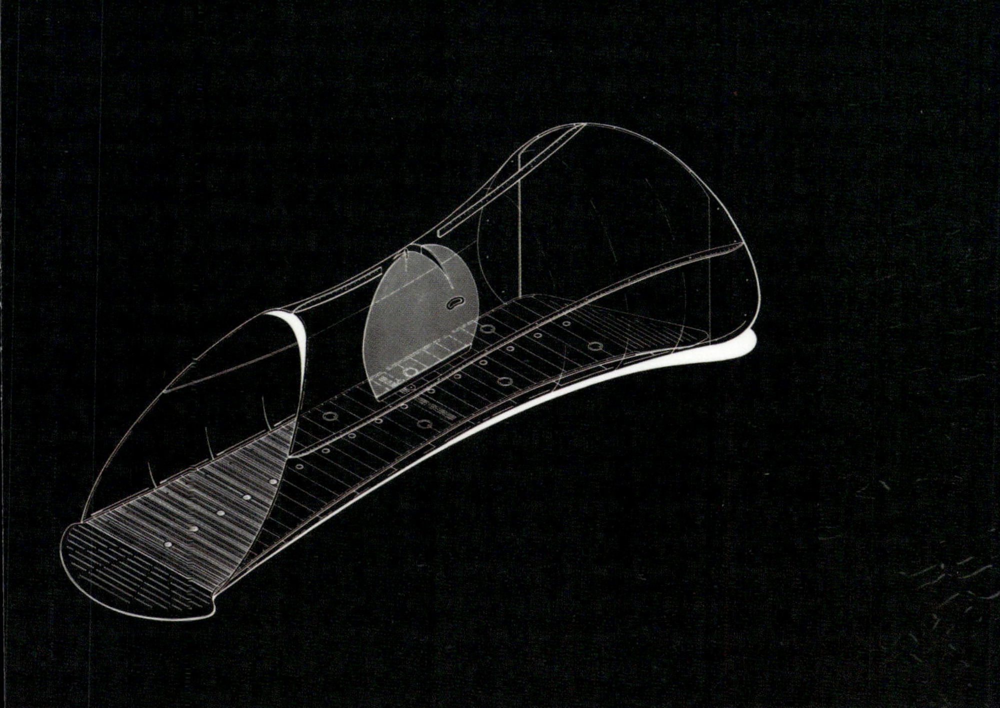

Heavenly BODY WORKS
691-1092
BAKED TO PERFECTION
• INSURANCE ESTIMATES •
Quality AUTO BODY
REPAIR & REFINISHING
HEAVENLY BODY WORKS

62 FUTURE SYSTEMS

Wild at Heart at the Great Eastern
Retail fit-out
Budget: £25,000
Completed: 2000
Rachel Stevenson: project architect

This tiny shop unit in the newly refurbished Great Eastern Hotel needed fitting-out for Wild at Heart both to sell flowers and to prepare and supply them to the hotel. We did not alter the existing unit, but simply inserted two pieces of furniture: a bright orange, tiered table where flowers are displayed, prepared and sold; and a long sink unit where flowers can also be stored. Both pieces are made of Corian on curved plywood; chosen for its bright colour and its tough, durable plastic finish, making the finished pieces seem almost like oversized plastic toys.

Vogue Table, Condé Nast International, London
Furniture design
Budget: £13,500
1999
Rachel Stevenson: project architect

This 3.6-metre long desk was designed for the private office of the publishing executive of Condé Nast International. Its curved form is constructed from a polystyrene-filled, glass-reinforced plastic skin, which was then lacquered and polished. Electrical and data connections run up through the main leg, which is supported at its other end by a braced stainless steel support.

Marni, London
Retail fit-out
Budget: £300,000
Completed: 1999
Rachel Stevenson: project architect

Future Systems was asked to design a concept for the Italian fashion designer, Marni, that could be used in both their international stand-alone stores and in department store concessions. Our solution was to present the clothes on a sculptural white island that sits in front of the brightly coloured background of the rest of the shop, and is reflected by a mirror-polished stainless steel ceiling of the same shape, removing the feeling of being in a rectilinear space. The background colour can be chosen to suit a particular collection and can be varied with changing seasons to give a fresh look from time to time.

Clothes and accessories are displayed on tall, delicate stainless steel branches and on a stainless steel rail, a dynamic element that curves around the perimeter of the island, changing from hanging rail to flat surface for display and serving counter. Clothes hang on specially designed plexiglas hangers and appear to float as sculptural elements, yet are accessible and tangible to the public.

63

64 STEPHEN GAGE

I came to the Bartlett in 1991 after many years of combining practice at Douglas Stephen and Partners with teaching at the AA and other schools of architecture. My previous design work included the construction of innovative primary care buildings in Highgate and Camden where passive ventilation and passive cooling significantly influenced the design strategies. This work left a range of unanswered questions that have led to a number of my subsequent research proposals. The research I have undertaken involves making large physical rigs, which have been treated as exercises in design research themselves. Research also continues in other physical projects, when time and available finance permit...

Isobel's Treehouse, North London (with Phil Ayres)
Design and build
Budget: £1,200
Completed: May 2002
Stephen Gage: conceptual design, client's agent
Phil Ayers: conceptual design, detail design, fabrication and erection

Most treehouse builders take their inspiration either directly or indirectly from the 19th century and specifically from Rousseau, constructing primitive huts in trees. The treehut can be noble in a grand tree in a large garden, but it gets progressively more absurd the more urban the garden and the smaller the tree.

For Isobel's Treehouse we found inspiration instead in a sophisticated treehouse first described by G K Chesterton in his book *A Club of Queer Trades*, published in 1905. He described 'an enormous, dark egg-shaped thing, pendant in the branches like a wasps nest' and 'hanging by a cunning mechanism' which caused it to 'swing only slightly' in a full gale. This treehouse is clearly a grand affair, requiring two large trees for support, but certain aspects are of considerable interest to the urban arboreal architect – specifically this is not a house in a tree – it is more like a nest which is interactive and responsive to its location.

We wanted to create a treehouse that changes shape as branches move in the wind, and deforms as its occupants play in it. A large object in a small tree can shade an already shady garden to a point where grass and plants find it difficult to grow. Consequently we made the enclosure translucent, to allow light transmission and to catch the moving shadows of the tree, the client and her friends. The initial idea was to construct a large translucent bud that would keep the weather out; this was vetoed because it would keep spiders in. The final concept is halfway between a flower and a boat, with two petals of translucent polycarbonate wrapped around a plywood base. The fluid geometry of the petals evolved through a series of model experiments by Phil Ayres. A translucent base was also considered – but was thought to be incompatible with the budget. The base, access trap and ladder were constructed out of 25-millimetre plywood sheets.

Isobel Gage is five years old, and is small and slender while her father is tall and beginning to spread. The base, access trap and access ladder are designed to accommodate both. Indeed the access trap is known as the 'Dad hole' and was prototype tested to ensure that a diet is rigorously maintained. Isobel bought the design when Thumbelina was used as a reference. Prior to this she was holding out for a roof.

The treehouse was fabricated in the Bartlett workshop and was erected by Phil, to the client's increasing elation, over a day in late spring 2002. It has proved to be a great success.

Top Down Ventilation and Cooling in Urban Areas Research (with Industry Partners and Bartlett Architecture Researchers – key research assistants: Phil Ayres, Tara de Linde, Chris Leung, Dan Townsend, Lydia Sheard)

Department for Education, Transport and the Regions Partners in Technology Research Project

Budget: £120,000

Completed: 1999

Stephen Gage: principal investigator

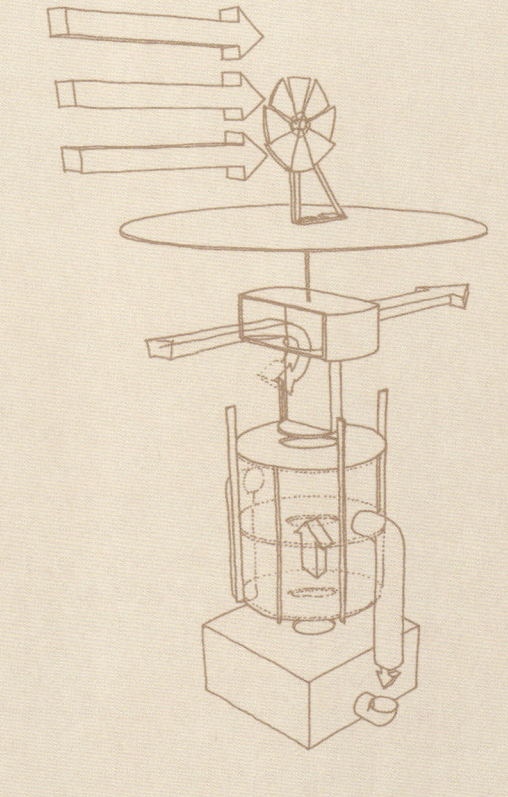

Poor indoor air quality is believed to be a cause of sickness and absenteeism at work. Pollution from the external environment is a major problem in cities, particularly in urban street canyons and car parks, while there are security risks and problems with noise when windows or louvres are opened at low level. Ventilation engineers are therefore advised to take air into buildings from roof level in urban areas, which has, up to now, required the use of fan-driven ducted ventilation systems that need a continuous supply of electrical energy. Fans also generate noise, and some concerns have been raised that this noise itself contributes to sick building syndrome. In a series of experiments we looked at ways of taking air in and out of buildings from the top without the use of fans, so that they are passively ventilated and cooled. We found however that intake air must be actively cooled on hot, still summer days. Our large-scale experiments demonstrated that it is possible to achieve this very efficiently using gravity down-draught coolers (peripheral chiller units at the top of air-intake shafts) that offer very little resistance to airflow, and that wind pressures on intake and extract terminals can assist ventilation airflow rather than opposing it. The introduction of small refrigeration units into an otherwise passive system requires an energy input, which can be achieved using solar power in most conditions.

Our research concluded with indicative drawings showing the implications of incorporating this type of ventilation into different building types and a note on the urban planning issues involved.

66 GENERAL LIGHTING AND POWER

Named after Section V of the NBS Minor Works Specifications, General Lighting and Power was founded in 1996 by Nic Clear, Jonny Halifax, Ezra Holland and Danny Vaia. Our original aim was to build a company that combined architectural design with computer imaging, animation and graphics – we really thought that we would become a cross between Hayes Davidson and Tomato. Luckily we failed miserably.

Our first real deviation came when we produced and directed a low budget pop promo for the Lo-Fidelity All Stars. Shot on a JVC camcorder and edited on a desktop Mac in Adobe Premier, only a week after completion the video was shown on ITV's Pepsi Chart show introduced by All Saints. Hmmm, easy peasy we thought. Further videos convinced us that this was more fun than specification writing and working drawing packages. As time passed we bought more kit, learned new programmes and generally moved further and further away from architecture. We started doing more work in advertising and TV and have recently completed a couple of short films. GLP has not taken on any commercial architecture projects for over two years.

Unit 15, run by Nic Clear, was established in 1995. The Unit has always sought to use digital technology to analyse existing urban conditions and modes of practice, generate formal strategies, develop and test architectural and spatial ideas and represent these ideas in exciting and innovative ways. In the first few years the emphasis was stills based. As GLP moved more into film and animation Unit 15 became the first to concentrate solely on time based work, initially hardcore modelling and animation. Now a much looser mixture of graphics, animation and video is produced.

As GLP has moved further away from explicitly architectural strategies the Unit has moved back towards them, disillusionment with 'virtual' projects resulting in more real-world sites and programmes. General Lighting and Power may never produce an architectural project again, but hopefully our influence will be felt through the output of our students. Over the years a number have passed through our office, but of particular note in 2000 we were joined by Unit 15 students Patrick Chen, Bastian Glassner and Chris McKenzie (who are now LynnFox), and then by Chog Burley. Steve Clements and former MArch student Allison Dring were also in residence for a while.

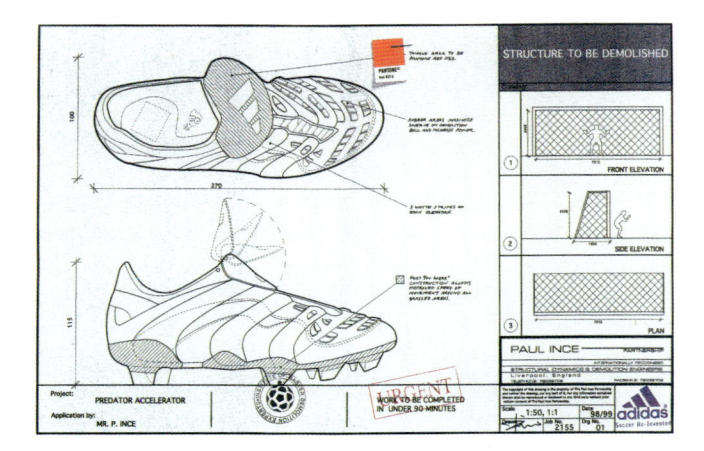

'Adidas Predator': art direction and illustration for Leagas Delaney national press advert, nominated for D&AD Award for Art Direction. Personnel: GLP ◄

'Maintel Telecommunications': concept, design and illustration for press adverts. Personnel: GLP, Chris McKenzie, Bastian Glassner ▲

'Who': specially commissioned illustration for *Dazed and Confused* magazine. Personnel: GLP, Patrick Chen, Bastian Glassner ►

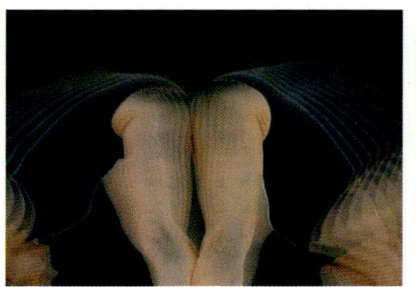

'Love Architecture': illustration for national poster campaign for the RIBA Gallery. Personnel: GLP, Bastian Glassner ▲

'Playstation': CGI graphic for national press campaign for TBWA. Personnel: GLP, Bastian Glassner, Chog Burley ▶

Groove Armada: I See You Baby: pop promo for Zomba Records. Personnel: GLP ◀

COME OUT OF YOUR PROTECTIVE SHELL

Still prepared to do 196mph with nothing between you and the tarmac? If you are, you're in for the ultimate race, around the world's fastest tracks, on the fastest bikes, MOTOGP, unarguable proof that two wheels are better than four.

www.uk.scee.com/motogp

68 KATY GHAHREMANI + MICHAEL KOHN

We met at the Bartlett in 1995, since when we have collaborated on conceptual design ideas and visualisations, including several competitions for speculative housing for the Millennium and beyond. We won Concept House 2000 with the HangerHouse, working with an inter-disciplinary team of designers, engineers and consultants. We were also awarded second place in the Living Sites competition in 1998, and were short-listed in Concept House '98 and '99. Our work has been exhibited nationally.

We both believe we benefited from the Bartlett experience through radical and continuous revision of our own design standards.

Living Sites, proposed for a three acre suburban site in Hampton Court ▼
Competition entry (awarded second place)
Budget: based on £500/square metre
March 1998
Katy Ghahremani and Michael Kohn: designers

The future of speculative house design lies in meeting the challenge of the changing attitudes of house builders and buyers. As a solution to the cultural void, we believe in 'sex appeal' to reinforce 'kerb appeal'. We believe in mass customisation. To achieve this, we believe in large spans. Pre-fabricated from concrete, steel or timber, large spaces can be customised to the consumer's design. We see the need for well-insulated, environmentally responsible housing able to take on appropriate technologies. Consumers will be able to marry their aspirations with the overall design intent of the development. The budget for the Living Sites project was based on £500 per square metre, a competitive comparison with today's volume house builders' figures.

HangerHouse, prototype built in Earl's Court, London ▶
Ideal Home Concept House competition winner
Budget: £100,000
March 1998
Katy Ghahremani and Michael Kohn: designers

The HangerHouse, developed with an inter-disciplinary team of designers, engineers and consultants, is a deliberately open vessel ready to be dressed up with varying lifestyles and technologies of the future, without compromising its own design integrity. As the only common element to the product, the frame is styled to give a very recognisable identity – familiarly domestic, yet funky enough to belong to the world of 'concept' and 'future' houses. It is on, in and around this frame that other elements of the house, such as the envelope, roof terrace and service column, can be hung. A specific HangerHouse can range from a budget-range spec to an outlandish luxury manor, depending on the kit of parts specified. The HangerHouse is an 'inclusive' piece of architecture, open to interpretation and appropriation.

The HangerHouse prototype was built and exhibited at the Ideal Home Exhibition 2000. The build budget was £100,000, although the project was greatly enriched with donations from suppliers of interesting and innovative construction materials. In addition we were able to display various product design prototypes from our design partners.

Roof clip-ons:
Clip-on a one lane swimming pool or additional photo-voltaics at any time.

Frame duvet:
Available in a choice of super-tog levels (from 5 to 25 togs), use this as an envelope to your frame or as an extra layer in winter.

Frame structure:
Our **engineer** can propose different frame configurations to maximise the opportunities on your particular site.

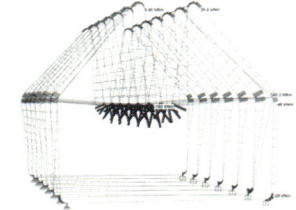

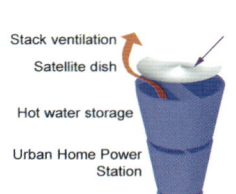

Stack ventilation
Satellite dish
Hot water storage
Urban Home Power Station
Batteries and Fuel cells
Adjustable grille
Incoming power supply management
Receivers and transmitters
Voice recognition microphone

Living Hub™:
Talk to our **energy expert** about your energy and communication requirements, in order to build-up a suitable specification for your flash-upgradable home nerve centre.

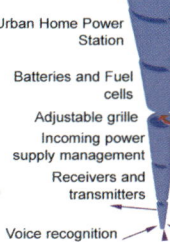

Wall, Facade and Roof cladding:
Choose from our expansive range of pre-fabricated claddings, from glazed systems and timber to titanium and more.

Pret-a-habiter:
Our ready-made cellular spaces can be highly-insulated and are available in a range of sizes from S to XL. Buy one of our pre-themed spaces or create your own. They can be used for cooking, bathing, sleeping, working, playing or just somewhere to escape.

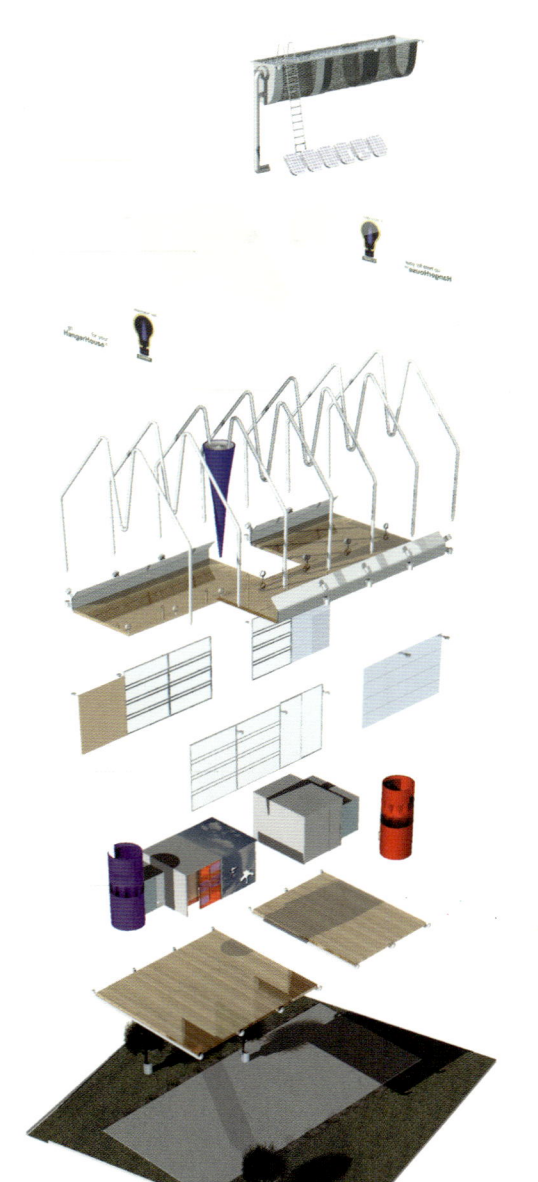

70 GLAS

Glas was formed in 1998 by Nazar Sayigh and Stas Louca. We met whilst studying in Diploma Unit 17 at the Bartlett under Niall McLaughlin and Phil Tabor. Over the last five years, we have built 26 projects and currently have 17 more on line. Each project is responsive to its unique context, both at an urban and at a material scale. We are fascinated by utilising and appropriating existing off-the-shelf systems and prefabricated technology to provide evocative, yet economic solutions.

2 Newham's Row, Bermondsey, London
Warehouse conversion and extension
Budget: £650,000
Completed: August 2001
Glas: architects

Three storeys have been added to this brick warehouse to create office space in an historic quarter of London off Bermondsey Street. Old and new cup together, the continuations and junctions between them determining several aspects of the architecture. New windows are playfully aligned with existing walls and vice-versa, resulting in a positive/negative configuration on the façades. The new upper 'interlock' is clad in copper panels that are currently reflective and contrast with the sturdy solidity of the masonry base, but over time will weather and transform.

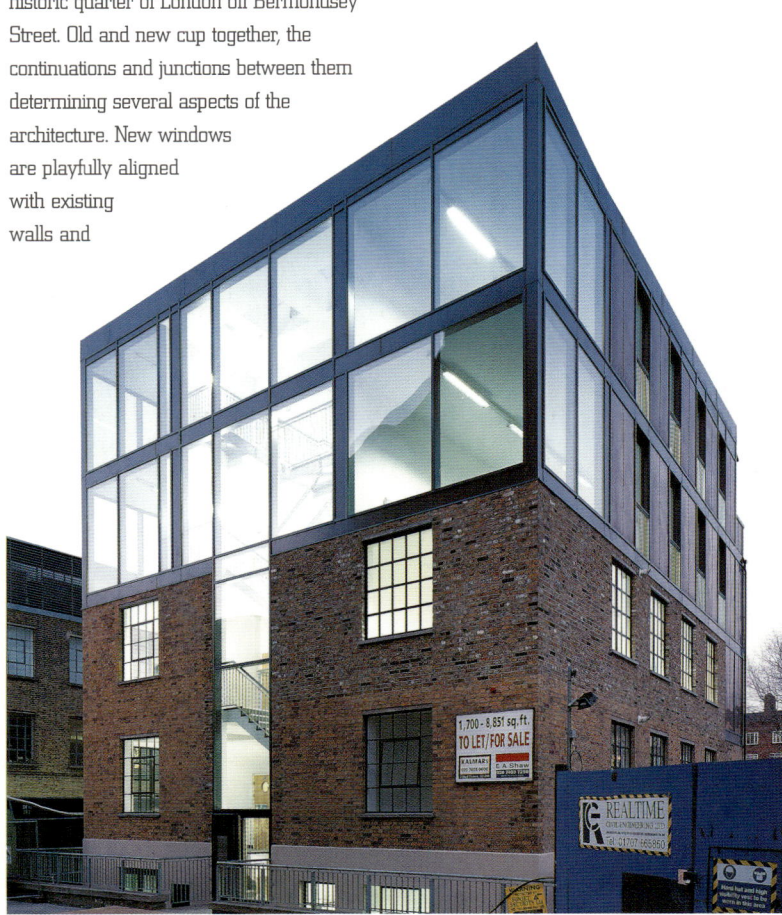

GOLLIFER LANGSTON

Gollifer Associates was formed in 1994 by Andrew Gollifer, and after Mark Langston joined as a partner became Gollifer Langston Architects in 2002. We are very focused on our clients' needs; we are keen to use each new project as a means of development, both in design and contract management. Our portfolio covers a wide range of work from small-scale domestic extensions to new buildings such as the Glass Centre in Sunderland, for which we are best known. Our current focus is on educational buildings.

City Learning Centre, South Camden Community School, Charrington Street, London
New build school extension
Budget: £1.2 million
Completed: September 2001
Mary Duggan: project architect

The new City Learning Centre sits on the end of the existing 85-metre long South Camden Community School, continuing the elevation parameters established by its host's concrete frame structure, with a cantilevering first floor clad in terrazzo-finished concrete panels. A double-height entrance lobby separates the new and existing buildings, allowing the City Learning Centre to be managed independently outside school hours. The ground floor is fully glazed, front and back, giving visibility right through to a courtyard and new dining hall (also designed by us) behind. Punched holes in the first-floor elevation create a more private environment for the resource centre and a punctuated end to the long elevation.

GRIMSHAW

Since being established in 1980 Grimshaw has built a global presence, now operating from seven offices worldwide. Our portfolio is characterised by legibility and structural integrity, and we have won over 100 awards. We believe that buildings should be understandable both spatially and organisationally, that they should reflect the activities within them, and that they should be flexible enough to respond to changing needs. Having made our name in the 1980s with a series of elegant and efficient industrial buildings for clients such as Herman Miller and Vitra, the practice has now established itself in other sectors such as transport, offices, education and the arts. Our most notable successes have been the International Terminal at Waterloo Station (1993) and The Eden Project (2001).

Education Resource Centre – The Eden Project Phase Four, St. Austell, Cornwall
New build education facility
Budget: £15 million
Completion: 2004
Jerry Tate: project architect

The Eden Project Education Resource Centre will house permanent and temporary exhibitions, multimedia facilities and web links and a café, and will host talks, lectures and interactive workshops. There are two major elements to the building, the roof and the ground. The timber roof is a spiral grid-shell structure, derived from the Fibonacci sequence of numbers. Fibonacci was a twelfth century mathematician who discovered a spiral pattern numerical sequence upon which many growth structures are based, evident in organic objects such as pine cones, cauliflowers and sunflowers. The roof is clad in a number of 'cellular' pyramid structures that collect energy from solar panels and incorporate opening ventilation louvres and glazed panels, producing a dappled daylight effect inside. Below the timber roof three floorplates with earth walls and floors at different levels accommodate the existing site levels.

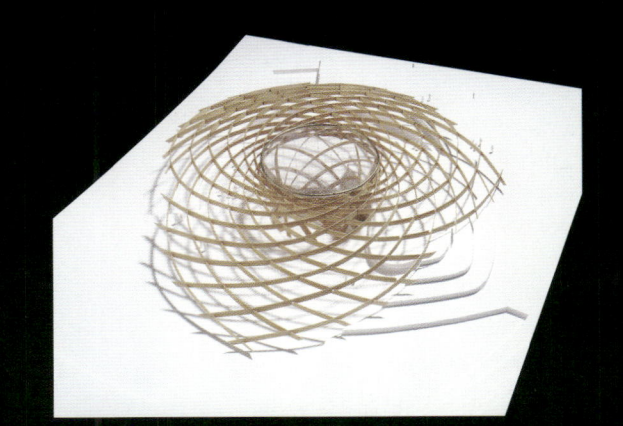

GRIMSHAW

CHRIS GROOTHUIZEN

Battersea Power Station
Multi-use redevelopment
Contract value: £225 million
Completion: 2007
Simon Beames: project architect

Battersea Power Station was built in three phases beginning in 1933, gaining its familiar silhouette of four chimneys in 1953. After powering the capital with electricity for 50 years, it ceased operations in 1982. Grimshaw is designing the redeveloped Power Station, as well as a new riverboat jetty and an 'airbridge' linking the site to a new railway station. Our plans highlight the building's architectural virtuosity, respecting and enhancing its Grade II listed status while making it suitable for new use. These plans include the restoration of the principal listed area, Turbine Hall A, to its full Art Deco glory, as a showcase for quality retailers and restaurateurs. The most sumptuous area, the Control Room, will be transformed into an elegant dining space with rooftop views over Kensington and Chelsea.

At rooftop level there will also be bars, an open-air cinema, and a hotel, offering views out over the Thames and down through the partially transparent roof (designed with the aid of non-linear mathematics) to the vast expanse of the Boiler House.

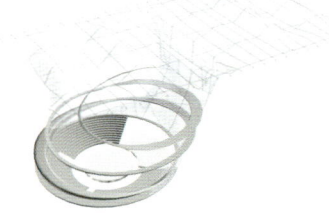

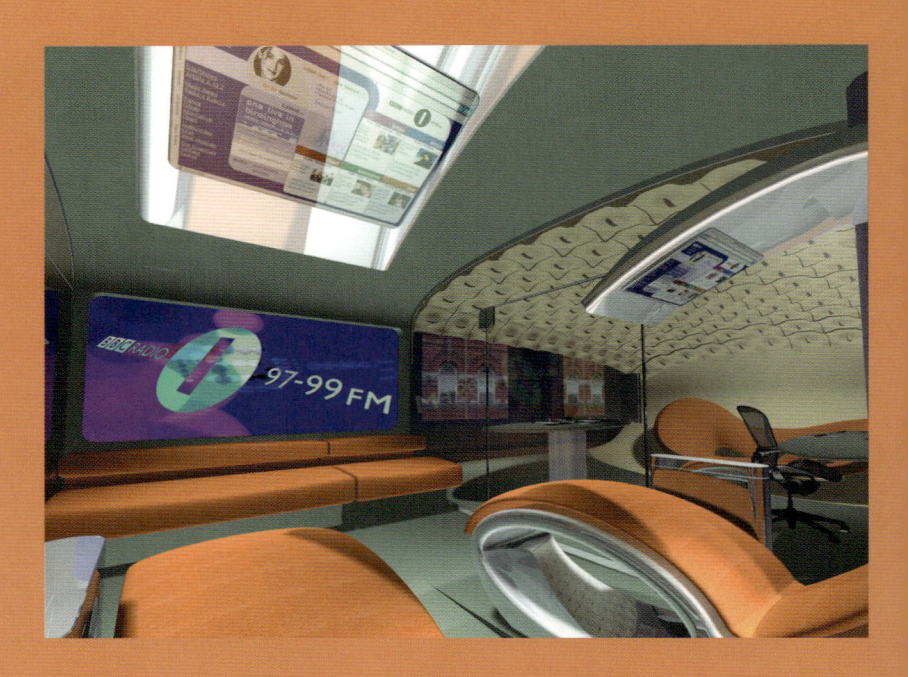

Studying Diploma under the tutelage of Neil Spiller and Phil Watson, I was given the freedom to redefine, for myself, the boundaries of what an architectural education could offer. I became interested in architectures that reflect upon the potential interaction between emergent synthetic 'life' and organic life, and on how virtual ecologies could enmesh themselves within 'torn' biological systems. I endeavour to bring these same interests and thought processes to play in my own practice and when teaching at the Bartlett. My practice is multidisciplinary, with outcomes equally likely to be in the form of animation, film, sculpture, lighting, product and furniture design and, increasingly, built architecture.

BBC Radio 1 Broadcast Studios, Central London
Digital studio design forum
Completion: Feb 2004
Christian Groothuizen: design consultant

Half constructed reality and half technologically driven think-tank, the BBC Studio Project is an ongoing forum where concepts and ideas on studio and recording architectures are discussed and tested to ensure that built studio design keeps pace with modern digital studio technologies. The forum group consists of BBC radio's brightest and most experienced technologists, operations managers and technicians, and includes myself in a design role. The image above expresses new concepts in studio design, utilising modern composite materials and digital interface technologies, and recent experimental methods of absorbing and isolating sound.

GUSTAFSON PORTER

Kathryn Gustafson is an internationally renowned landscape designer who has worked for 15 years in Paris, and also has a practice in the United States. She frequently works with architects, such as Ian Ritchie and Norman Foster, and set up Gustafson Porter with architect Neil Porter to work on multi-disciplinary projects. In my own diploma work at the Bartlett I was interested in the relationships between landscape and architectural design, an interest which I have continued to develop working on projects such as this.

Peter Culley

Great Glass House Internal Landscape, National Botanic Garden of Wales, Carmarthen
Landscape design
Budget: £1.8 million
Completed: 2000
Peter Culley: project architect

For the interior landscape of Foster and Partners' new National Botanic Garden of Wales Great Glass House, Kathryn Gustafson designed a ravine, gradually cutting down by six metres below the perimeter level, establishing a series of horizons, outcrops, shear walls and terraces. She designed the form with a clay model, from which we poured a plaster duplicate in London. The model was a key presentation *and* design tool. We made a 3-D triangular surface scan of it and imported it into Form-Z to tweak pathways, ramp gradients and watercourses, and to form an x,y,z setting-out schedule for stone and metal work, but the built scheme is almost exactly true to the model.

Looking to the landscape of the Mediterranean, historic stone cultures and processes of natural erosion informed the treatment of vertical surfaces, and inspired the basic use of steel, mesh and timber for handrails, bridges and boardwalks. Stone walls with a variety of textures and reliefs are like cuts in a quarry, where man-made forms intervene in nature. A watercourse leads visitors to the lowest level where on one side a vertical sheet of water falls into a stone-lined pool, with a weeping 'seepage' wall covered in mosses and lichens on the other. A distinct and very separate sense of place is achieved with bleached stone finishes replicating the glare of the Mediterranean sunlight in the lush green countryside of South Wales.

74 CHRISTINE HAWLEY

I joined the Bartlett in 1993 as the Director of the Architecture School and at a moment in its history which enthusiastically embraced change. This was a period of growth, experimentation and perhaps some danger. I felt that I was in the right place at the right time surrounded by enormous optimism and talent. Ten years later and now Dean I still feel much the same although my overview is much broader: the Bartlett is an enormous repository of imagination, enquiry, creativity and sheer energy. I think that it is inevitable that if you exist in such a world, your own work will benefit.

Centro Congressi Italia, Rome, Italy
Competition entry (shortlisted from 700 entries)
1999
Christine Hawley: architect
Abigail Ashton, Andrew Porter: designers

This project is a competition entry for an international congress centre in the EUR district of Rome, able to accomodate up to 10,000 people in one single event, with conference facilities, theatres, exhibition halls, shopping centres and public spaces. It is essential that a building of this scale is both clearly legible to the public as a landmark, and relates seamlessly to the urban fabric. The building's identity is established by its deliberately simple surface, broken only by significant points of public entry and by indicators of the events taking place inside. At lower levels the skin is clear, allowing those outside to identify the sculptural forms and major spaces of the interior.

Internally the centre is organised in four distinct layers, with access, exhibition, conference and infrastructure spaces clearly articulated to enable visitors to comprehend the space. Public piazzas within the building are distinctly 21st century spaces, but echo and continue the orthogonal geometry of urban open spaces in the surrounding city, integrating the hall into its context.

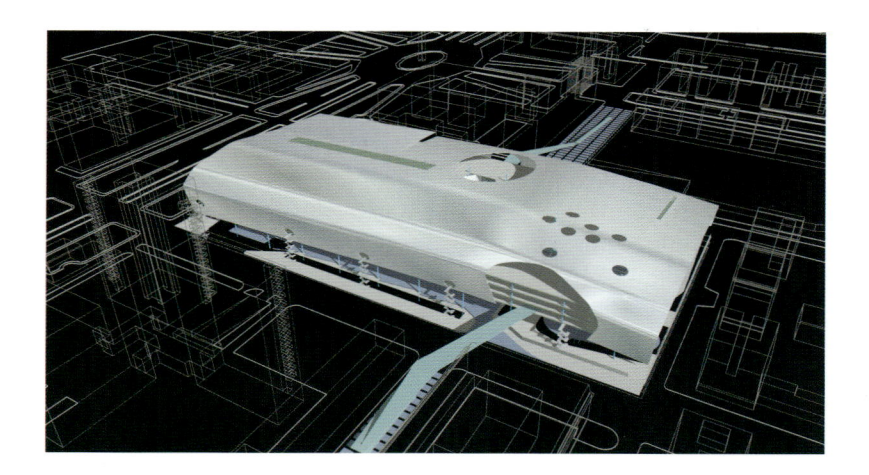

Gifu

New build social housing

Completed: 1999

Christine Hawley: architect

Abigail Ashton, Andrew Porter: designers

Patrick Weber, Eduardo de Oliveira Rosa: model making

Gifu social housing was the result of a collaborative invitation from Arata Isozaki Associates and the Gifu Prefectural Government in Japan. The four architects involved were all female – two from Japan, one from the USA and myself from the UK. The project was initiated to develop a critique of social housing in Japan, and to provide alternatives to universal templates that had remained unchanged since 1945.

The apartments are predominantly arranged as duplexes with some triplexes and single-storey flats. The character of social housing in Japan is characterised by bland neutrality; it is both relentless and anonymous. The building challenges this model by manipulating a series of double-floor volumes to create both sculptural eccentricity and a façade that should be read as a painter's canvas. The living areas are open plan, many with double-height spaces, offering clear views to the landscape and a greater sense of space.

Canteen, Städel Academy, Frankfurt am Main, Germany (by Cook & Hawley) ▲
New build café
Completed: 1991
Peter Cook and Christine Hawley: architects

This new canteen is located within the courtyard of the existing 19th century Städel Academy, and its glass skin is a direct contrast to the heavy stone materiality of its surroundings. Existing stone columns were used for basic structural support, superimposed with a roof constructed from a set of arched steel beams whose bottom members are post-tensioned with steel cables. Two-thirds of the roof canopy is openable along its entire length when activated by hydraulic rams, allowing rapid cooling and creating a space that is substantially open to the air in summer.

Lützoplatz Social Housing, Berlin, Germany (by Cook & Hawley) ▲
New build housing
Completed: 1989
Peter Cook and Christine Hawley: architects

This apartment block containing 13 flats was developed as part of a publicly funded programme. Facing the park of Lützoplatz the more public western façade uses the Berlin tradition of the glazed winter garden to extend the living area of the apartments. Several of the larger flats have double-height living spaces that extend into the winter gardens, bringing additional light into the depth of the block and amplifying the panoramic view across the city.

North Osaka Station Development, Japan (with Andrew Porter) ▶
Competition entry
2003
Christine Hawley, Andrew Porter: architects/designers
Tom Holberton: assistant

Our proposal for a cultural centre in Osaka includes a theatre, exhibition spaces, cinemas, restaurants and a retail boulevard, raised on a plinth, so that visitors can enjoy a safe pedestrianised environment, and leaving the ground for service access, plant and car parking. Rather than adopting a traditional street and block structure the design is organised as a series of activity nodes in a quasi-natural landscape, free from the surrounding relentlessly linear organisation. Activities are not stacked vertically, but are laid out in a relaxed composition that is perceived as a permeable cultural and physical landscape. Movement around the site is assisted by pedestrian travelators.

CHRISTINE HAWLEY

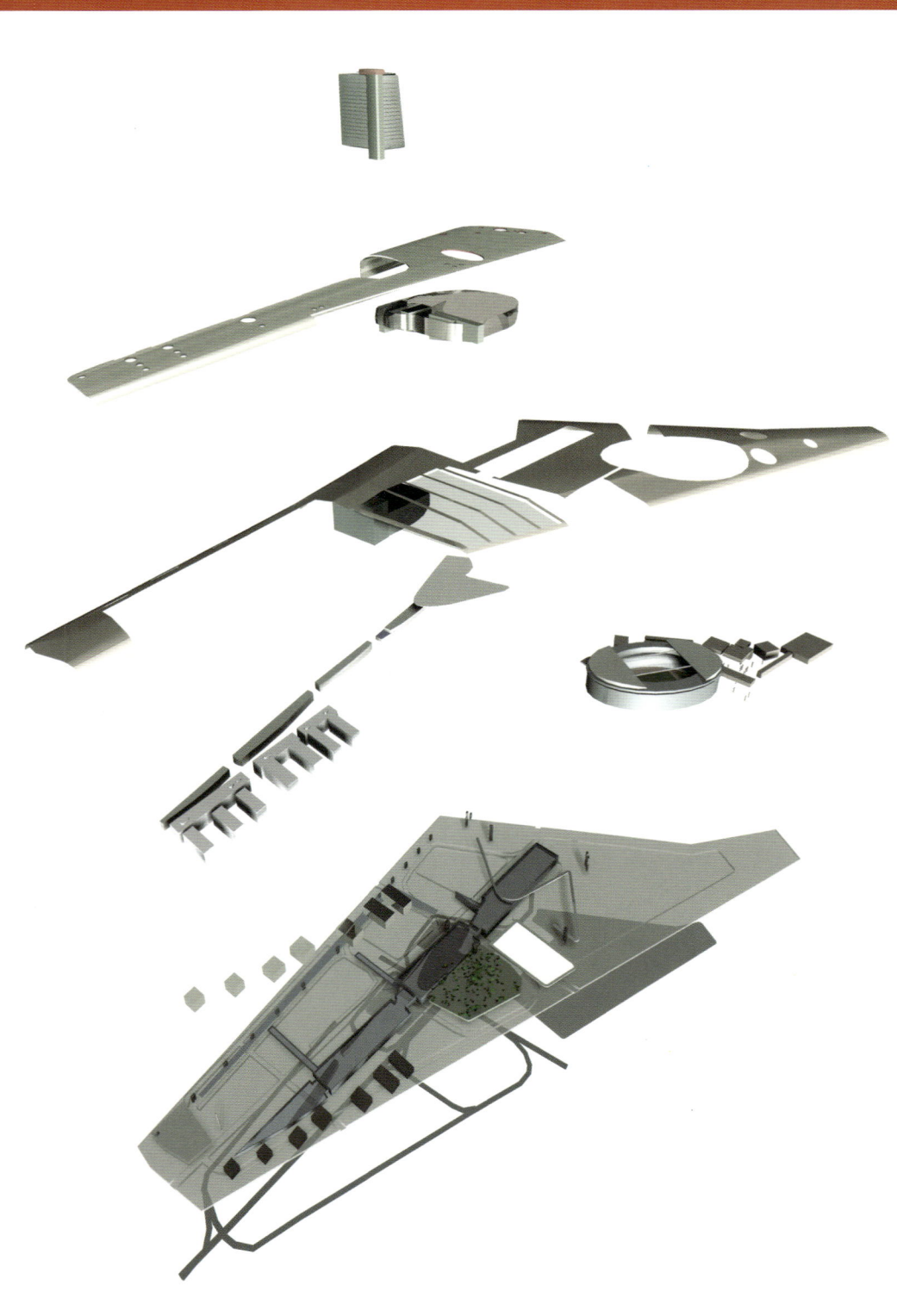

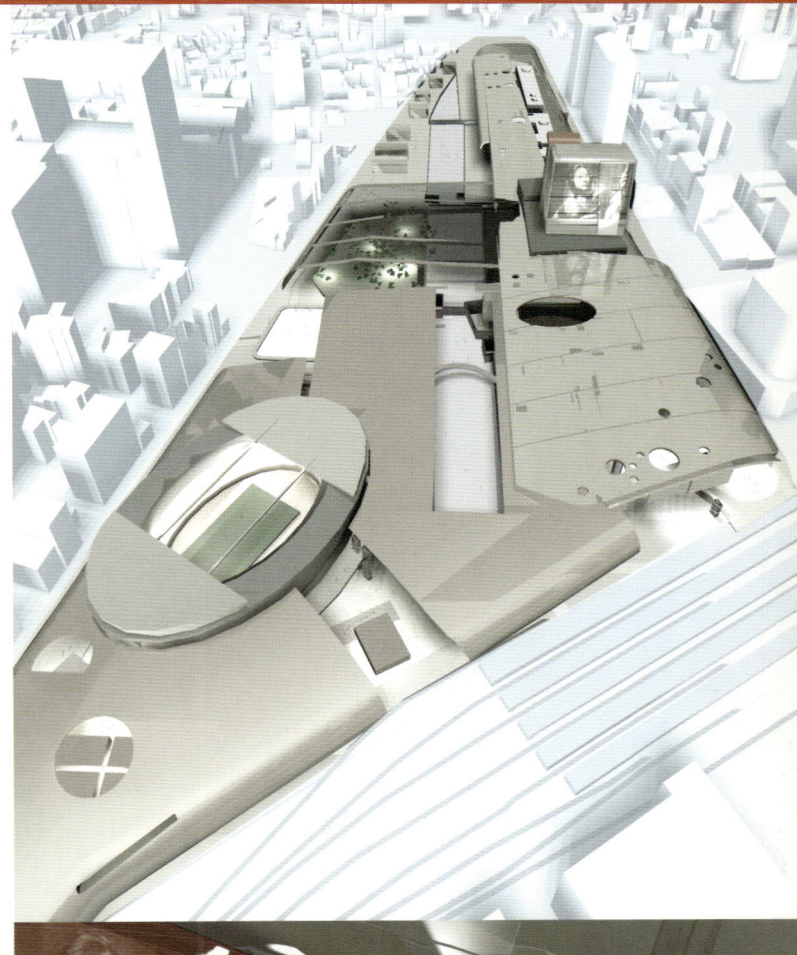

78 WAYNE HEAD

My childhood paralleled Thatcher's rise, and the decline of the precious Welfare State. My mother encouraged me to be a drug-taking rock star, but Grandad, a sailor with a twinkle in his eye, gave me a hankering for romance and broader horizons. So I became an architect. I went through the Bartlett in Unit 10. My tutors claimed they were famous. And so I graduated, heavily in debt, eager to clog my trainers with concrete and, I was told, with all kinds of transferable skills that the coming years would reveal to be of inestimable value. Now, I'm grateful I'm not a child of the Blair years, about to enter a glamorous school of architecture after 2006. Grandad would have to go back to sea to pay for the inflated fees...

'Moving Home!' Inderoy, Norway
Relocating a house
Budget: £40,000 including purchase of original house and new plot, transportation and refurbishment costs so far
Completed: January 2003
Wayne S Head: architectural consultant

This timber-frame house was built in Norway in 1917, mainly from reclaimed materials. It was later purchased by the local Kommune (council), which had no interest in the building and only wanted the land. They said they would be willing to sell the house, without the land, for £3,000, so the idea emerged of re-locating it. Two engineering companies proposed different methods to transport the house – one wanted to construct a platform underneath and then to lift the platform, the second, Verdalskrana Als, to use two steel 'H' carriers in place of the platform, which looked less safe but was half the price. Verdalskrana Als was duly awarded the contract.

The house had to be prepared for the move. To avoid anything collapsing the spaces between floors and ceilings were secured with beams and engineering jacks. The chimney and balcony, both in bad shape, were removed to make space for the carrier beams. And a few trees had to be removed locally and the soil on site strengthened to withstand heavy-duty machinery.

The team at Verdalskrana Als assured us that they could move the house without spilling a drop of water from a glass placed inside. We didn't put this to the test, but our fears of ending up with a large pile of firewood were unfounded. On the day of the move two cranes lifted the house onto a multi-wheeled remote-controlled vehicle, which was then hooked onto a seemingly ordinary truck, and towed in a sedate zigzag fashion ten miles to the new location.

LOUIS HELLMAN

80 LOUIS HELLMAN

IN 1961 HELLMAN DOES GRAND TOUR... BUMMING AROUND FRANCE AND ITALY DISCOVERING ARCHITECTURE EXISTS OUTSIDE OF BANNISTER-F AND BANHAM

1962 HELLMAN QUALIFIES !... ...BY MARRYING FELLOW STUDENT... SOON THERE ARE TWO LITTLE HELLMANS...

HAVING BEEN MISLEAD (BY HIMSELF) THAT ARCHITECTURE CAN BE RATIONALISED SCIENTIFICALLY, HELLMAN JOINS WELL KNOWN FUNCTIONALIST FIRM —

"ALL YOU HAF TO DO ISS APPLY ZER FORMULA!"

1963 CAME THE CULTURAL REVOLUTION — QUESTIONING THE VALUES OF THE TECHNOLOGICAL SOCIETY... A NEW ROMANTICISM AND INDIVIDUALISM...

1965 HELLMAN'S ENLIGHTENMENT/ DISILLUSIONMENT — MOD ARCHITECTURE IS MERELY A STYLE... AND IT'S USUALLY UGLY (GASP!)

1967 AS A RESULT FIRST SATIRICAL CARTOONS IN ARCHITECTS' JOURNAL...

HELLMAN NOW ABLE TO INDULGE IN HIS MANIC OBSESSION — CUTTING UP MAGAZINES AND NEWSPAPERS AND BUILDING SECRET FILES — AND GET PAID FOR IT!

1972, NOW WORKING FOR THE GLC, OUR HERO TAKES ON THE WHOLE BUREAUCRACY OVER MACE (ROCK BOTTOM SYSTEM BUILDING FOR SCHOOLS), AND WINS!

1974 MAKES ANIMATED CARTOON FILM FOR BBC TV
JOINS SPASTICS SOCIETY TO DESIGN BUILDINGS FOR DISABLED PEOPLE —

1975 "A IS FOR ARCHITECT — The Best of Hellman" PUBLISHED
1979 EXHIBITION AT THE ARCHITECTURAL ASSOCIATION

1980 FINALLY MAKES IT — EMBARKS ON PRIVATE PRACTICE...

DEEP END

JONATHAN HILL

After completing my Diploma at the Architectural Association and qualifying as an architect I undertook the Architectural History MSc at the Bartlett, where I've taught design and history and theory for over ten years. In 2000 I completed a PhD by Architectural Design, the first person to do so in the UK, and now run this programme at the Bartlett, one of very few such doctoral programmes in the world. Architects tend to talk, write and draw a lot as well as build. If everyone reading this text listed all the architectural works that influence them, some would be drawings, some would be texts, and others would be buildings either visited or described in drawings and texts. Studying the history of architecture, it is evident that researching, testing and questioning the limits of architecture occurs through drawing and writing as well as building. My research touches in particular on one of the most potent of architectural traditions: the authored book that is both critical and propositional.

To acquire social status and financial security architects need a defined area of knowledge with precise contents and limits in which they can prove expertise. Therefore, the architectural profession furthers the idea that only architects make buildings and spaces that deserve the title architecture. Architects are caught in a vicious circle; in order to defend their idea of architecture they often adopt practices, forms and materials already identified with the work of architects, and learn little from other disciplines.

In stating that architecture is far more than the work of architects, my aim is not to deny the importance of architects in the production of architecture but to see their role in more balanced terms and to acknowledge other architectural producers, especially the user. In 'The Death of the Author' Roland Barthes questions the authority of the author, and recognises that the journey from author to text to reader is never seamless or direct. He states that reading can be a creative activity that constructs a text anew, and argues for a writer aware of the creativity of the reader. 'The Death of the Author' suggests a new writer as much as a new reader, both having a role in the creation of a text. Barthes' text does not refer to art and architecture. It is, however, an important influence on artistic production, encouraging less didactic subject-object and artist-viewer relations than ones familiar in the gallery. The relevance of 'The Death of the Author' to architecture is equally strong but largely unnoticed. My work questions the authority of the (professional) architect and argues for another architect aware of the creativity of the user.

My principal means to disseminate and develop these ideas are books, such as *The Illegal Architect, Occupying Architecture, Architecture—the Subject is Matter* and *Actions of Architecture*; and exhibitions, for example at the Haus der Architektur in Graz and the Architektur-Galerie am Weissenhof in Stuttgart. Two projects, 'The Institute of Illegal Architects' and 'Weather Architecture', feature in both the books and the exhibitions. Each begins with a critique of an architectural idea and an architectural institution in which the idea is manifest, and leads to a counter proposition.

Sited directly in front of the headquarters of the Royal Institute of British Architects, 'The Institute of Illegal Architects' challenges the idea that architects alone make architecture. Questioning the binary opposition of architect and user, it proposes a third entity: the illegal architect, a hybrid producer-user, who questions and subverts the established codes and conventions of architectural practice and acknowledges that architecture is made by use and by design.

To imply that they can predict use, architects promote models of experience that suggest a passive user. One of the most prevalent of such models, the contemplation of the artwork, is exemplified in the history of the Barcelona Pavilion. Designed by Mies van der Rohe, the Pavilion is an architectural icon, not only because it is seductive and much copied, but also because it has most often been perceived in conditions similar to that of the artwork. Between 1929 and 1930 it was an exhibition building, between 1930 and 1986 it was known only through photographs, and since 1986 the reconstruction's status as an historical monument discourages everyday use. Questioning this status, 'Weather Architecture' inserts Berlin weather from 1929-30 into the 1986 Pavilion. Made of frost, fog, snow and ice, 'Weather Architecture' proposes a reassessment of architectural matter that undermines the status of the Pavilion as an object of contemplation and focuses, instead, on its potential for user appropriation.

(See Roland Barthes, 'The Death of the Author', in Roland Barthes, *Image-Music-Text*, trans. Stephen Heath [London: Flamingo, 1977] pp142-148).

Jonathan Hill
'Weather Architecture', 1999
(Berlin 3.29pm 20 January 1930 – Barcelona 3.29pm 20 January 2000)

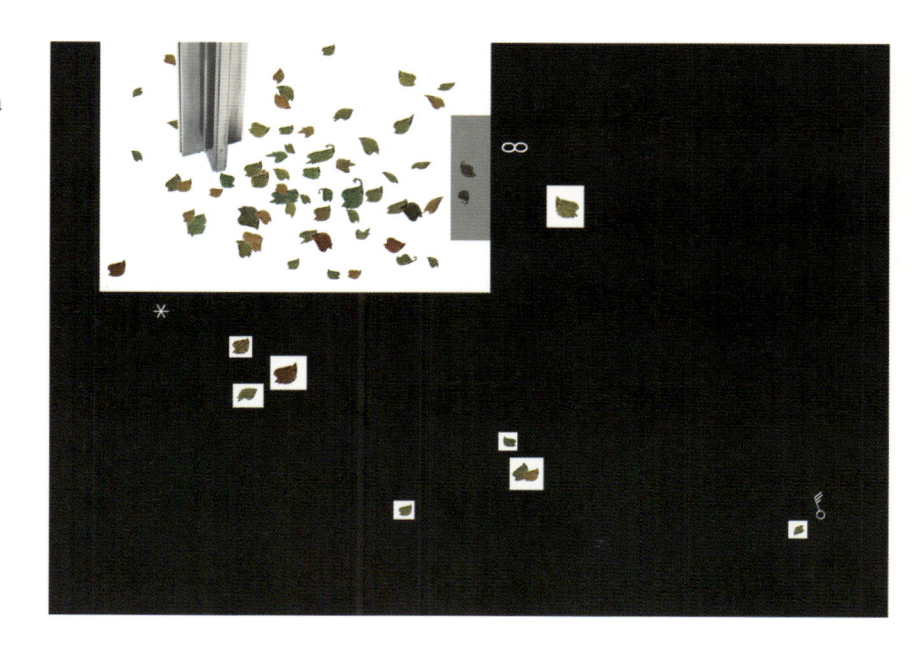

82 JONATHAN HILL

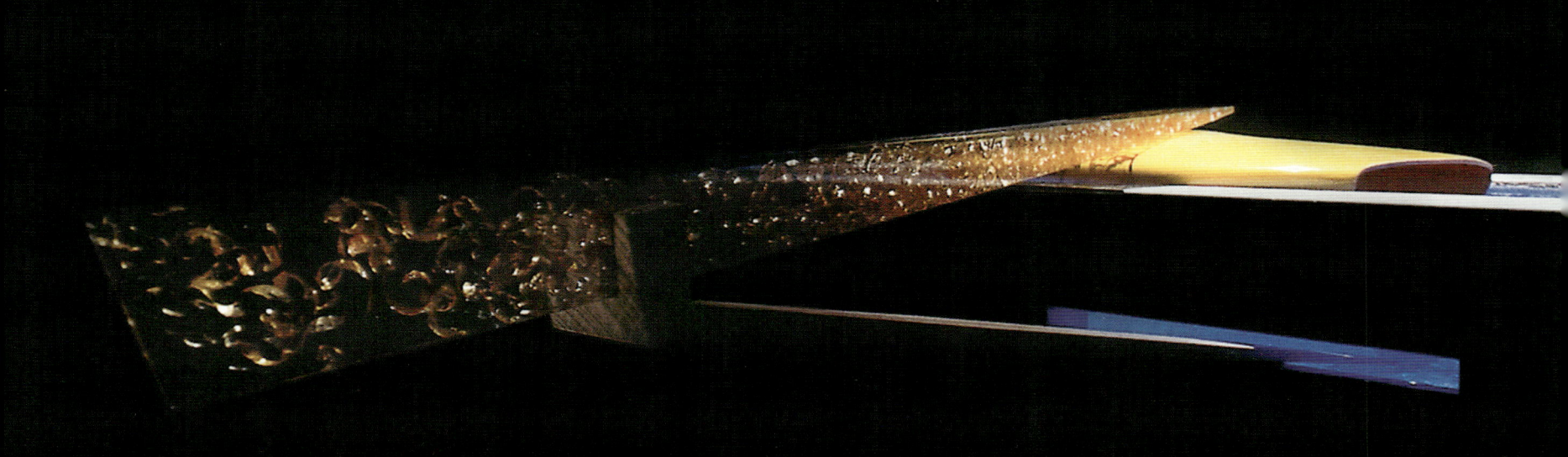

Jonathan Hill
'The Institute of Illegal Architects', 1996

WILLIAM HODGSON ARCHITECTS   83

William Hodgson Architects was formed in 2000 and Elm House is our first real project.

Reflecting on how the Bartlett has affected my work, it is clear that I was encouraged to have a particular attitude towards problem solving. Former institutions had taught me to draw or understand construction, or kindled interests in the work of particular designers, but had rarely made me see the need for a clear set of principles as the underlying rule of good architecture. Today this is set against the obvious constraints of the kind of low-budget projects generally available to sole practitioners in the first few years of architectural practice, but faced with discussions of style, it is always great to respond with challenging questions of principle.

William Hodgson

Elm House, Broadheath near Worcester (with Louise Smith Design)
Rebuilding private house
Budget: spiralling out of hand
Completed: November 2002
William Hodgson: architect – design concept to contract cleaner

Anne and Melvin Smith bought Elm House for its excellent location in the Worcestershire countryside with views to the Malvern Hills, though the house itself was ugly and too small for their needs. We removed most of the existing internal walls to allow for a series of interventions: glass staircase, sliding bookcase, timber garage, shading device, glazed link, canalised pool, fireplace and chimney. New internal and external spaces are organised around these interventions. We had planned more, but the decidedly parochial local planning authority outlawed any scheme 'out of scale with the original dwelling', preventing any large-scale extension or fundamental remodelling. Melvin Smith carried out most of the works himself. He rarely looked at the drawings and liked to improve things where he saw fit!

84 ANDREW HOLMES

The River of Stars, Great West Road and Furnivall Gardens, Hammersmith, London
Urban design
Budget: within annual borough financial allocation
Completion: as long as it takes
Andrew Holmes: designer

The Architecture Foundation asked a group of designers to make proposals for a number of critical sites identified by the Borough of Hammersmith. Furnival Gardens and the Thames are cut off from the rest of Hammersmith by the Great West Road, and are only accessible from King Street via three forbidding pedestrian underpasses. I propose to replace the underpasses with pedestrian crossings, and to create visual links by extending the planting of the Gardens into King Street. The Gardens will be illuminated in the evening and at night to create a riverside walk.

The aim of the design is to reveal the sources of Hammersmith's prosperity in the past (industry relying on ships and water) and the present (computers and satellites). The presence of the Thames is conveyed by planted waves of white trees that blossom in spring, and flowers. Satellites are expressed as a constellation of white lights in the branches of the trees.

Work has started on the landscaping of the Gardens whilst discussions continue with the government about the Great West Road.

I am interested in the art of architecture, and teach students who wish to be designers to convey their intentions and know something of the ways in which their ideas can be constructed, revelling in the nitty-gritty of that process. I studied at the Architectural Association and have worked as an artist, architect and designer for 30 years. I taught at the AA for 15 years and have been teaching at the Bartlett for two.

I don't differentiate between these activities.

'Asphalt Paradise', Laurent Delaye Gallery, London
Art exhibition
Exhibition: 1999
Andrew Holmes: artist

'Gas Tank City' is a project of 100 drawings started in 1972. Each colour pencil drawing is the same size, 510x790 millimetres, mounted in a square moulded plastic frame maintaining the proportions of a 35-millimetre slide mount. 20 of these drawings formed the exhibition 'Asphalt Paradise' with a video installation 'The Golden Hour'.

The work reflects a vernacular city that is loosely structured, fluid and expansive. The commercial street, bordered by transit sheds, supermarkets, fast-food outlets and used-car lots is itself an elongated transit space, devoted to a steady flow of traffic composed of mobile enterprises, delivering, collecting, hauling and distributing, and controlled by traffic lights. As architecture it cannot be encompassed by plan or rendering. Only through glimpses of temporary fragments can it be represented. The process of drawing invests photo-like fragments with the sense of their sublime, ungraspable whole, through subtle decisions on emphasis, contrast and simplification.

86 HOPKINS ARCHITECTS

At Hopkins Architects we aim to design cost-effective, agile and beautiful buildings that enable clients to maximise the potential of their site, programme and budget. During more than 25 years of practice, we have completed a varied and memorable range of built projects, made possible by our teams of talented and enthusiastic individuals.

We have developed a good relationship with the Bartlett and have recruited many Part One, Two and Three students, who have often chosen to stay with our office for long periods of time. In common with the practice, they share a desire to achieve design excellence through rigorous process, sensitive use of materials and an efficient yet poetic aesthetic.

The following projects showcase some graduates' work and illustrate how the innovation and creativity fostered within them at the Bartlett has matured and developed to result in valuable contributions to the final designs.

The Evelina Children's Hospital, Lambeth Palace Road, London
New build hospital
Budget £41.8 million
Completion: May 2004
Simon Goode: architect

The Evelina Children's Hospital is situated at the southern end of the St. Thomas' Hospital complex, adjacent to Lambeth Palace Road and opposite the Houses of Parliament. The radical design moves away from traditional hospital blueprints, often based on Victorian principles, and turns for inspiration instead to other building types, such as offices and student halls of residence, to provide a positive environment to assist with the healing process and minimise the recovery period.

Standard components, rather than bespoke systems, have been used in an innovative manner throughout the building to achieve an overall high level of design within an extremely constrained budget. The built evidence so far suggests that the Trust will be getting a building that will meet its objectives and, hopefully, one that will substantially raise the expectations of patients, staff and Government as to what can be achieved.

New refectory and library extension, Norwich Cathedral
Additions to historic buildings
Budget: £3.15 million
Completion: December 2003
Sophy Twohig: job architect
Emma Frater: architectural assistant

This project, won through an invited competition in 1996, involves both renovation of the existing fabric and a new-build refectory and reading room within the mediaeval cloister walls of Norwich Cathedral. The roof of the new refectory is supported by nine pairs of laminated English oak columns, each with four laminated props connecting up to the soffit via stainless steel bosses. The columns are set away from the mediaeval walls and rise through the double-height space. A timber box sits between them, containing toilet and kitchen facilities on the ground floor and forming a 'platform' for the refectory itself on the first floor.

88 HOPKINS ARCHITECTS

Wildscreen at Bristol, the Harbourside, Bristol
New leisure and education building
Budget: £3.15 million
Completed: 2000
Tom Holdom: project architect

With their diverse and experimental construction techniques, the Wildscreen World Botanical House and Entrance Foyer areas, for which I was responsible, gave me a good introduction to making buildings. We had constructed a working model with a rigid steel beam structure, but the use of lightweight and flexible ETFE pillows prompted the evolution of a flexible cable-net roof. Fresh from a design session with Michael, I sat down with Mike Cook of Buro Happold. Armed with a pair of Marks and Spencer's ladies' stockings and a box of pins we began dismantling the model, and in about an hour a new design was taking form; having removed the steel ribs, we laid the stockings over the roof, made a couple of holes through which masts were placed, and then with a needle and thread started weaving in cables and tying points along a potential ridge, which was then pulled up to the top of the mast.

Detailed development was a close collaboration between architect, engineer and Ben Morris at Vector, which won the contract to build the roof.

Tom Holdom

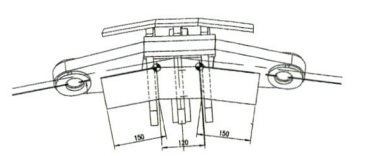

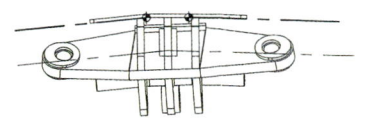

Wellcome Trust Headquarters, 215 Euston Road, London
New build offices
Completion: Spring 2004
Tom Holdom: project director

Located a stone's throw from the Bartlett, the new Headquarters building for the Wellcome Trust consists of a ten-storey block in Euston Road and a six-storey block in Gower Place, separated by an internal street under a sweeping roof.

The design process has largely been one of reduction. Through a process of constant simplification, building components have been evolved into a system of elegant functional simplicity. The steel frame, braced by muscular steel plates that cut in like bookends to the twelve-metre façade bays, remains visible through the glazed elevations, responding to the client's brief that the building should present an open façade to its surroundings, whilst still having a sense of solidity and permanence. A ventilated cavity between the two enveloping glazed skins acts as a buffer zone between the internal and external environments, and allows for a fully glazed façade without the traditional problems of excessive heat transfer. The three-metre wide by four-metre high glazing panels reflect the size of the cellular office units behind. With no external capping pieces or any mechanical fixings, the envelope is held in place with structural silicone, pushing the boundaries of the use of glue in building in the UK.

90 HÛT ARCHITECTURE

Scott Batty formed hût architecture in 2000. Andrew Whiting joined as a partner in 2003. We work today to the same principles of rigorous testing of our propositions that we both encountered at the Bartlett, and in the work we've done since – Scott's five years in the office of Simon Allford and Paul Monaghan (which together with two years spent in their Diploma Unit felt like a seven-year Bartlett education!), and Andrew's UCL Research Scholarship with Pringle Brandon. As a practice we always try to test our ideas, through drawings and models, and by fabricating full-size prototypes. A feedback loop is integral to this design approach.

Scott Batty and Andrew Whiting

British Council E3 Electronic Entertainment Expo Pavilion, Los Angeles, USA (designed with graphic designers Studio Myerscough) ▲ ◄
Demountable exhibition stand
Budget: £325,000
Completed: May 2003
hût architecture: designers

This 225-square metre pavilion served as a focal point for representatives of the best British software and computer games designers at the E3 Electronic Entertainment Expo in Los Angeles in May 2003. The demountable walls, floor and ceiling are constructed from twin-wall polycarbonate sheet and are internally lit. Spaces, ranging from formal meeting rooms to a casual plug-in café, provide a number of different types of environment for users to meet and conduct business. Double-skin curved plywood gaming pods feature seating ergonomically designed for virtual gameplay.

The pavilion was made in Oregon and then crated and transported for reassembly in LA. It has now been demounted and stored for future use.

30D Kitchen Extension, Clerkenwell, London ▶
Domestic rooftop kitchen extension
Budget: £70,000
Completion: August 2003
hût architecture: designers

The client's brief was for a 'log cabin' on her Clerkenwell roof. We designed a flexible new space for her to cook and relax up amongst the busy roofscape, featuring a retractable roof to allow views out, and sunlight in. The cabin was designed as a prefabricated flat-pack timber 'kit of parts', limiting on-site work to extending the existing stairwell and installing the structure in its new rooftop location. Variants of the modular design could be produced for other sites. The project has a strong emphasis on sustainability, with solar panels, wood-burning stove and thermal insulation made from sheep's wool.

IMAGINATION

Imagination is a design and communications company with offices in London, New York and Hong Kong. Our work calls upon almost every design discipline, from architecture and lighting to multi-media, and includes projects for, amongst others, Tate Modern, Guinness, Ford and the Millennium Dome. Specialising in permanent installations, as well as events and exhibitions, we couple environmental design with the techniques of theatre and live performance to create truly memorable experiences.

Orange Imaginarium, At-Bristol Science Centre
Interactive exhibition
Budget: approximately £200,000
Completed: August 2002
Paulo Pimentel: 3D designer

The At-Bristol Science Centre is a new space for young people to learn about technology. The Orange Imaginarium, developed in collaboration with a team of researchers and futurologists from sponsor Orange, is an interactive learning environment aimed at 4-16 year olds that explains wirefree technology from a child's point of view. The experience begins with a series of animated stories linking everyday needs and technology. Three more learning areas follow a pattern of 'search and find', letting visitors experience and be creative with technology. Wildfire voice recognition and activation technology recognises a child's voice and tells a joke at their request; visitors move through clusters of fibre optics, turning them from white to orange in a representation of how technology can personalise your space; and directional speakers controlled by voice-recognition technology throw back voices at different pitches.

'Predators', The Natural History Museum, London
Travelling exhibition
Budget: approximately £360,000
Completed: June 2001
Paulo Pimentel: lead designer

With The Natural History Museum's in-house researchers, we developed an overall creative strategy for the 'Predators' exhibition, including the theme, storyline, environment, graphics, identity and lighting; and concepts for an integrated marketing campaign. 'Predators' is an exploration of attack and defence in the natural world. Rather than trying to reproduce realistic environments, abstract imagery creates a sinister world where visitors learn what 'survival of the fittest' really means. Visitors can try on the ear of a bat-eared fox to discover how a keen sense of hearing can improve their chances of finding prey, test their predatory skills by operating the eyes and long sticky tongue of a four-metre robotic chameleon, and play a high-speed interactive game where they either survive or become extinct. The 500-metre long modular exhibition has been designed to tour internationally for up to four years.

92 DARYL JACKSON ARCHITECTS

Jackson Architects work in many locations, both within Australia and internationally. Each project is produced in an office in the city where it is to be built, to respond to regional and cultural differences. I involve myself directly in the design of each project, but rely upon the talents and energy of my regional partners and design teams. I see my role as like a film director, working on the plot, lining up the cameras, editing and producing. As in filmmaking a host of talents are brought together, and my job is to keep the plot intact.

I believe that both theory and practice are critical to designers; I enjoy collaboration and continue to learn as well as lead, exploring further ideas about architecture. Exchanges with Bartlett students and staff continue to fuel my enthusiasm.

Daryl Jackson

CSIRO Discovery Centre, Canberra, Australia (with Daryl Jackson Alastair Swayn)
Scientific research and information centre
Budget: Australian $16.8 million
Completed: 1998
Daryl Jackson: principal designer

The CSIRO Discovery Centre comprises research laboratories, a conference centre, retail areas, exhibition hall, bank, café and science education centre. The centrally located atrium is a focus for public activities and gives the building an introspective configuration. This naturally ventilated winter garden space looks up to the sky, and has views from one end towards Canberra, and from the other to the bush covering the mountains behind the city.

The two blocks on either side are markedly different. On one side is a highly serviced three-storey laboratory box with a taut gridded concrete frame. Bridges in the atrium allow the public to watch the scientists inside at work. On the other side the conference centre, cafeteria and communications exchange are housed in a sharp, fragmented, teased-out and expanded enclosure with balcony antennae that stretch out to meet the landscape – the opposite of the controlled architecture of the laboratories.

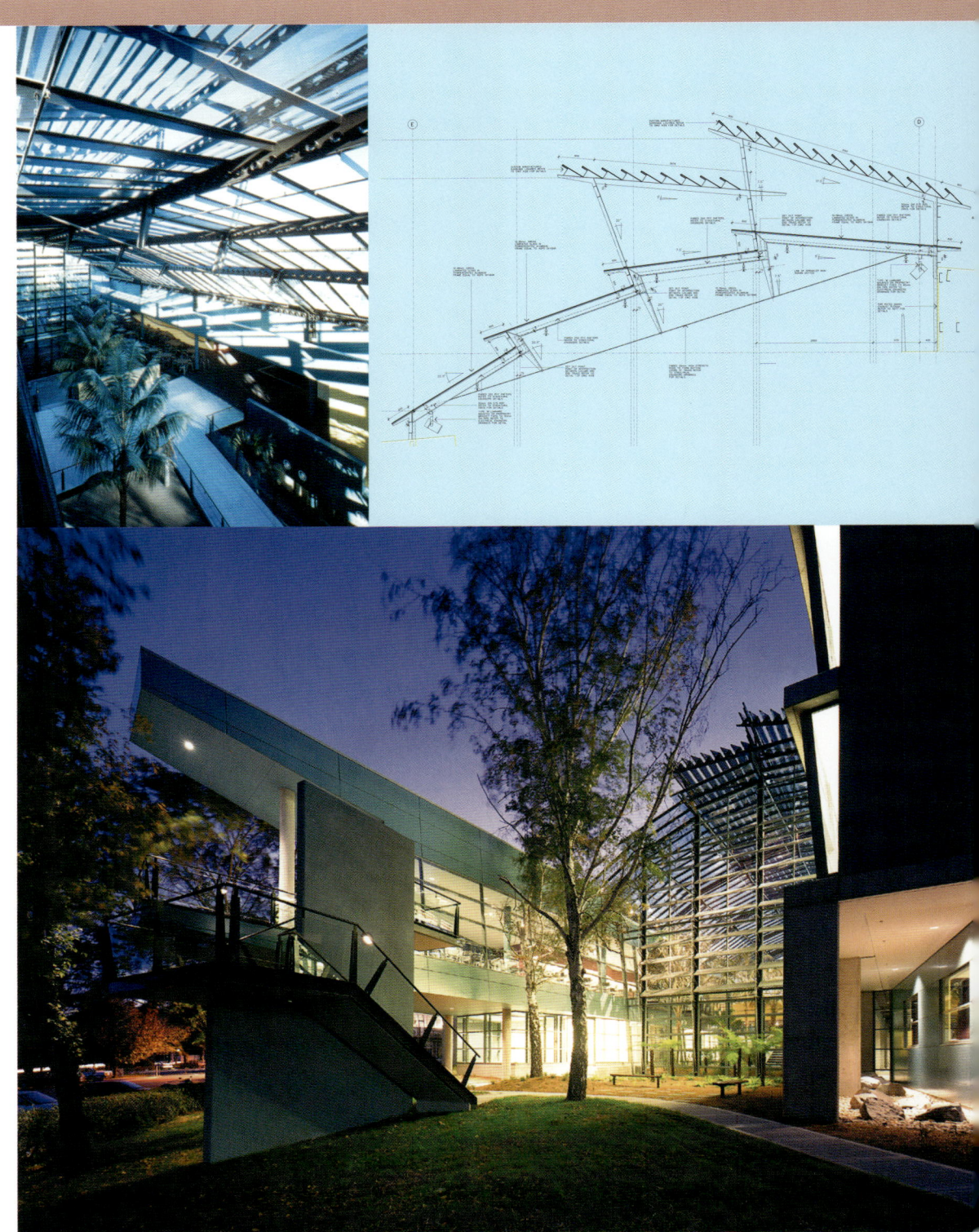

JESTICO + WHILES ARCHITECTS

I trained at the Bartlett in the mid 1970s during a decade of student marches, energy crises, flares and flowers. The smoke-filled haze of student life cleared during the 1980s and as a career loomed I continued to develop a passionate interest in the environment and the beauty of natural things. This interest endured through the tough days of running my own practice and eventually found expression at Jestico + Whiles, a committed practice where I am now a director. The environment and our impact upon it remain central to my work. A theoretical zero-energy office building and the competition-winning House for the Future have become models of this approach. I believe passionately in the considered use of the earth's natural resources to create an architecture that is delightful, enduring and above all socially responsible: the challenges of the 1970s remain.

Heinz Richardson

House for the Future, Museum of Welsh Life, Cardiff
Concept House
Contract Value: £120,000
Completion: 2000
Heinz Richardson: architect

Winner of an international design competition, the House for the Future adds to the Museum of Welsh Life's collection of historic structures. It challenges the traditional view of the family unit by responding to economic and technological change and an increased desire for flexibility, and the timber-frame structure can be reproduced in both urban and rural locations. The House for the Future relies on a strategy of sensible energy use, assisted by passive technologies with easy-to-use control systems, and has been designed to make no net contribution to CO_2 emissions. It is highly insulated and heating is by a ground-source heat pump and wood-pellet heater, as well as by passive solar gain. A solar photovoltaic and water-heating unit is mounted at roof level.

The project was awarded Best House for the Future in the National Homebuilder Design Award 2001. As a testimony to its popularity, the house has attracted over a million visitors a year since opening.

94 EVA JIRICNA ARCHITECTS

Eva Jiricna Architects is based in London with an international portfolio of residential, commercial and retail interiors; furniture, product and exhibition designs; and private and public buildings. The practice is at the forefront of innovation in form and technology, with highly-crafted and detailed designs employing classic elements – glass, steel and stone – in a thoroughly modern language. Lightness, transparency and truth to materials are the hallmarks of our design approach. Georgina Papathanasiou joined us in 1996 and became an Associate in 2000.

Berkeley Tower Penthouse Flat, Canary Wharf, London ▸
Interior design
Completed: 2002
Georgina Papathanasiou: project architect

This two-storey apartment with spectacular views over the Thames was formed with as open a plan as the building's structure and building regulations would allow. As a speculative development the design was not directed to a specific client, and the conceptual approach was to be as simple as possible, providing views and vistas and creating an atmosphere of light and magic. Special features include a glass and steel staircase; a kitchen with lacquered cupboards, enamel baked white glass doors and sparkling white reconstituted glass worktops; a purpose-made, lacquered finish, rotating bed with leather insets and bolsters and bespoke glass dressing table in the master bedroom; and a custom-designed glass bath in the master bathroom.

Faith Zone, Millennium Dome, Greenwich, London ◂
Exhibition pavilion
Budget: £6.5 million
Completed: 1999
Georgina Papathanasiou: project architect

This project endured a long cycle of arguments, discussions and changes which, given that religion and faith are complex and sensitive issues, was somehow inevitable. The original name for the exhibition zone, for which Eva Jiricna Architects were commissioned to develop a proposal, was the Soul Pavilion. The concept for this first brief was to house an exhibition covering three areas – 'the search for humanity', 'the celebration of life' and 'the garden of joy'. The main structure was to include an enclosure in which approximately 1,000 people could gather in a peaceful atmosphere with an ambient background of lights, music and artistic performances, to contemplate and celebrate, regardless of their subjective views on religion or faith.

This proposal did not satisfy some of the religious groups involved who felt it was too 'new age'. Consequently we were instructed to develop an alternative brief based mainly upon the development of Christianity in the UK, alongside a presentation of eight other mainstream religions. We designed a tensile structure to cover the exhibition area, pulled together around its supporting mast into a steel 'crown'. On top of this a tall enclosure was created which formed the 'contemplation zone' with a light sculpture installed by American artist James Turrell.

PATRICK KEILLER

People sometimes ask me how it was that having become an architect, I began making films. The answer usually involves some idea of the films being a way to pursue architecture by other means, but in any case I studied architecture probably not so much because I wanted to be an architect, but because it offered a more than usually wide-ranging, practical education. The Bartlett School of the late 1960s was somewhat ahead of its time in advancing the notion that architecture might not be an exclusively vocational subject, though what someone who had studied architecture might be expected to do other than become an architect was never very clear.

Architecture schools were very different then. There was, for instance, no end-of-year exhibition. If the design briefs offered by the staff failed to match our supposedly radical aspirations, as they often did, we would write our own. While these were generally tolerated or even welcomed by most of the staff, rewriting projects naturally involved a fair amount of time and effort so that, while the more conformist students usually managed to produce more or less convincing designs for what were sometimes rather bureaucratic buildings, others, myself especially, gained more experience in the use of the typewriter and the photocopier. This was not always much use as a preparation for architecture, but was extremely good training for a future filmmaker, and set a pattern for a subsequent career in which a considerable amount of time has been spent preparing proposals for films. Whereas researching and writing architecture projects rarely left one with enough time or energy to carry them out, the completion of a film proposal is generally followed by a long pause, during which one can recoup one's energy in case the project has to be realised. If not, architecture (with its competitions, selection bids and so on) has accustomed one to failure.

Robinson in Space
Film shot in England
Released 1997
Patrick Keiller: director

Robinson in Space is a film about the UK's landscape in the 1990s. It was photographed in 1995, released in January 1997 and later adapted and extended as a book, published in 1999. The project set out to explore English appearances, material culture and so on as the visible results of various characteristics of the UK's economy, in a series of seven journeys around England, suggested partly by Daniel Defoe's *Journey through the Whole Island of Great Britain*.

It was commissioned by the BBC as the sequel to another film, *London*, which had introduced a character called Robinson, a fictional part-time lecturer in a suburban polytechnic, who was researching what he called the 'problem' of London. In *Robinson in Space*, exiled to Reading after the publication of the earlier project, Robinson is commissioned by 'a well-known international advertising agency' to investigate the 'problem' of England. *London* having been the subject of the earlier film, the subjects of *Robinson in Space* were largely the spaces of England-outside-London, in particular some of the landscapes characteristic of an international, computerised consumer economy, that in some ways evoked predictions of the 1960s.

In this respect, the film drew on the architectural culture of that period, with many images – container landscapes, airship hangars etc. – that would have been recognised by readers of the magazine *Architectural Design* circa 1969, or Reyner Banham's articles in *New Society*. Robinson's move to Reading was suggested by its having been Rimbaud's last known address in England, and by the imprisonment of Oscar Wilde there, but it is also a reference to Professor Sir Peter Hall, formerly of Reading University, whose essay 'The Geography of the Fifth Kondratieff', which describes the emergence of high-tech industry in the M4 corridor to which Reading is the gateway, I had read before setting out to make the film. Peter Hall was one of the contributors, with Paul Barker, Cedric Price and Reyner Banham, to the proposal *non-plan*, which some of the landscapes in the film (and its successor, a film about housing) to a certain extent recall.

When I was a first-year student at the Bartlett School, we were taught history of architecture by Reyner Banham. At the time, he was writing *The Architecture of the Well-tempered Environment* (1969) and *Los Angeles* (1971). I think we understood even then what an exceptional privilege it was to be taught by him. We also soon discovered that his influence extended a long way beyond the subject of architecture. When I subsequently migrated to art school and filmmaking, this brief contact with Banham, in addition to his writing, was one of the factors that made me think it would be possible.

96 PATRICK KEILLER

L&V KIRPICHEV LAB-7

We both graduated from the Moscow Architectural Institute, where we later went on to teach. In 1977 we set up the Experimental Children's Architecture Studio in Moscow, which children attended after normal school hours, to learn about art and architecture. We now live in Frankfurt, but continue to run workshops like the Camden Summer Workshop for school children all over Europe, including in the UK, Germany, Scandinavia, Italy and Poland, and to teach in architecture schools. Vladislav also won first prize in the 1972 UNESCO competition of the second UIA Congress, and was responsible for the design of the Moscow River Shipping Headquarters.

Camden Summer Workshop
Design workshop for young people
August 2002
Luidmilla and Vladislav Kirpichev: organisers

This five-day summer workshop was initiated by the London Borough of Camden in collaboration with the Bartlett, and took place in one of the studios in Wates House. The workshops allowed young people to experiment in the field of architectural processes, opening up new opportunities for them. They channelled their creative energies into designing a Vertical City, which involved a discussion of many spatial and construction issues. We plan to continue the workshops in future years.

LAB-7

The two spiritual leaders of Lab-7 are Patrick Poon, who studied fashion design and architecture, and myself. Our paths crossed while teaching at the Architecture Department of Ming-Chuan University. Aware of the discrepancy between theoretical academia and practical professional practice, we decided to establish Lab-7 together in Taiwan, hoping to integrate technology and design in an appropriate aesthetic for the new century. We always employ the Integrated Design System (IDS) strategic design concept, formulated by Patrick Poon, to combine the strengths of different professionals in architectural, interior, landscape, planning and multimedia design projects, and in project management and marketing.

Shuheng Huang

'ACTION Center', Far Glory Group, Taipei, Taiwan
Customer service centre and museum
Budget: approximately £1.4 million
Completed: April 2001
Lab-7: planners, designers, contractors

This project exhibits and celebrates the successes of our client, a large corporation, and seeks to fuse space and media. The Customer Service Centre consists of six parts telling the story of the corporation's different interests ('A' for air cargo, 'C' for construction, 'T' for travel and leisure, 'I' for insurance, 'O' for Ocean Park, 'N' for net technology). The central staircase with its recombinant DNA structure penetrates and links the three floors, orientates visitor circulation and symbolises an everlasting vital spirit. The circulation route creates a narrative space through the careful arrangement of a series of interactive devices that integrate exhibits, graphics, multimedia displays and architecture. Visitors passing through a time tunnel, a pinball station and a 'blueprint of life' are left feeling a vital pulse and with fresh images.

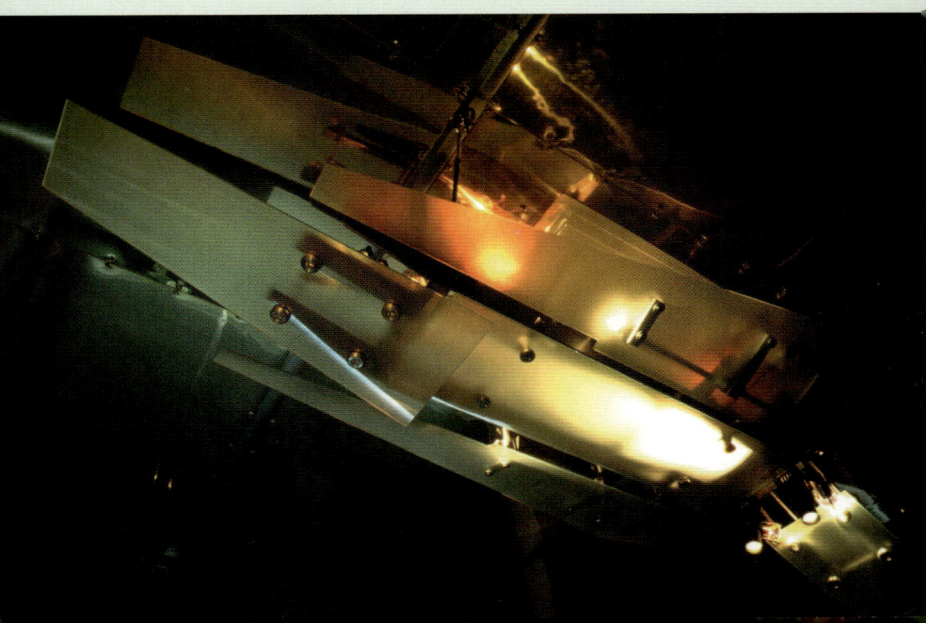

Lab-7, Taipei, Taiwan
Office design
Budget: approximately £50,000
Completed: September 1998
Lab-7: designers

The vitality of Lab-7 is evident in two pieces of hand-made kinetic furniture designed for our office, which are symbolic of building and innovation and our underlying culture and philosophy. The meeting table and ceiling lamp carry the 'spirit' and 'energy' of Lab-7 as a space and practice as it sets sail. The dynamic table is constructed with a steel structure and a glass top capable of rotating through 360° horizontally and 90° vertically, so it can be used as a TV screen or bulletin board, or folded up to create space for gatherings. The lamp hanging directly above is made of steel with frosted glass panels that can be adjusted to reflect light onto the copper ceiling. With its versatility and transitory quality the lamp is a stimulus for us in our exploration of a new aesthetic.

Star Tech, Taipei, Taiwan
New office building
Budget: approximately £8 million
Completion: June 2003
Lab-7: architects, interior designers, media kit producers

This project explores possibilities for the workplace of tomorrow within the constraints of commercial real estate. Combining eastern and western architectural vocabulary and the rules of Feng-Shui, the building is designed for the pursuit of introspection, and seeks to open up a dialogue between nature and technology. Sunlight upon water and the wind become parts of the material of the building, whose composition and configuration are constantly changing. A glass access bridge reflects rippling water; a canopy in the tall lobby space moves with the sun and creates a resonating play of light and shadow on the white walls; while the elevator waiting area looks out onto a bamboo forest which is illuminated at night to take on the aspect of a Chinese watercolour painting.

100 THE LIGHTHOUSE

The Bartlett is one of the few places where it is possible to study a Diploma at research level in the true sense of investigating ideas on architecture, what it is and could be. Consequently my career since doing the Diploma has been diverse, though at the same time everything I've done is related. I have worked in an architecture office (and would probably like to again) but this was never the main aim. I taught at Southbank and Kingston and, since moving back to Scotland in 1998, at Strathclyde, The Edinburgh College of Art and Edinburgh University. I have also designed theatre sets and continued installation work, which are good foils to teaching – balancing academic and hands-on making, something that the Bartlett and Unit 12 highlighted. With the National Programme for The Lighthouse, as with all aspects of my work, I feel that my attitude towards architecture results in an expansive approach to any discussion or project.

Morag Bain

National Programme
Architecture awareness programme
Budget: £300,000 annually
Ongoing
Morag Bain: National Programme development officer

When interviewed for the post of National Development Officer I was asked what I thought the most interesting and most difficult aspects of the job would be. The answer was the same for both – the amount and diversity of things to be done.

I am responsible for delivering the National Programme, a series of activities informed by the Scottish Executive's Policy on Architecture. The aim is to involve communities nationwide in issues relating to architecture and the built environment. Central to this is the ambition to broaden accessibility, awareness and understanding of architecture and the design process through a variety of projects and events which make connections and encourage collaboration between the profession and the public at all levels. I am interested in the creative energy which comes from putting people together in new situations – in the common interests as well as the differences which emerge between architects, artists and others when they work together, and in the possibility this opens for unexpected new ideas.

There are five major initiatives:

1: Touring exhibitions start at The Lighthouse and then travel to venues throughout Scotland. The first exhibition in 2002 was 'Anatomy of the House' which looked at the diversity of housing in Scotland. In 2003 the exhibition is 'Common-place', an examination of public spaces demonstrating the wide-reaching, and often unacknowledged, effects of the built environment.

2: Community programmes across Scotland take on different formats depending on their themes; they have included a seminar and education programme aligned to the touring exhibitions, workshops to design a wind shelter, and a student competition.

3: The Innovation Fund encourages projects at a local level. The emphasis is on creative new ways of thinking about architecture and on promoting a network of people and ideas. Past projects have included a film, a research programme, the redesign of a public space and setting up a website.

4: www.ScottishArchitecture.com is a central hub for information and communication. It is a public educational resource for lifelong learning, outreach work, activities and events, linking communities around Scotland, and features, among other things, projects and virtual exhibitions.

5: Student awards entitled SIX, in collaboration with the Royal Incorporation of Architects in Scotland. The awards will be for the best third and fifth year architecture work and for the best Urban Design project, and will be exhibited and judged at The Lighthouse, offering a high public profile and an exceptional chance to showcase the six Scottish schools together.

It is vital that documentation of the process and content of projects is visually effective so that the work can be developed into tools, legacies or exhibitions, reaching as many people as possible. The National Programme team, which includes a curator and a website developer, work very closely with extremely good exhibition and graphic designers, photographers and film makers to communicate what we do.

101

Future

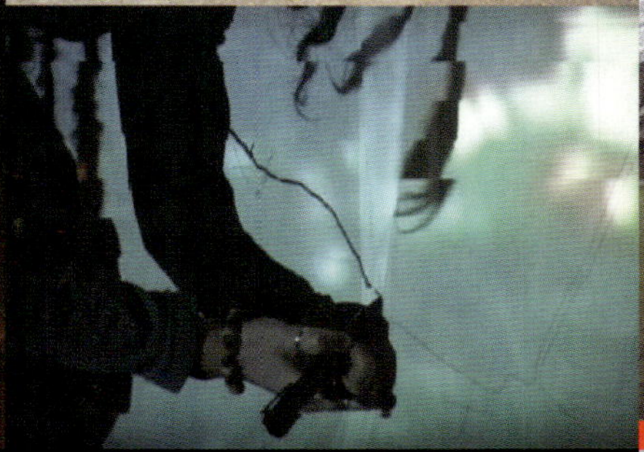

ScottishArchitecture.com

L4

We made temporary wind breaks with shrink wrap. We used posts to support the material, this makes a shelter and keeps out the wind and rain and only takes 10 minutes to make.

co-op
GLAS

102 CJ LIM/STUDIO 8 ARCHITECTS

Our research projects are 'test beds' for ideologies and spatial speculations, while the more restricted architectural competitions we enter are vehicles to implement the abstract speculations – both constantly exploring the phenomena and complexities of social culture and architectural narrative. The intensity of research is furthered by the symbiotic discourse I have through my teaching within the Bartlett.

cj Lim

Dialogue with Nature – Country House Lancashire (with Bartlett Architecture Lab)
Competition entry
2000

Rhys Cannon: co-designer
cj Lim: designer

This country house is devised as a modulating garden wall through which occupants can refer to the landscape. The datum is established from the site's summit – tips of the hedged horizon emphasise the slope of the land, and a grid of recessed lights stretching out below describes the contours of the undulating landscape at night.

A series of inhabitable horizontal concrete platforms forming the main house extend from the garden wall, replicating the stepped landscape. The garden wall starts with an office unit, away from the main house, allowing privacy and security, and doubling as the gatehouse. From here, the stone drive leads to the entrance viewing deck overlooking the sunken courtyard garden below. Visitors arrive amongst a carpet of mechanical flowers with heat and smells of domesticity vented from the spaces below. The flowers present a fluctuating landscape to the building's upper surface, responding to the activities below – closing, opening and tilting as desired.

How Green is Your Garden? (with Bartlett Architecture Lab)
Monograph of projects by Bartlett Architecture Lab
£20 per copy
Published: 2003 by Wiley-Academy
cj Lim: author
Edward T H Liu: co-author

Alicia was feeling bored. It was raining cats and dogs outside, and her elder sister Edith was impersonating *Adult Edith*, her nose deep in some ever-so-dry treatise on architectural history from father's library of ever-so-dry first editions. Alicia made the silent wish that her over-serious sibling's enunciation of the words *'entablature'*, *'neo-classical'* and *'pilaster'* would dry out the horrid wet weather so that she could search for disorientated felines and canines in the community garden downstairs. When it soon became clear that the wish would remain ungranted, she sighed and turned her attention to her decrepit toy rabbit…

Follow the adventures of Alicia Liddell in *How Green is your Garden?* as she mounts an expedition through the uncharted landscape of the family Victorian flat. Peering from beneath our heroine's flights of fancy lie questions of an ecological bent, focusing on the impact of the environment on architecture rather than architecture on the environment. Is it possible for buildings to learn from organic systems? And can the banal interactions of flora and fauna in the domestic flat be scaled up into hybrids of growing edifices and engineered gardens of gargantuan size?

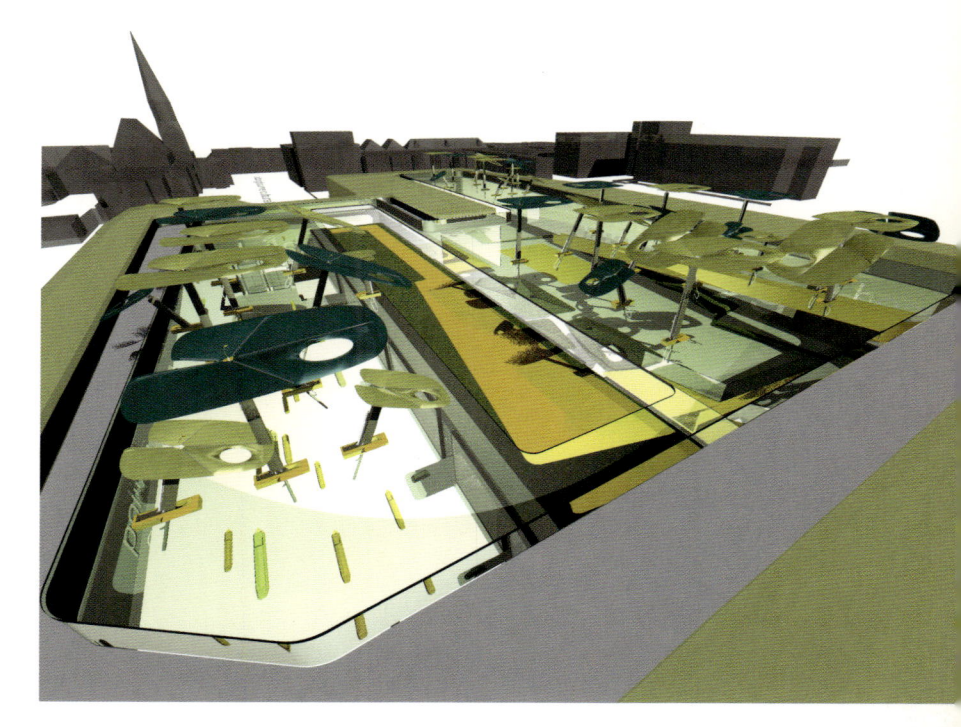

104 CJ LIM/STUDIO 8 ARCHITECTS

Folkestone Seafood Stall (with Bartlett Architecture Lab),
Folkestone, Kent

Competition entry

2000

Michael Kong: co-designer
cj Lim: designer

The Folkestone Seafood Stall sets out to reconcile the functional simplicity of a food-vending outlet with the romantic lyricism of a coastal location. It comprises two components: a kitchen/stall core and a modulating 'shell-wrap'.

The working area of the stall is an exercise in stripped-down simplicity. Continuous stainless steel work surfaces contain refrigerated displays, sinks and servery, with storage and cooking facilities fully integrated within the structural housing. In stark contrast the functional core is wrapped, not only figuratively, but also dynamically, by an ultramarine shell that extends out into a sinuous tail overhanging land and water. The cyclical nature of the tides and seasons is mirrored by the periodic unfurling of the protective shell, which initially assumes the shape of its host, and as the day progresses, reconfigures to assume the line of the retaining wall and surrounding landscape to accommodate changing occupancies. The tail cantilevers over the sea when the stall is closed, the silvered underside catching the light reflecting off the water's surface in a caustic celebration.

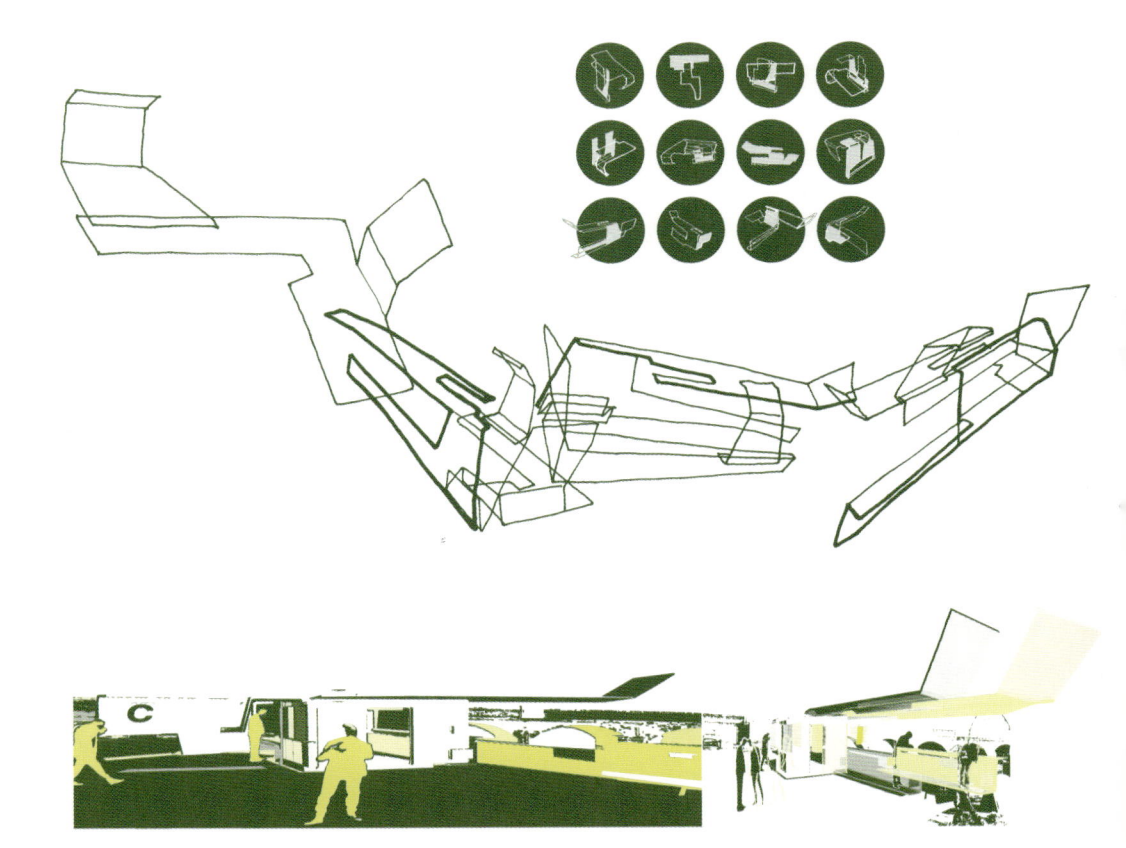

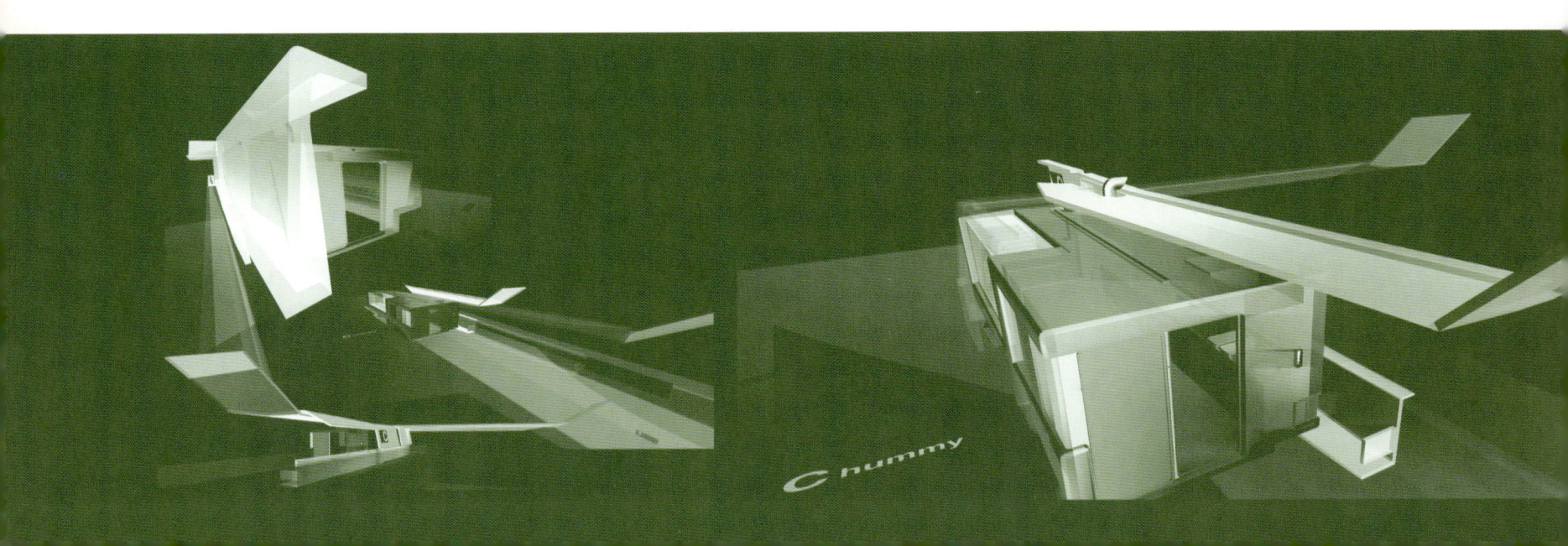

Clonehouse (with studio 8 architects)
Concepthouse 2000 Ideal Home
Exhibition competition entry
(awarded second prize)
Entry: December 1999
cj Lim: designer
Edward T H Liu: co-designer

The central theme of the Clonehouse, simultaneously conceived as a polemic and as a central showpiece for the Ideal Home Exhibition, is habitual repetition. Whether daily, weekly, yearly or generational, it proposes new patterns of domestic interaction. Clonehouse is centred around four identical and interchangeable chambers. There is no hierarchy to these units, with a cloned view shared between them, achieved through the use of mirrors and optics. Each chamber contains a bed, computer workstation, movable wall and liquid-crystal glass ceiling. Collectively, they may be hoisted or stacked up to dramatically reconfigure the space around them. Communications between household members become both more intimate and more distant via devices that enable occluded conversations – a non-verbal intercourse consisting of glimpses, half-heard dialogues, echoes, unmade beds and vestigial odours. As the units are interchangeable, the lingering presence of the last occupant is always apparent.

Clonehouse is colour-coded to create the illusion of inhabiting a three-dimensional diagram. Red designates kinetic elements that volumetrically re-order the indefinite space, an all-purpose area for living, dining and entertaining.

sins + other spatial relatives
(with studio 8 architects)
Publication, 252 pages
£18 per copy
Published: December 2000
cj Lim: author
Edward T H Liu: co-author,
book designer

sins + other spatial relatives is an architectural novel published under the Studio 8 imprint in 2000. Based on the seven cardinal sins, it comprises a series of seven projects designed by a fictional architect for a fictional metropolis that question the morality of our current social programme through satire and parody. Notable features include a vertiginous cow-farm in the city, a play-ground for voyeurs, a mile-high casino and a mobile garden for harvesting marijuana. The book reached the dizzy heights of being the 19430th best seller in the country.

Working on *sins* and its constituent projects was an unparalleled joy. This book provided me with the opportunity to purge myself of the delusion that I could write a book, to create a fictional architect with the biggest ego since Ayn Rand's Howard Roark, design spaces with deranged agendas, and direct a screenplay involving actors in wigs and cow-suits.

Edward T H Liu

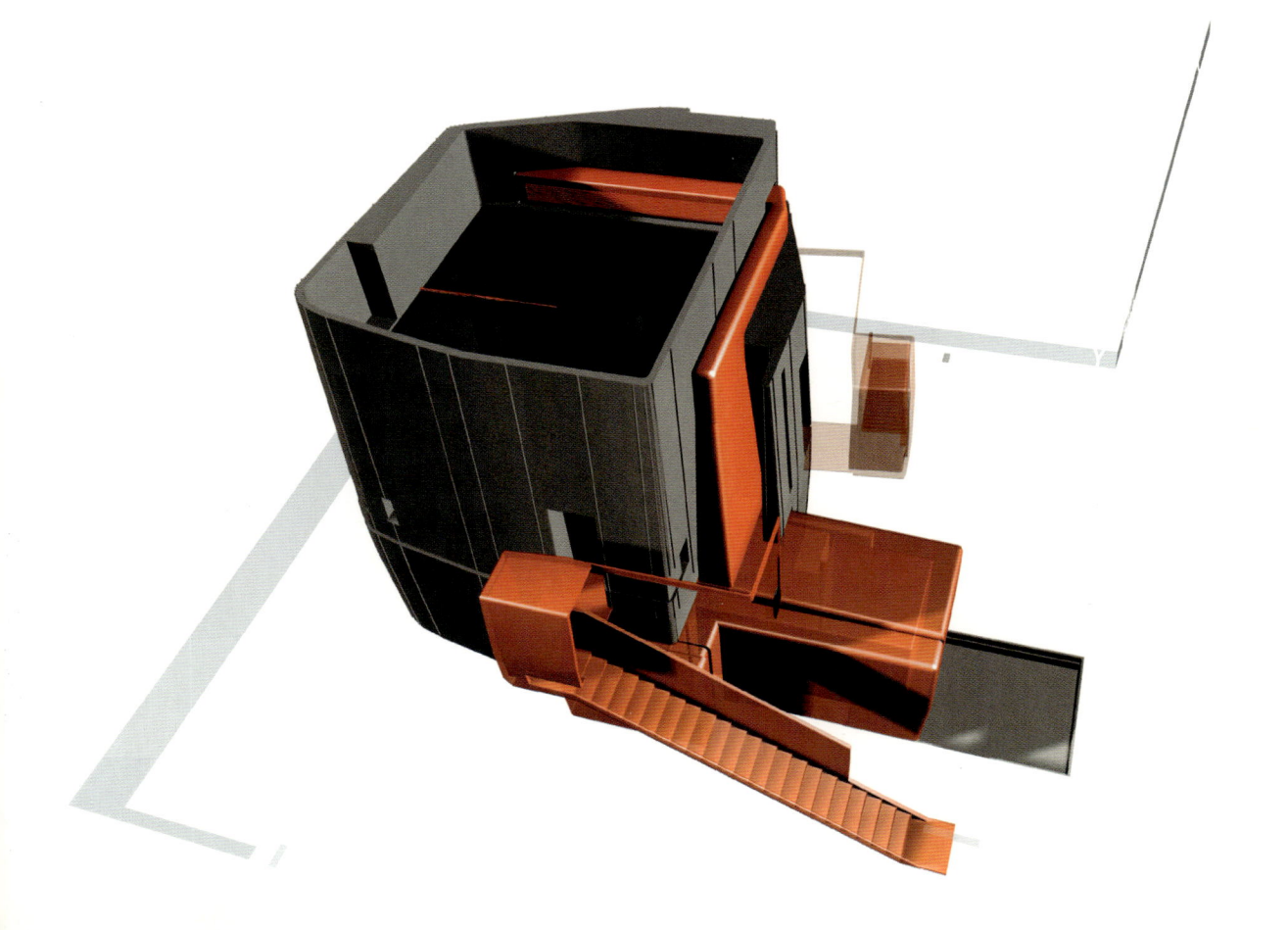

106 JOHN LYALL ARCHITECTS

I set up John Lyall Architects after twelve years in practice with Will Alsop. Based in Shoreditch, we are known for our large urban regeneration projects, and have an award-winning reputation for the design of railway stations. I am passionately interested and involved in architectural education (as a design tutor, occasional lecturer, external examiner, course validator, and employer of year-out students). I relate well to the Bartlett, possibly because it maintains the range of diversity and unpredictability that I enjoyed as a student and teacher at the AA in the 1970s and 80s. Teaching and examining at the Bartlett have two main effects on me: ever-new demands are made on my architectural judgement, and I am challenged by the better students at strategic and philosophical levels. This must have a healthy effect on my work and on the culture of my office.

John Lyall

Tottenham Hale Station, North London
Transport interchange
Budget: approximately £8 million
Completed: 2000
John Lyall: partner in charge, co-designer
Morag Tait: phase two project architect

The construction of Stansted Airport was the catalyst for Tottenham Hale to become an augmented transport interchange, providing a direct link into London's West End via the Victoria Line. The station took ten years to complete with three different clients. We started with a new overground station framed in large steel portals clad in glass and aluminium, with a curved bulge at the side housing the waiting room (variously dubbed the 'bike shed' and the 'caterpillar'). The oversailing canopies were then extended to embrace the 1960s underground station, and finally an illuminated beacon and a glass-enclosed fountain developed with artist Bruce McLean transformed the forecourt bus/taxi interchange.

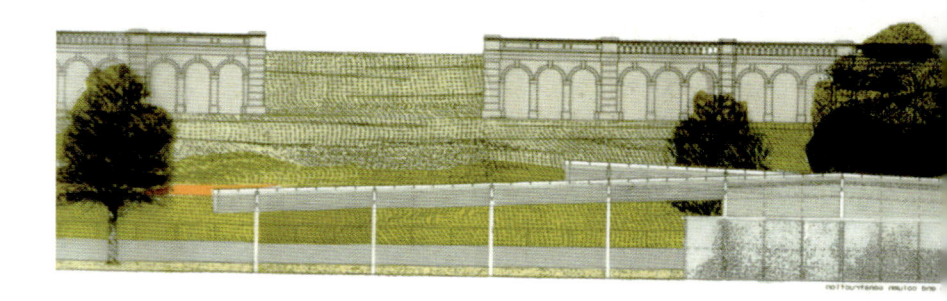

Crystal Palace Park, South London (with Gustafson Porter)
New build park buildings
Budget: £4 million (including landscape)
Completed: 2002
Peter Culley: job architect
John Lyall: director of architecture, chief designer for buildings
Zoe Quick: architectural assistant
Philip Turner: architectural assistant

In 1996 John Lyall was in the team led by landscape architect Kathryn Gustafson that won the competition to redesign Paxton's historic Crystal Palace Park. Two new pavilion buildings on opposite sides of the park follow the same design idea and are intended to work with Gustafson's landscape and to suggest how future superstructures could be developed. The first is a visitor centre for a new city farm, located to mark the end of one corner of the park. The pavilion is constructed, appropriately, in materials typically found in agricultural structures: raised above the ground on a gabion wall base, with a monopitch steel roof structure straddling a spine wall of in-situ concrete and propped on raking steel posts. Cedar wood walls enclose flexible spaces with clerestory windows between them and the oversailing roof overhead. The second building, a base for park maintenance vehicles, has the same basic structure, but elongated and with different non-structural materials.

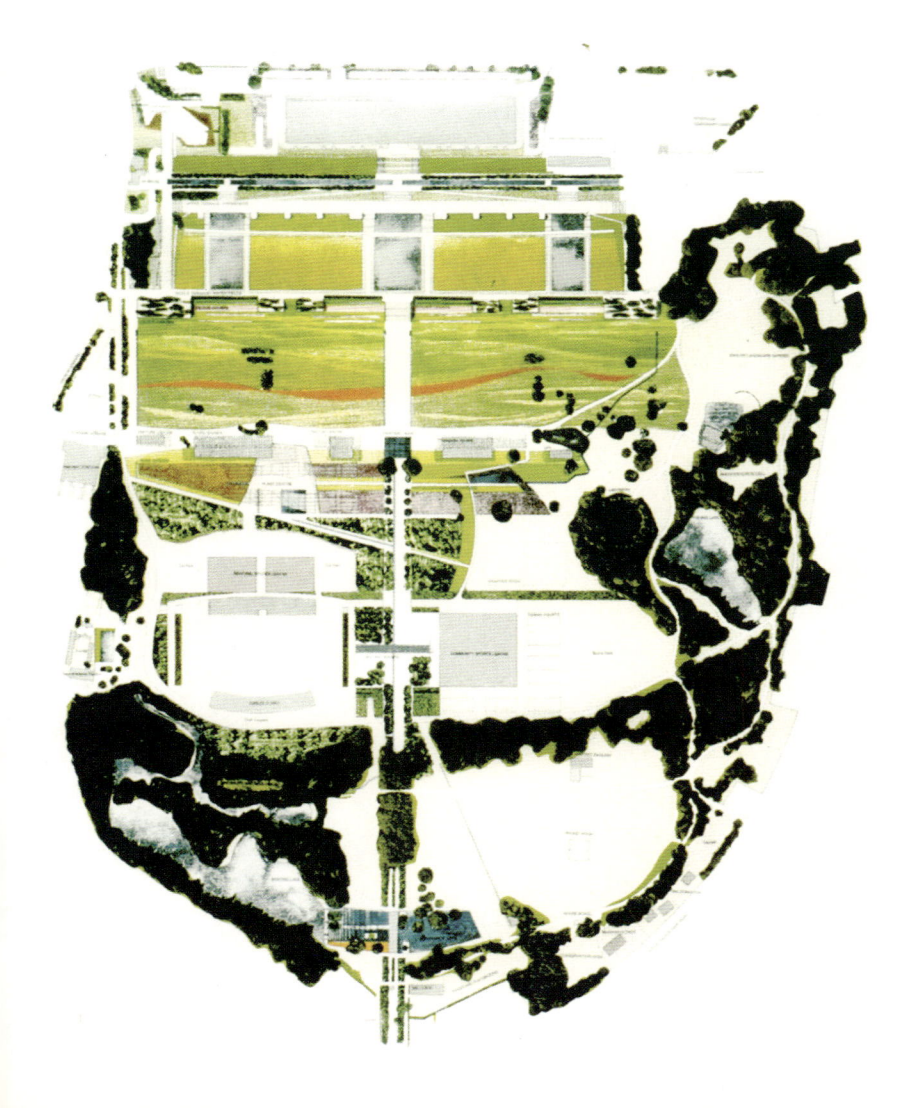

North Greenwich Underground Station, London (architects: Alsop Lyall & Stormer with Jubilee Line Extension project team)

New build underground station

Budget: £122 million

Completed: 1999

John Lyall: partner in charge, co-designer

While still working in the Alsop Lyall & Stormer practice John Lyall was partner in charge for the new North Greenwich Underground Station for the Jubilee Line. The station is described as the 'largest underground station in the world' and was shortlisted for the Stirling Prize in 1999.

As one of twelve new Jubilee Line Extension stations designed by various celebrated architects under master of ceremonies Roland Paoletti, North Greenwich was first conceived as a trench open to the sky above. Unfortunately contractual pressures meant that a lid had to be put on the trench, but the design principle of having a lower concourse or 'pier' from which banks of escalators cascade down to the platforms remained. The predominant colour is blue, and the design is defined by large walls of glass mosaic and by towering V-shaped columns that march rhythmically down the cathedral-like space. At the time of its conception an office development was planned for the site above – nobody imagined a Millennium Dome (by Rogers) and a new bus station (by Fosters) sitting on top!

108 LYNNFOX

LynnFox are Christian McKenzie, Patrick Chen and Bastian Glassner, all ex-Unit 15 students. Formed in October 2001, we are primarily music video directors, but have dabbled in commercials and concert visuals. The transition from architecture to making videos was completely accidental; we just went down the wrong path. One day we might enter the odd architectural competition – when we are 50 or something. The Bartlett has given us skills to take an image, or object, chew it up and spit it out into something completely unintelligible.

FC Kahuna: Hayling
Computer-animated video
Music video (City Rockers)
Completed: 2001
LynnFox: directors

This video is an attempt to translate the unfolding of a classical love-story into an abstract succession of sensuous atmospheres. We gradually follow the courtship process from the initial shy and fragile glance to the careful establishment of bodily contact. Over the duration of the track we watch the invigorating stimulus of a giant and versatile organism as it is coupling with a cosmic epicurean light source. It is Romeo and Juliet's moment of attraction transferred into an abstract Eden of epic proportions.

The 03.45 minute fully computer-animated video was completed in December 2001 after an intensive four-week production. Since delivery it has been screened in video festivals all over the world and received wide press coverage.

Björk: Nature is Ancient
Music video (One Little Indian)
Completed: 2002
LynnFox: directors

This promo retells the story of Adam and Eve, delicate and beautiful embryonic beings in the primordial soup as the earth cools. We watch them mating, a complex and magnificent dance. The climax comes with the revelation of the first human growing inside Eve's womb.

Working with Glassworks we devoted a lot of time to developing the appearance of Adam and Eve. We based their design on reassembled human embryos, which have a fragility and delicacy that we were keen to preserve. With revolutionary new software that uses particles to create form, rather than conventional nurbs or polygon geometry, we created the amniotic membranes and chorion layers, bringing an incredible organic roughness that would be very hard to achieve using traditional modelling techniques.

The primordial soup was largely shot in a glass tank with spotlit suspensions of cleaning fluids and milk. Additional floating debris was captured for foreground plates, enhancing the non-computer-generated quality of the composite. Spunk plates of Jeyes cleaning fluid emitted from pipettes were used during Eve's arousal and Adam's ejaculation sequences, as well as for mist banks and to build the landscape inside Eve's womb. The human baby in the final shot is derived from a 3D scan of Björk herself, her eyes, nose and mouth triangle compressed, and her cheeks and head bulging out.

The completed 4.11 minute-long promo is the final track on Björk's forthcoming DVD compilation.

110 MARCOSANDMARJAN ARCHITECTS

We established marcosandmarjan architects in 2000. We met during the MArch course at the Bartlett in 1998. It was Peter Cook who first drew a parallel between our seemingly opposite design interests, namely softness in architecture (Marjan) and visceral qualities in architecture (Marcos). We continue to develop our work in parallel research, into digital-cuddly (Marjan) and bio-technological (Marcos) interfaces in the MPhil/PhD by Architecural Design programme, and through teaching in Units 5 and 20, testing ideas against each other and finding points of interconnection in marcosandmarjan projects – competitions, publications, exhibitions and built design.

Involving others in our projects is important to our design approach. Collaborators have included Andres Aguilar, Orlando de Jesus, Jia Lu, Shao Ming, Yu-Ying Hu, Shie-Wei Pan, Ute Pernthaler, Steve Pike, Jens Ritter and Hui Hui Teoh.

Marjan Colletti and Marcos Cruz

New England Biolabs, Massachusetts, USA
Competition entry
Budget: £20 million
2001
marcosandmarjan: design leaders

The New England Biolabs competition, developed with Chinese architect Shao Ming, was the first in a series of projects developed in collaboration with other former Bartlett students. An immense volume is submerged into the topography. Laboratories are integrated into 'Lab-cones' that form a structural skeleton supporting the table-like roof overhead, while research offices are located in tiny capsules like eyes in the roof, allowing scientists to sit under the 'big American sky'. The winter garden spaces between cones are used for circulation, resting zones and support equipment.

The 'inlucent' resin skin of the cones and roof plays host to all major services and appliances and blurs light penetration into the enclosed lab areas. The resin surface with incorporated photo-chromatic chemicals provokes a 'soft perception' of space. Its properties vary across its extent, from rigid structure to opaque surface to flexible transparent membrane.

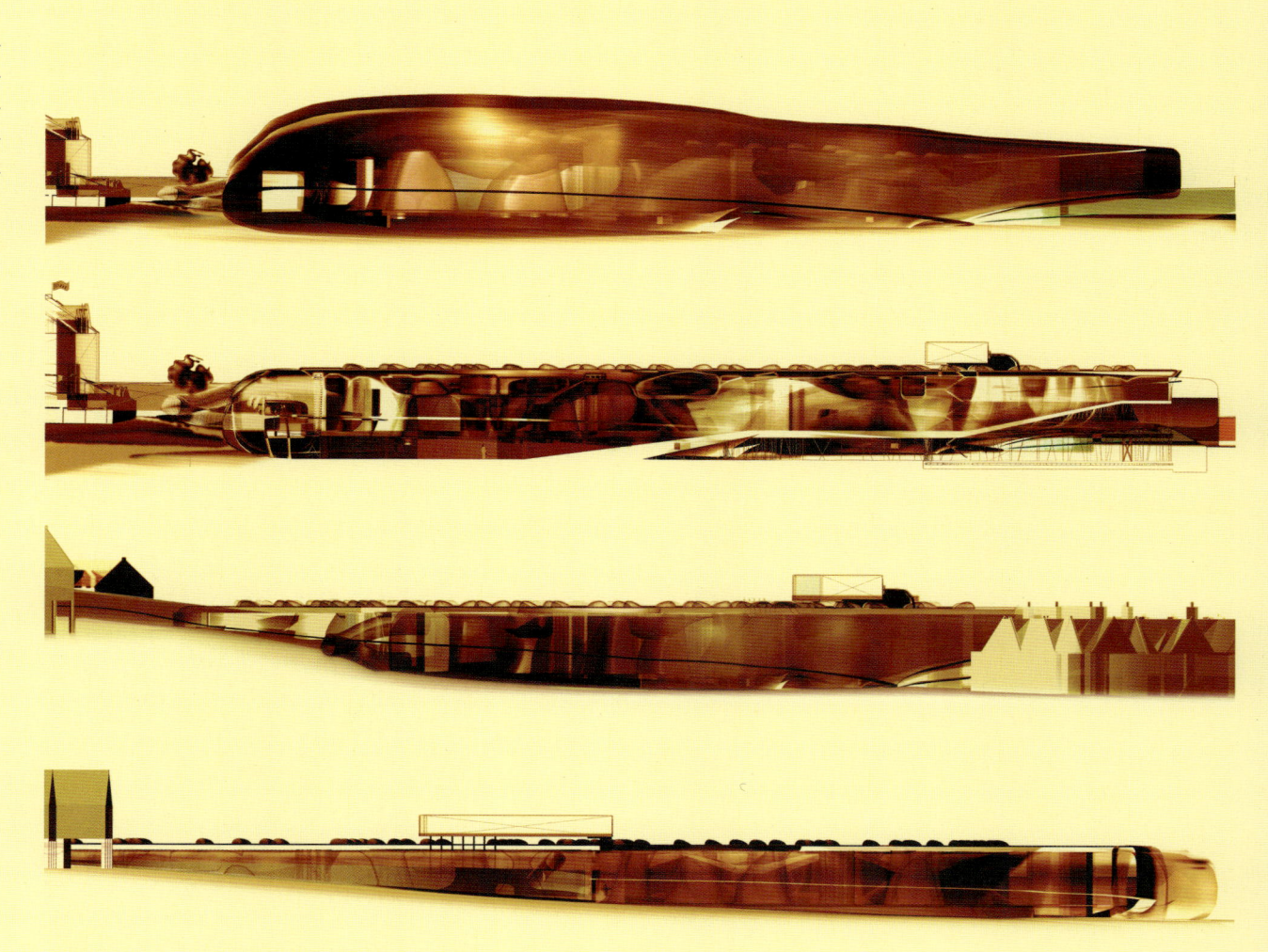

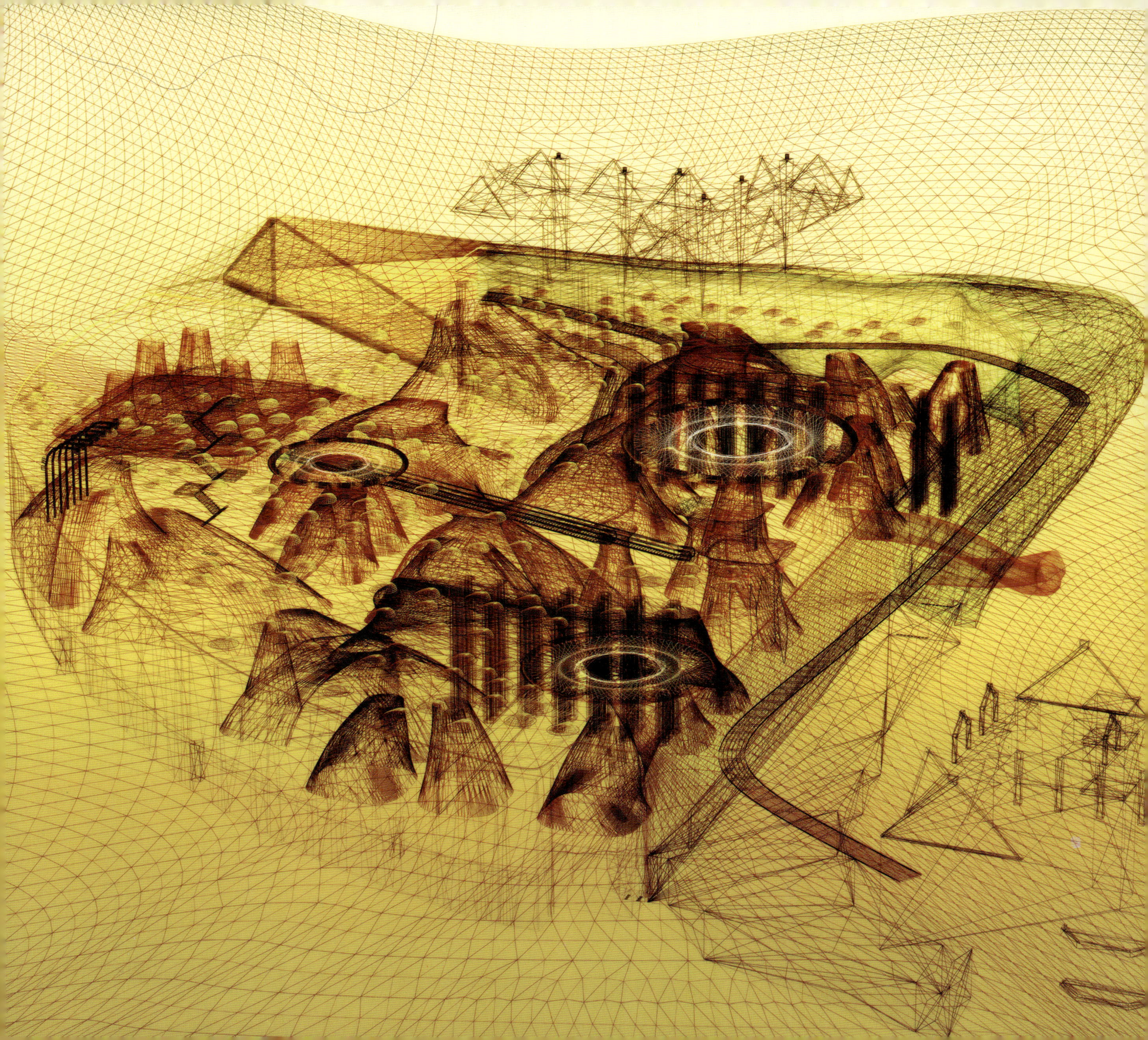

112 MARCOSANDMARJAN ARCHITECTS

The Bagpipe/Garden of Vessels, New Tomihiro Museum, Azuma Village, Japan

Competition entry

Budget: £6.4 million

2002

marcosandmarjan: design leaders

To visit the New Tomihiro Museum of SHI-GA (poems and watercolour paintings) is to enter a reinterpreted landscape. Following the meandering route through is a process of discovery: a metaphorical life journey of Tomihiro himself. Passing through and between exhibition vessels the experience is one of incidences of confluence and activity, interspersed with moments of contemplation and intimacy. The external envelope coalesces transparent and occasionally translucent elements, and is interrupted by intruding light cones. Exhibition vessels consist of a timber structure with a dual layered skin. An opaque internal layer controls light and humidity, creating an environment appropriate for presenting and preserving Tomihiro's work.

An internal garden separates the exhibition spaces from the rest of the Museum, and makes visitors aware of seasonal changes, as rain, snow, and blossom fall 'within' the museum. Paths continuing beyond the physical boundaries of the museum lead to the forest above and the lake below, encouraging the possibility of a real encounter with nature.

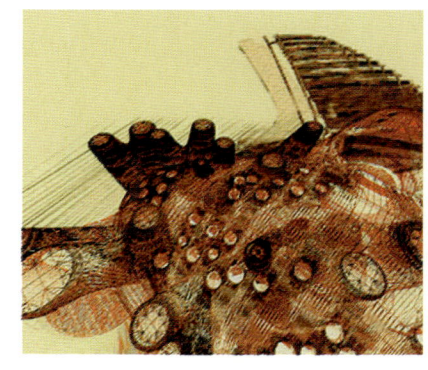

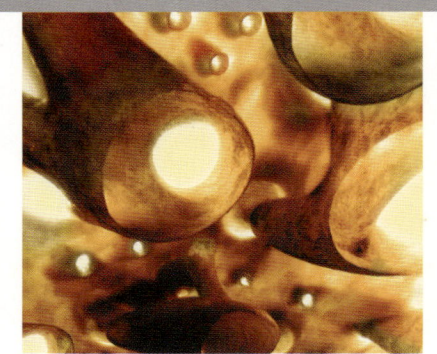

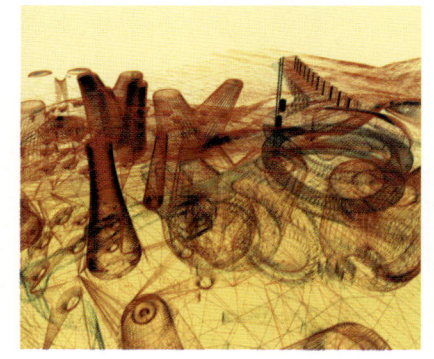

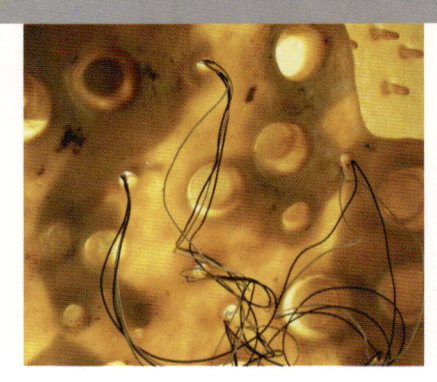

RICK MATHER ARCHITECTS 113

Rick Mather Architects was founded in 1973. Its work spans both new build and renovation, with a special interest in the cultural and education sectors. Many of the projects form outdoor 'rooms' to extend both use and setting. As with my previous work at the Bartlett, John Lyall Architects and Gustafson Porter, at Rick Mather I have pursued an interest in balancing built form with themes of natural and cultivated public space – in the Virginia Museum of Fine Arts seen in the incorporation of the four-acre sculpture garden into the architecture.

Peter Culley

Virginia Museum of Fine Arts, expansion and sculpture garden, Richmond, Virginia, USA (with SMBW)
Museum renovation and expansion
Budget: $100 million (£60 million)
Completion: 2007
Peter Culley: project architect, associate in charge

The Virginia Museum of Fine Arts opened in Virginia's capital, Richmond, in 1936. Since then it has had major additions built in a variety of styles every 20 years or so. Our scheme removes the current entrance wing built in 1976 and replaces it with a large extension, opens up significant areas of the existing building to public use, and replaces the current parking-lot at the centre of the site with a tilted sculpture garden with parking beneath. The extension houses galleries, the new main entrance, library, café and restaurant, shop, conservation department and offices. An atrium connecting the new and existing buildings has an all-glass roof supported by 600-millimetre cantilevered glass fins capable of resisting seismic loads.

A twelve-metre high by 22-metre wide window gives views out from the exhibition lounges onto the adjacent boulevard and over Richmond's downtown, reinforcing the message that this is a public gallery for all in a city which was racially segregated until the latter part of the 20th century.

114 NIALL McLAUGHLIN ARCHITECTS

We have been in practice since 1991. For us, practice is understood as a range of activities all necessary to each other: design of buildings, fittings and furniture; making buildings, installations and models; connecting speculation and practice, lecturing and writing about architecture; collaborations with craftspeople, artists and consultants.

We use a great range of materials in our building projects, and enjoy inventively combining traditional and new construction techniques. Our work is less about the expression of technology by bolts, junctions and gaskets, more about the overall presence of a space, in particular in the way materials alter it by modulating light: combing, diffusing, storing, reflecting or dulling light.

Most of our projects are developed in relation to particular narratives – the history of the site is frequently the starting point for architectural speculation. These stories are absorbed into the architecture and are only ever implicit; they are ways of bringing the project into being, not of explaining it when it is there.

Digital Studio, Oxford School of Architecture ▸
Budget: £80,000
Completion: June 2003
Matt Driscoll: architectural assistant
Spencer Guy: project architect
Niall McLaughlin: principal architect

The School of the Built Environment at Oxford Brookes University held a competition for the redesign of their top-floor design studios. Despite an extremely tight budget, they were very ambitious, inviting entrants to rethink the principles of architectural education in the digital age. While digital technology allows for working from home and decentralised workplaces, we took the view that good architectural education depends on physical proximity between students. In Oxford, students had started drifting away from the shared studio culture and working by themselves at home, largely due to a lack of flexible and secure workspaces. Our solution was to design a new desk. Simply pushing the lid down locks the whole thing, allowing students to secure it even when popping out for coffee, while the computer and screen are secured to the structure. When raised the lid forms a pinboard for work. The space of the studio was imagined as a thicket of data cables, power lines and clothes hangars descending like rain from the ceiling, with desk and wall surfaces kept clear for pinning-up work.

We are watching closely to see if the pattern of work at Oxford changes – the success of the project will lie, not in its visual manifestation, but in whether it changes the culture of studio working in the school.

Bandstand, De La Warr Pavilion, Bexhill

Mobile bandstand
Budget: £60,000
Completed: 2001
Sandra Coppin: project architect
Niall McLaughlin: principal architect

The De La Warr Pavilion, designed by Erich Mendelsohn, is one of the most famous modern buildings in Britain. The commission for a new bandstand was the outcome of an RIBA competitive interview. It is important for the community to feel a sense of possession of their own public buildings, and we were interested in entering into a collaborative process with local people. We involved children from six local schools as co-designers; the design was developed through a series of workshops with the pupils. The success of the collaboration was marked by the number of parents and adults who also became involved.

The bandstand canopy is a fibreglass-coated stressed ply skin, which sits on a steel base structure. The bandstand can move about on the terrace to accommodate different performances. Its shape was based on computer analysis of sound projection.

House, Jacobs Ladder, Oxfordshire

New build house
Budget: £450,000
Completed: 2000
Sandra Coppin: architectural assistant
Niall McLaughlin: principal architect
Silke Vosskötter: project director

Owning a very beautiful piece of mature woodland – on an escarpment in the Chilterns commanding a beautiful view across the South Oxfordshire plain – our clients asked that the architecture of their new house should frame the surroundings, but not draw excessive attention to itself. With its suspended ground floor, only the steel columns disturb the woodland floor below.

As one approaches Jacobs Ladder the view is framed by an opening in the trees, but after crossing the bridge into the first floor entrance it is concealed. This approach is similar to that to Mies Van der Rohe's Tugendhat House, which inspired the design. Descending through the curved staircase enclosure (an echo of Tugendhat) into the living room the view is revealed again – the promise of the landscape, given and withheld, is the thread that draws circulation through the building. This journey ends with a sightline along the swimming pool projecting out of the house. The pool is tiled black to reflect the tree canopy – when you dive in you swim straight out into the view.

NIALL McLAUGHLIN ARCHITECTS

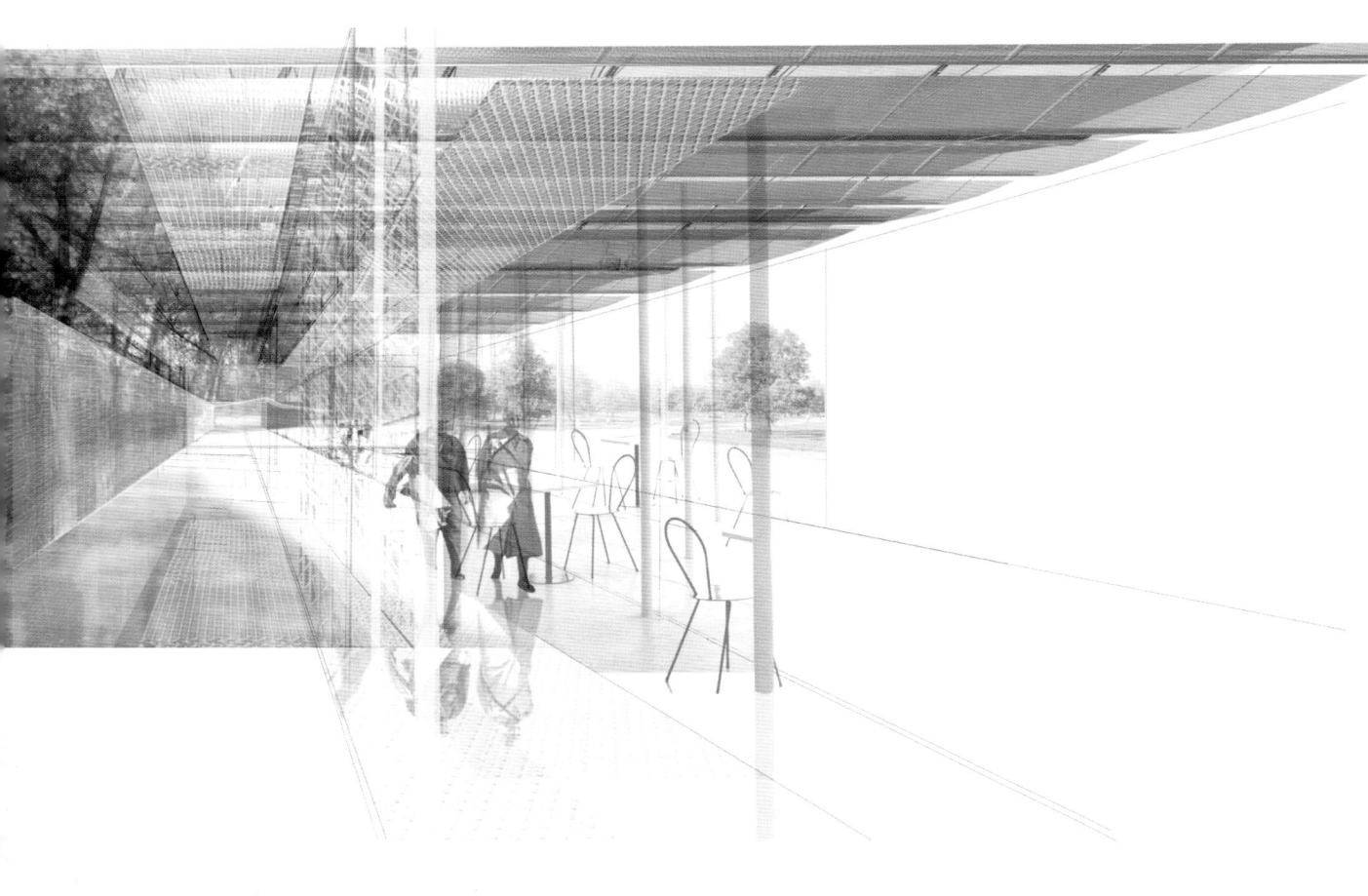

Finsbury Park Community Building, North London ▲
New build community building
Budget: £750,000
Completion: 2002-04
Hannah Corlett: architect
Spencer Guy: project architect
Niall McLaughlin: principal architect
Emma Wales: architect

This new community building is like a gate lodge to Finsbury Park. The building is like a grove of trees, representing the idea of the community coming together at the boundary between city and park. Its disparate functions are collected beneath a light-filtering canopy, which casts complex dappled shadows, and is translucent to allow views out to the sky. Existing trees are retained and grow up through the canopy: trees and architecture are so interwoven that they seem to grow into each other.

Layers of transparent materials and a maze of fine lines create a space from which you look out as if from a hedge or thicket. Following the theme of weaving – a fundamental principle of making, crossing cultural and gender boundaries, and with powerful connotations of unity coming from collective activity – the canopy is supported by a forest of very fine columns bound together for support.

Temple Quay Pedestrian Bridge, Bristol ▶
New pedestrian bridge
Budget: £1 million
Completed: 2002-04
Beverley Dockray: project architect
Niall McLaughlin: principal architect
Simon Tonks: architectural assistant

This bridge will link Bristol's Temple Meads Station and the Floating Harbour as part of the ongoing development of Temple Quay. The bridge is a stressed skin arc of stainless steel, landing on haunched abutments on either side. The balustrade forms part of the structure, making the bridge particularly slender. Its shape changes across its length, twisting and becoming higher and thinner, introducing beautiful curved surfaces that reflect light from the changing sky and water. Towards the centre the bridge becomes narrower and the balustrade slopes in, making it easier to lean over and look at the water below, accentuating the drama of crossing.

Small laser-cut perforations are cut in the stainless steel skin, with LED lights behind making the bridge glow at night, and subtly revealing the ghost of the internal structure.

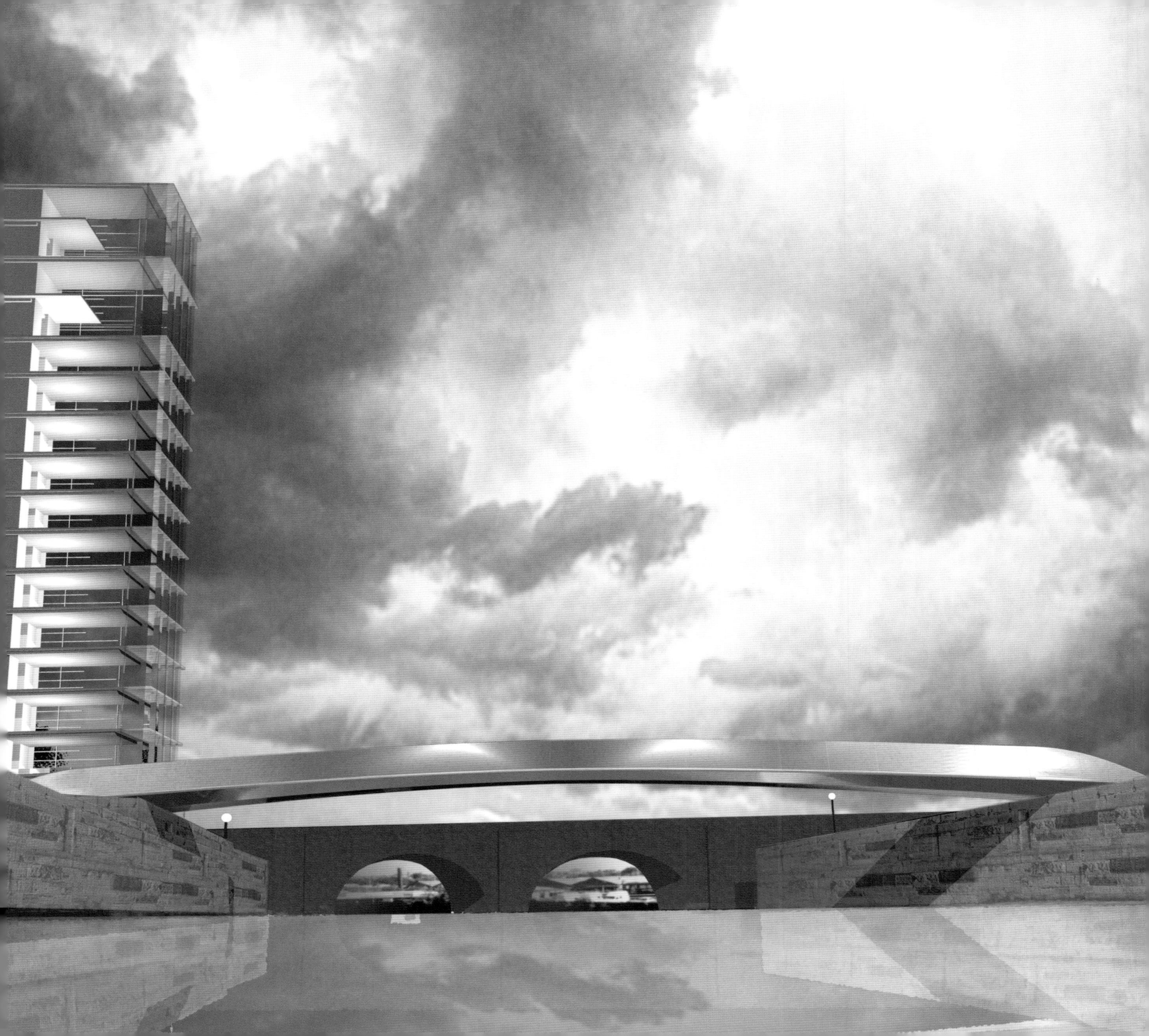

118 BRIGID McLEER

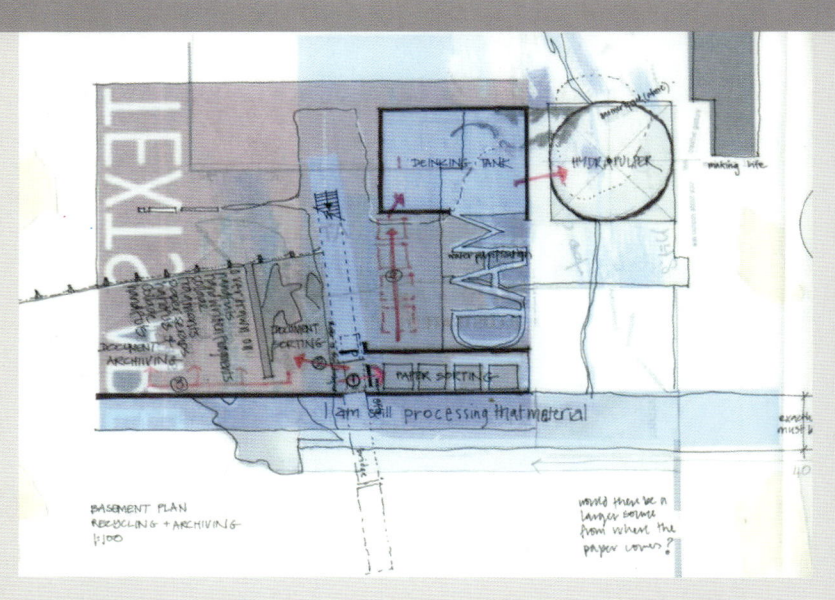

I am an Irish visual artist and writer based in London. My work moves between creative and critical practices in fine art, experimental writing, architecture and performance. It is also often collaborative. I did a postgraduate degree in Fine Art at the Slade, UCL, and have taught at a number of art, design and architecture schools in the UK. This coming year I will be working with Jane Rendell on the development of the new MA in Art, Architecture and Writing at the Bartlett.

Brigid McLeer

'In Place of the Page' (with Katie Lloyd Tomas)
Art project
We've spent £1,500 so far
Ongoing, 2000-04

Brigid McLeer: artist, conceived and organised project
Katie Lloyd Thomas: collaborator

'In Place of the Page' explores the relationship between our real experiences of place; both in terms of geographic location, and a more emotional desire for belonging; and the ways in which place is imagined and constructed through such modes as writing, architectural drawing and digital media. The project began with email correspondences with ten people, discussing 'place'. From these emails I generate graphic 'textplans' – not exact representations of the emails, more a changed material outcome, where text is transformed into a related but distinct new form. In the most recent phase of the project architect Katie Lloyd Thomas imposes a scale and reading (as plan, section or elevation) onto the textplans, and from these derives architectural drawings. With each new textplan we have gradually been 'finding' a building from her plans.

MIRALLES TAGLIABUE

The office of Enric Miralles and Benedetta Tagliabue in Barcelona is working on a series of major public buildings in Europe, including the new Scottish Parliament, Utrecht Town Hall, the Market of Santa Caterina (Barcelona), a new architecture faculty in Venice and the new headquarters of Gas Natural (Barcelona).

I have been involved in the work of the office for more then ten years: on competions such as the Rosenmuseum Frankfurt and the Bremerhaven city plan; as project architect for the music school in Hamburg and Trinity Quarter in Leeds; and as site architect on the Scottish Parliament. I also taught with Enric Miralles and Peter Cook at the Städelschule in Frankfurt am Main until 1999.

Karl Unglaub

The Scottish Parliament
New build parliamentary building
Under construction
Karl Unglaub: EMBT site architect in Edinburgh

The new Scottish Parliament building is located in the Old Town of Edinburgh at the foot of the Royal Mile, next to Holyrood Palace and Arthur's Seat. The location and questions such as what a parliament should look like and how it should relate to the history of the nation were key considerations in the design development. The parliament is part of the city but its main concern is with the whole country.

The new building rests on a piece of landscape, which the public can freely use. All the different parts of the Parliament form a conglomerate, not only a building. These parts are connected by a glazed foyer, which opens a view to the sky. The structure integrates an existing building (Queensberry House) and is related to the Royal Mile by a wall, which works like a 'pinboard' for the history of the country. The Debating Chamber rests on a grass-covered concrete vault structure. The roof of the Chamber is made of oak, and the key façade material is Kamney Granite.

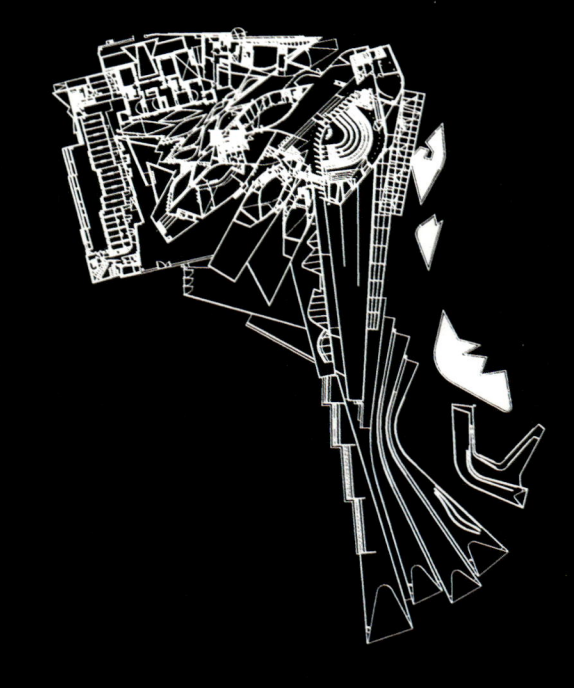

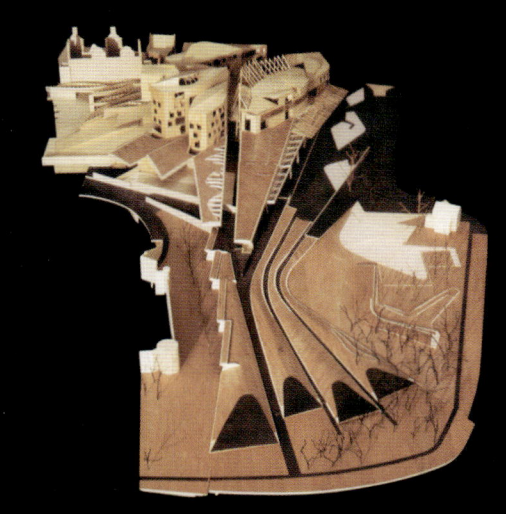

120 MIRALLES TAGLIABUE

NAAU

NAAU – New Architecture & Artists Union – is a group of architects, artists and filmmakers. We believe that by pooling diverse talents and transferring creative processes across disciplines we can produce powerful architecture and art forms that are truly of our time – a return to the ethos of the Renaissance, when the skills of craftspeople and artisans produced a unique whole. Today's craftspeople are not stonemasons and wood carvers; but filmmakers, computer animators, sound engineers, contemporary artists and photographers. The Bartlett exposed us to these new media and encouraged us to make leaps of the imagination with them, both then and now.

Dream more! Demand more!
Film
Budget: £30,000
Completed: June 2000
Rahesh Ram: producer and director

This film about people and architecture was produced to raise awareness of the urban environment and to encourage the public to demand better, braver architecture. We aimed to break down the barriers between architects and the public by encouraging debate during Architecture Week 2000 through the popular medium of cinema. The film was shown in 100 cinemas and reached an audience of approximately 500,000.

The voiceover reads: 'This is your world, a place for your imagination, transform it and create your future. Dream more, demand more… think architecture!'

122 NOODLEJAM

We met as undergraduate architecture students in Oxford and founded noodleJam immediately after graduating in 1997. Our partnership is based on a common interest in the juxtaposition of the spectacular and the ordinary in our environment. While studying for the Diploma at the Bartlett we worked on two photography projects, 'Eine Se(h)kunde' and 'Cruising', which deal with the commonplace and the beauty of the marginal. Although we are principally interested in journeying, in the possibilities of a determined yet aimless mode of drifting, we are currently working on a body of images taken in and around London since the city became our temporary home in 1999.

Nina Vollenbröker and James Santer

'Eine Se(h)kunde' – 'One Second' or 'The Art of Seeing'
Photographic documentation
2000
Nina Vollenbröker, James Santer: photographers

Photographing for seven months, we made a journey of almost 35,000 kilometres through 37 US states, to get away from the country's image as a dominating political, economical and cultural world power.

We don't assume the role of photographers. A photographer holds a camera to the eye, which in itself alters and falsifies the moment. The camera sterilises, irritates, interrupts the story. We assume the role of thieves. Taking photos from the hip, without looking through the viewfinder, secretly acquiring fragments of our surroundings without being noticed. Our pictures are not composed; they are free from drawn-out perspectives and constructed arrangements. They invite the coincidental, the fragmented, the arbitrary; their centres are often vacant and undefined.

Now we are inserting our stolen perspectives into new contexts: in exhibitions; generating narratives from them with literary groups; collaborating with America's influential contemporary composer, Gloria Coates, who performed her work amongst them during an exhibition in a derelict factory.

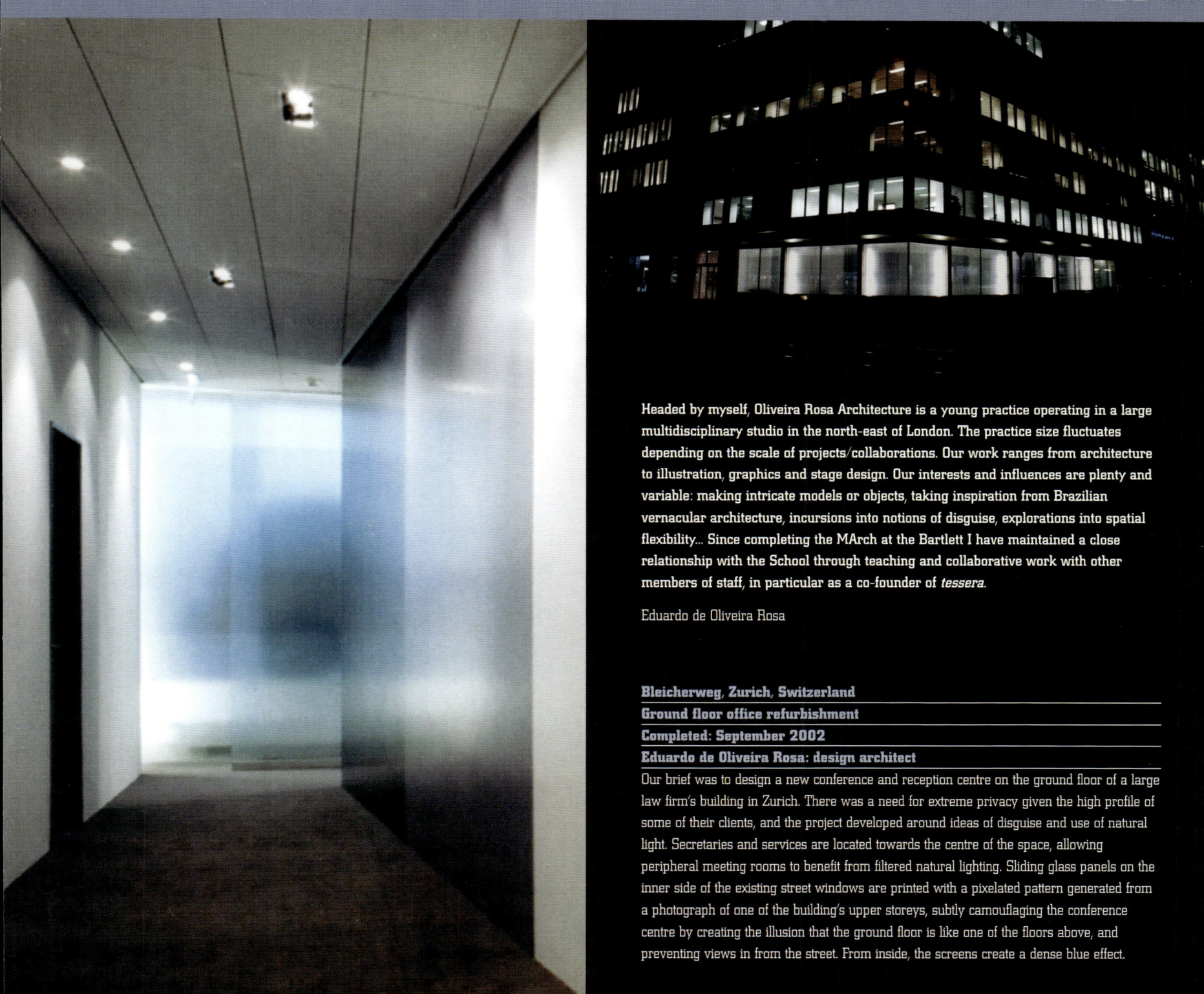

OLIVEIRA ROSA ARCHITECTURE

Headed by myself, Oliveira Rosa Architecture is a young practice operating in a large multidisciplinary studio in the north-east of London. The practice size fluctuates depending on the scale of projects/collaborations. Our work ranges from architecture to illustration, graphics and stage design. Our interests and influences are plenty and variable: making intricate models or objects, taking inspiration from Brazilian vernacular architecture, incursions into notions of disguise, explorations into spatial flexibility... Since completing the MArch at the Bartlett I have maintained a close relationship with the School through teaching and collaborative work with other members of staff, in particular as a co-founder of *tessera*.

Eduardo de Oliveira Rosa

Bleicherweg, Zurich, Switzerland
Ground floor office refurbishment
Completed: September 2002
Eduardo de Oliveira Rosa: design architect

Our brief was to design a new conference and reception centre on the ground floor of a large law firm's building in Zurich. There was a need for extreme privacy given the high profile of some of their clients, and the project developed around ideas of disguise and use of natural light. Secretaries and services are located towards the centre of the space, allowing peripheral meeting rooms to benefit from filtered natural lighting. Sliding glass panels on the inner side of the existing street windows are printed with a pixelated pattern generated from a photograph of one of the building's upper storeys, subtly camouflaging the conference centre by creating the illusion that the ground floor is like one of the floors above, and preventing views in from the street. From inside, the screens create a dense blue effect.

124 OLIVEIRA ROSA ARCHITECTURE

La Fromagerie, Marylebone, London
Specialist food shop design
Completed: October 2002
Eduardo de Oliveira Rosa: architect

The new Marylebone La Fromagerie (a specialist food shop from North London) brings their famous cheese room to the front of the shop. The new premises in Moxon Street had two possible entrances, one of which was adapted to house the cheese room, a refrigerated display and storage area where cheeses are handled. The design of the shop and its furniture arose from preoccupations with flexibility. From the stackable shelves and the collapsible market stalls (the latter typical of street vendors in Brazil) to the grid-like cheese display wall, the furniture allows for an almost infinite set of possible displays.

Inselweg 11, Hurden, Switzerland
New build single family house
Completed: August 2000
Eduardo de Oliveira Rosa: architect

This house was built on a plot of land directly on the Obersee, the upper part of the Zurich Lake. It was designed as a summer retreat for a couple with two grown-up daughters. The living area connects the couple's quarters on the northeast side with the guest accommodation, a long flexible volume on the first floor with large hinged panels modulating the space. Bordering a busy road, the masonry façade along the back of the building has a strong monolithic appearance, while the wooden front facing the lake presents itself as very open and permeable. During hot summer days, the wooden shutters offer shelter against the sun, and during the long winter they enclose and secure the empty house.

ORMS

The duality inherent in the architectural process has always fascinated me: on the one hand is the built manifestation almost subconsciously generated by the interaction of those involved in constructing it, and on the other is the realm of paper architecture that encourages intellectual exploration and radical ideas. Combining teaching and practice gives a unique opportunity to critically think through what I design, and simultaneously to set theoretical ideas into a context that is not divorced from reality.

Since I joined ORMS I have run a number of projects primarily based in Germany. Working for a UK company in Germany and teaching as a German in the UK not only involves some linguistic amusement, but is also a cultural challenge that offers stimulating insights into different and equally valid approaches towards the same profession.

Julia Backhaus

Health Club am Gendarmenmarkt, Berlin, Germany
Interior design of health club
Completed: October 2002
Julia Backhaus: project architect

The Health Club am Gendarmenmarkt is a cocktail of material sensations occupying three storeys of the renowned Quartier 205 building. Throughout the club a mixture of active and passive spaces are carefully interlinked. Gloomy walls and sequential screens separate different zones and moods. Perspectives are always controlled, either allowing or denying views, to inform the distinct spatial qualities. The palette of materials and subtle use of light give the illusion of reversed and infinitive spaces, confusing the notions of ceiling and floor, up and down. The pool hall is a silent, timeless space that relies on the primary experiences of bathing, relaxing and cleansing the body – antidotes to the fast tempo of the city. A cantilevered vision slot bursts out of the dividing wall between it and the foyer, the pool appearing like a shimmering aquarium from the entrance, confusing the boundaries between private and public, water and street level.

PASTINA MATTHEWS

In every project we seek not only to fulfil the client's commercial and pragmatic requirements, but to extend their ambitions, encouraging their involvement in the design process and unlocking unforeseen potential in even the most modest of commissions. In a cycle of editing and re-appraising, we always look to include rather than exclude, emphasising the dissimilar characteristics that this process creates, resulting in an architectural language that uniquely addresses each project's context.

66-68 Sclater Street, London
Residential conversion and extension
Budget: £450,000
Completed: October 2002
Chris Matthews: job architect

We have converted and extended an 1877 Spitalfields railway tenement block into three two-bedroom apartments. The existing front to Sclater Street has been restored, and the rear rebuilt and expressed as a new 'front', facing the Bishopsgate Goodsyard site, due to be redeveloped soon. To avoid an ugly network of pipes, timber screens mask drainage connections, and absorb horizontal windows set at different heights into a coherent façade. Low kitchen windows allow views out from seats in the lounges beyond, while higher bathroom windows provide greater privacy.

PATEL TAYLOR

Established in 1989, we are a successful medium-sized practice, large enough to tackle most projects and yet able to maintain a consistency of quality. We work at many scales, encompassing architecture, urban design and landscape, including major regeneration projects such as the Thames Barrier Park; masterplans for Ayr, Reims, Antwerp and St Paul's School; and education, leisure and housing designs. Many of these have been won through international competitions, which together with numerous awards and a variety of publications testify to the quality of our work.

Thames Barrier Park, Silvertown, London
Landscape design
Budget: £12.5 million
Completed: November 2000
Andrew Taylor: partner in charge

We won the commission for this new park, built on the north shore of the Thames on a former industrial site by the Thames Barrier, through a competition that sought proposals which would act as a catalyst for development of the surrounding area. We adopted a clear and bold landscape strategy, inspired by the history and context of the site, which will in turn determine the future architectural composition of the area.

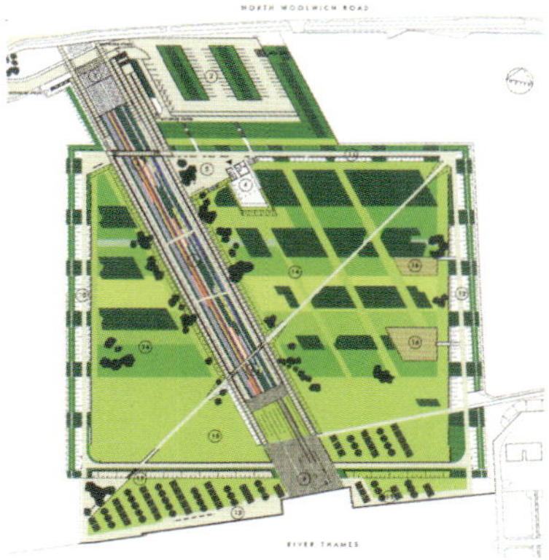

PENOYRE & PRASAD 127

Recalling the scale of dock structures, the 'Green Dock' slices through it and shelters the 'Rainbow Garden'. At its landward end the 'Dock' is approached through a dramatic water plaza, while a pavilion of remembrance, contemplation, reading and relaxing forms a focal point at the river end, framing views of the Barrier. The 'River Promenade' is for strolling by the Thames.

A series of settings are created for activities throughout the year. The 'Plateau', for informal recreation and public events, extends across the site, with contrasting open and closed spaces structured by lines of trees and wild flower meadows.

The completed park is already having a significant positive effect on the surrounding area, with nearby developments progressing and bringing affordable housing, a primary school and shops.

Since it was established in 1988, Penoyre & Prasad has gained a reputation for high quality, inventive architectural design. The practice has received wide recognition through many awards, publications and competition wins. Our mission: out of today's complex needs to produce an effective, sustainable architecture that is simple, sensual and thought-provoking.

The Charter School, Red Post Hill, London
Renovation of existing school
Budget: £17 million
Completed: April 2003
Wayne Head: phase one assistant architect, phase twi project architect

We have completed the transformation of the original 1950s Charter School into an exemplary modern comprehensive school for 1,400 pupils. In the first phase two existing blocks have been converted. A central courtyard has been roofed over to form a new entrance and foyer – the 'new heart' of the school. A central steel tree-like structure supports the partially-glazed roof, with natural light flooding dramatically in around it. The roof collects both solar energy and rainwater for recycling – a visible manifestation of the school's commitment to a sustainable future. The school has won a regional RIBA award and the Aluminium Imagination Award for the most original use of colour.

128 PÉREZ ARROYO + HURTADO ARCHITECTS

Salvador Pérez Arroyo is Professor of Building Technology at the ETSAM, Madrid´s School of Architecture and Visiting Professor in Milan, Venice, Cracow, Copenhagen, Rotterdam and the Bartlett. Eva Hurtado teaches at the CEES Universidad Europea de Madrid, and regularly attends Bartlett crits. We see our practice, based in Madrid, as a research exercise into the contemporary world and the complexity of living in it. We do not distinguish between restoring old buildings or designing new ones, designing objects or sculpture, and writing. Teaching is an activity that helps support this continuous and non-rigid way of thinking.

The following students and architects from the Bartlett have worked in our office: Kit Lewis, Julia Von Rohr, Tomás Amat, Laura Colmenares, Gwenola Kergall, Timothy Matthew and Karen Willcox.

Tomelloso Swimming Pool, Ciudad Real, Spain
New build public sports centre
Budget: £1.8 million
Completed: September 2002
Pérez Arroyo + Hurtado Architects: architects

This covered swimming pool responds to the environment in an area where the land, colours and sun are the strongest elements. The primary need was to provide shade. The pool hall is an asymmetrical space designed around light and shadow, its organisation and architectural language refined to be as simple as possible. Circular holes punched in the roof set up a dialogue with the rounded holes in the sculptural concrete legs and beams, sharing a language of form. Glass doors hang from all the façades and completely disappear when opened.

The roof is covered with stones, showing continuity with the landscape, and is inspired by a particular tradition we discovered in this region, whereby farmers piled up the stones found in their fields into a series of artificial hills that can be observed throughout the countryside.

Ground Zero, New York
Speculative design proposal
February 2003
Pérez Arroyo + Hurtado Architects: architects

A newspaper invited practices to submit alternative proposals to the official competition designs for the site of Ground Zero. The trace of lived events remains in a place. Ground Zero is a point of return, of infinite words and visits. New York's skyline belongs to everyone now, and Ground Zero will always belong to the Twin Towers and will be inhabited by ghosts. Like a ghost, our design occupies the atmosphere without compromising acts of remembrance. It occupies the air and shares its qualities: sometimes still, sometimes moving. This construction, close to the natural in the heart of Manhattan, invites reflection.

Our design is both idealistic, and a point of departure for research into developing a real building that could move, change colour and texture in response to its environment.

7+4 Housing Towers, Oviedo, Asturias, Spain
New build private housing
Budget: £10.9 million
Completion: summer 2003
Pérez Arroyo + Hurtado Architects: architects

We won a competition to design these eleven towers constructed above a railway line in dense urban surroundings. The towers provide housing, offices and shops. An application of 'pixels' is evident in the façade treatment and controls the whole project. The pixellated design allows a great amount of freedom in resolving the structure, dimensioning and detailing. Variations in the layouts at different levels and between towers are easily absorbed by the pattern.

The upper floors rest on four supports at second floor level that protect them from the vibrations of trains passing below. Below the towers the design integrates an environment that is split into two levels: the railway platforms and the street. At street level big 'corten' steel vertical waves help to dampen the sound of the trains and two extremely light triangular staircases lead to the platforms.

130 PHAB ARCHITECTS

I am a practising architect based in London, and a Bartlett design tutor. Formerly a partner of PHAB Architects, I now practice as Peter Hasdell Architects. The work of the practice involves consultancy for cities and urban planning, cultural and public art projects, as well as small-scale architectural projects. I am also involved in research and have published various pieces.

Peter Hasdell

Multifuctional Station, Mendrisio, Switzerland
Europan 6 competition entry (awarded a special mention and exhibited in the Europan Exhibition)
2001
Peter Hasdell: principal architect

Italy being in the EU, and Switzerland outside it, leads to specific forms of commuting and regional development. Our design strategy in a competition entry for the Swiss border town of Mendrisio took advantage of the cross-border rail travel, intertwining infrastructural flows and vectors operating at different scales. We proposed bringing regional commuters together with local transport users, through the redesign of the station and the reprogramming of the valley floor as a 24-hour service and commuter centre to complement the traditional hillside town above.

Our proposed station node compresses the east-west sectional experience and extends trajectories in a north-south direction through a series of linear strips. The strips intensify landscape and urban conditions adjacent to the railway infrastructure, transforming the area into a buffer zone and linear public space. Strips to the west incorporate high density housing, clean industry, media and technology programmes as future commercial attractors.

The station itself is a linear building and a functional and programmatic hybrid, stretched and made as thin as possible. The translucent structure is designed in response to envisaged 24-hour future use, and glows from within at night whilst allowing sightlines through. In contrast, adjacent factory buildings are broad flat structures, creating an interesting roofscape when seen by day or night from the city centre on the hillside above.

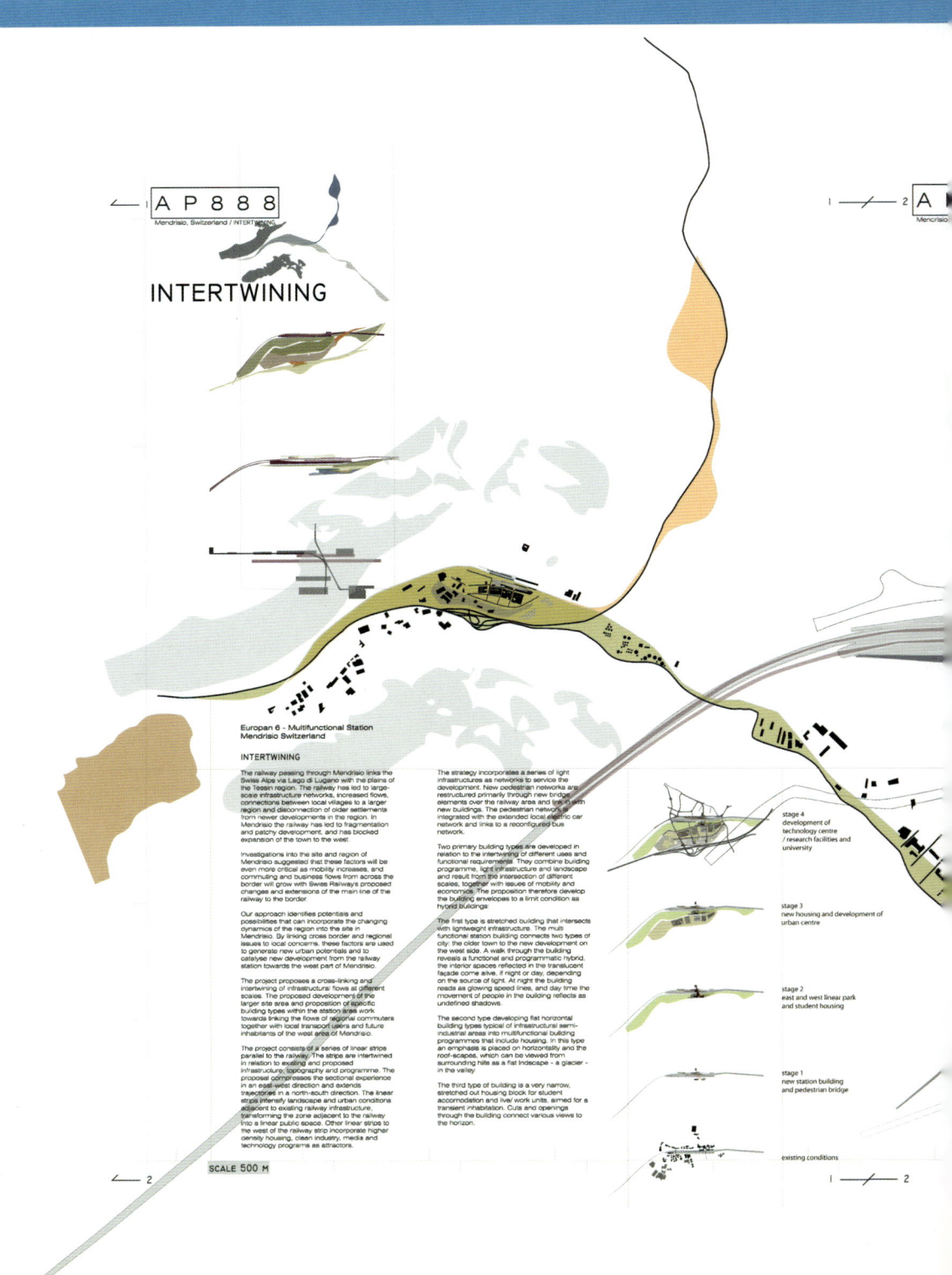

131

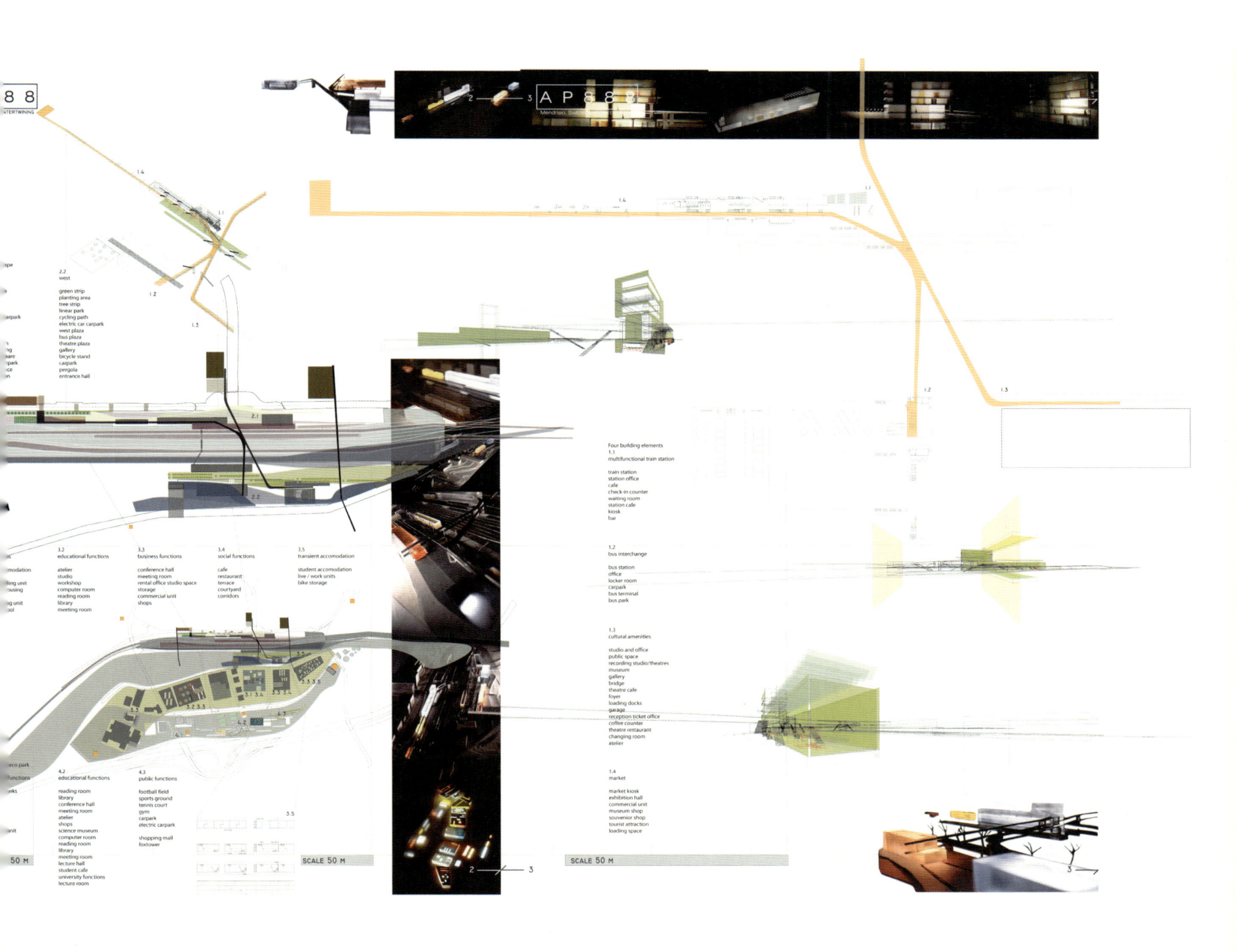

Four building elements

1.1 multifunctional train station
- train station
- station office
- cafe
- check-in counter
- waiting room
- station cafe
- kiosk
- bar

1.2 bus interchange
- bus station
- office
- locker room
- carpark
- bus terminal
- bus park

1.3 cultural amenities
- studio and office
- public space
- recording studio/theatres
- museum
- gallery
- bridge
- theatre cafe
- foyer
- loading docks
- garage
- reception ticket office
- coffee counter
- theatre restaurant
- changing room
- atelier

1.4 market
- market kiosk
- exhibition hall
- commercial unit
- museum shop
- souvenir shop
- tourist attraction
- loading space

2.2 west
- green strip
- planting area
- tree strip
- linear park
- cycling path
- electric car carpark
- west plaza
- bus plaza
- theatre plaza
- gallery
- bicycle stand
- carpark
- pergola
- entrance hall

3.2 educational functions
- atelier
- studio
- workshop
- computer room
- reading room
- library
- meeting room

3.3 business functions
- conference hall
- meeting room
- rental office studio space
- storage
- commercial unit
- shops

3.4 social functions
- cafe
- restaurant
- terrace
- courtyard
- corridors

3.5 transient accomodation
- student accomodation
- live / work units
- bike storage

4.2 educational functions
- reading room
- library
- conference hall
- meeting room
- atelier
- shops
- science museum
- computer room
- reading room
- library
- meeting room
- lecture hall
- student cafe
- university functions
- lecture room

4.3 public functions
- football field
- sports ground
- tennis court
- gym
- carpark
- electric carpark
- shopping mall
- foxtower

SCALE 50 M
SCALE 50 M

132 PIERCY CONNER ARCHITECTS

After my studies at the Bartlett I co-founded Piercy Conner with Stuart Piercy. In 2000 we won the Velux lifetime homes competition with a fully modular flexible housing scheme (now being developed with the Circle 33 Housing Trust) and were shortlisted for several concept housing competitions (The Ideal Home Show Concept House and Wates Built Homes Living Sites Competition). In 2001 we launched the Microflat affordable housing concept, specifically aimed at the intermediate housing market in central London. Our ideas continue to focus on the creation of new hybrid building typologies that reflect the diversity of our changing society.

Richard Conner

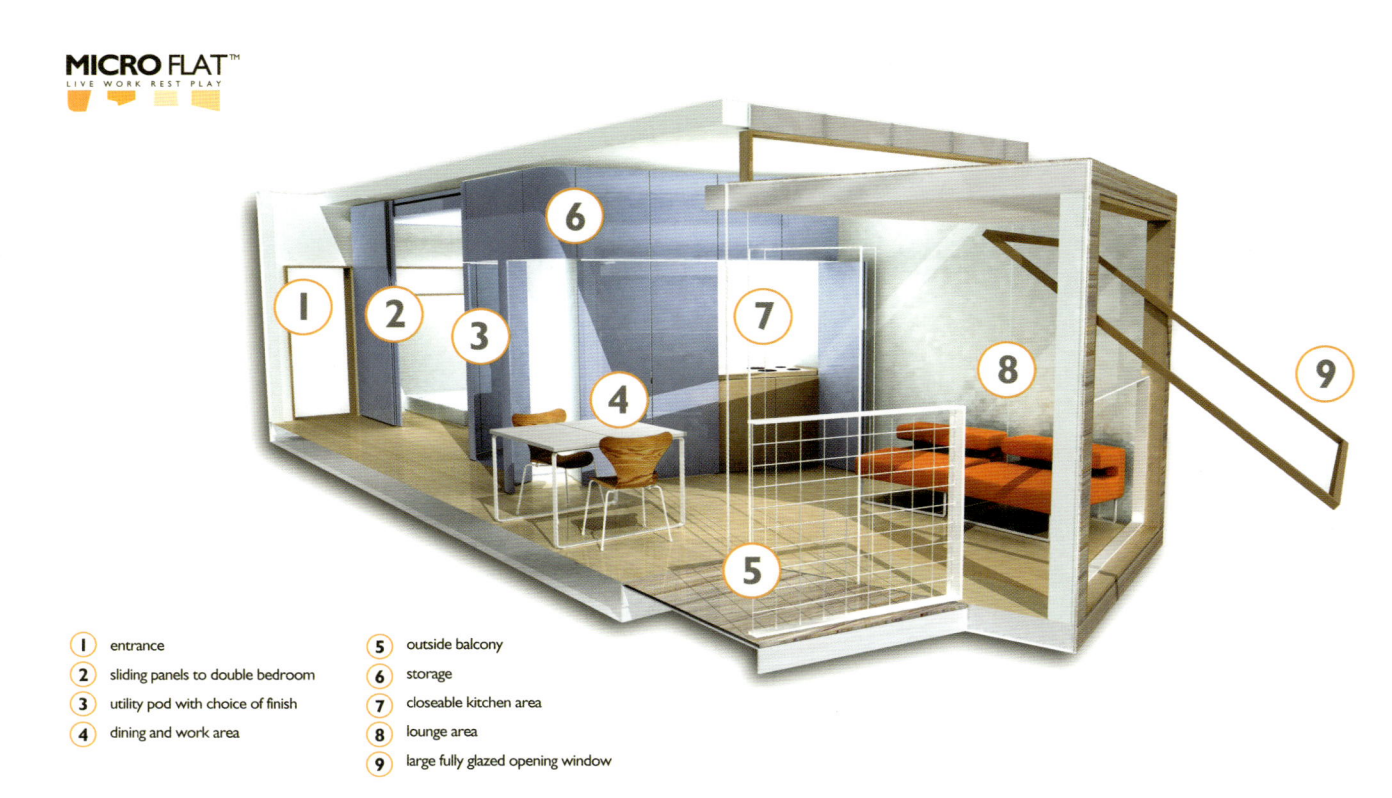

MICRO FLAT
LIVE WORK REST PLAY

1. entrance
2. sliding panels to double bedroom
3. utility pod with choice of finish
4. dining and work area
5. outside balcony
6. storage
7. closeable kitchen area
8. lounge area
9. large fully glazed opening window

Microflat, Central London (for The Microflat Company)
Proposed affordable urban housing
Richard Conner: design director

A radical rethink of dwelling typologies, intelligent construction and simplified planning procedures is necessary to stem the migration of young city dwellers to the suburbs, driven out by high house prices and the lack of accommodation for keyworkers and young professionals. Microflats are a pragmatic response: a typical flat has a customisable interior and can be configured into several massing and material options depending on site conditions.

The Microflat was originally conceived as a solution to the difficulty we ourselves faced in getting on the property ladder. We decided to team up to buy a small site, and to design compact flats, which would work properly as small units. We soon realised that the idea works extremely well for the intermediate market here in London, and set up the Microflat Company, generating worldwide interest and media coverage, including being featured on the TV chatshow, Richard and Judy. We have a financial backer and have already made two offers for sites.

Microlife, Selfridges, Oxford Street, London (for The Microflat Company)
Shop-window installation
Budget: £100,000
Constructed: January 2002
Richard Conner: design director

Microlife was a prototype affordable inner-city Microflat. Two 'Micronauts', Helene and Warren, lived for two weeks in the fully functional flat, constructed in the window of Selfridges' Oxford Street store, practising yoga, entertaining guests and enjoying the proximity to the centre of London. The installation aimed to raise the profile of the Microflat concept – a lifestyle that benefits from drastically reduced commuting times, ease of access to facilities, vibrant city life and affordability – and generated valuable design feedback from Helene and Warren.

PIERCY CONNER ARCHITECTS

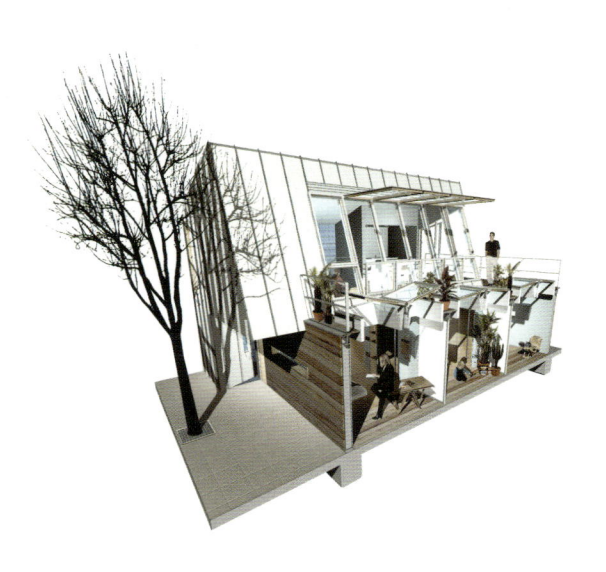

Martello Tower Y, Bawdsey Beach, Suffolk
Conversion of historic structure for residential use
Budget: £250,000
Under construction
Richard Conner: design director

Martello Towers were constructed at the beginning of the 19th century to protect the coast of England from any possible attack from the French. Despite being a huge investment, the towers were never used in a conflict. All are now Scheduled Monuments. Tower Y was one of the last to be built, in 1812. It is constructed of around 750,000 bricks, with four-metre thick walls, only four windows, an entry door at first floor level, and a rooftop with three gunning platforms.

Our proposed new roof form and interior fit-out had to make as little impact as possible on both the structural fabric and the landscape setting. The new roof, a lightweight steel and laminated plywood structure, will float above the existing parapet, supported on five 50-millimetre diameter V-shaped columns anchored into the brickwork. A 700-millimetre skirt of frameless curved glass below the roof will provide a 360° view of the landscape and sea.

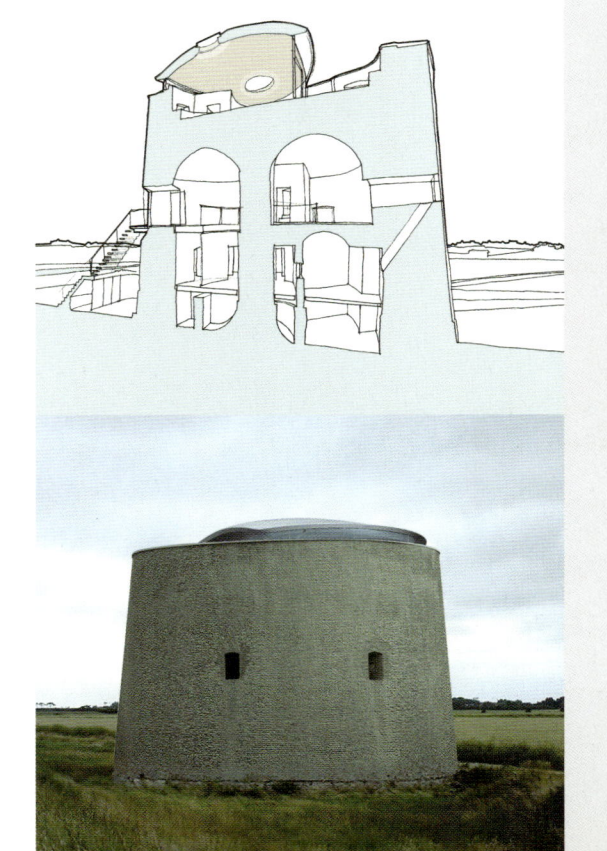

FLO houses, Oliver Road, Leyton, London
Velux lifetime homes competition winner
Budget: seven houses approx £1.5 million
Site purchase currently under negotiation
Richard Conner: design director

Contemporary cellular housing fails to react to the complex and rapidly changing patterns of urban living. FLO (Flexible Living Opportunities) housing, winner of the Velux lifetime homes competition, embraces the idea of change as a generator for a new type of mass housing. The scheme acts as an interface between the apparent spatial conflicts of privacy, flexibility, permeability and security, offering a fine balance between retreat and interaction.

Each dwelling has two distinct faces: an urban façade responding to the street, and a more permeable and transparent elevation opening onto a small secure community garden. A combination of live-work spaces, studios, four-bedroom family homes and one- or two-bed flats is possible from the modular unit, and the flexible floor plan allows different combinations of bedroom, study rooms and lounge configurations as circumstances change.

A scheme is now being developed with Circle 33 Housing Trust for a site in North London.

ALICIA PIVARO

Question: how to be involved in the world of architecture if you do not have the desire actually to build buildings? How to engage with its culture and processes, still be creative and contribute to its development?

Useful things from the Bartlett = Masters in History (Adrian Forty and Iain Borden) – the power of the written word and history – understanding of buildings as a manifestation of ideas; cultural, political, social, economic – Diploma Unit 15 (Kevin Rhowbotham, Clive Sall, Nic Clear) – the power of the cultural statement and provocative action – exploring territories for architectural activity beyond 'building'.

I've been testing and learning through roles at the Design Council, the Arts Council, the RIBA and now the Architecture Foundation – exploring ways of pushing forward thinking in architecture and communicating architecture to the public.

Answer: this is what I do.

Architecture Week
Public events
1997-ongoing
Alicia Pivaro: created and launched Architecture Week

Whilst at the Arts Council I had the opportunity to create and launch Architecture Week as the national celebration for architecture, working with Claire Pollock and supported by the Director of Visual Arts, Marjorie Allthorpe-Guyton. With limited funds the emphasis was on providing an 'umbrella' under which anyone – a gallery, school, community group or architecture practice – could run an event. The Architecture Unit provided administration and advice, a national guide to events, a website, launch event and some PR.

Many in the industry and media were supportive (the RIBA joined as a partner), some of course were typically cynical, but mostly we were inspired by the response from around the country – people got it. They understood the spirit in which the Week had been created – it was uncontrolled and even slightly anarchic – and that was what was most enjoyable. Over the years, thousands of people who would never go to an architecture exhibition or ever meet an architect have participated in an event and engaged with architecture – somehow. And they might now think of architecture as something relevant, interesting, even enjoyable.

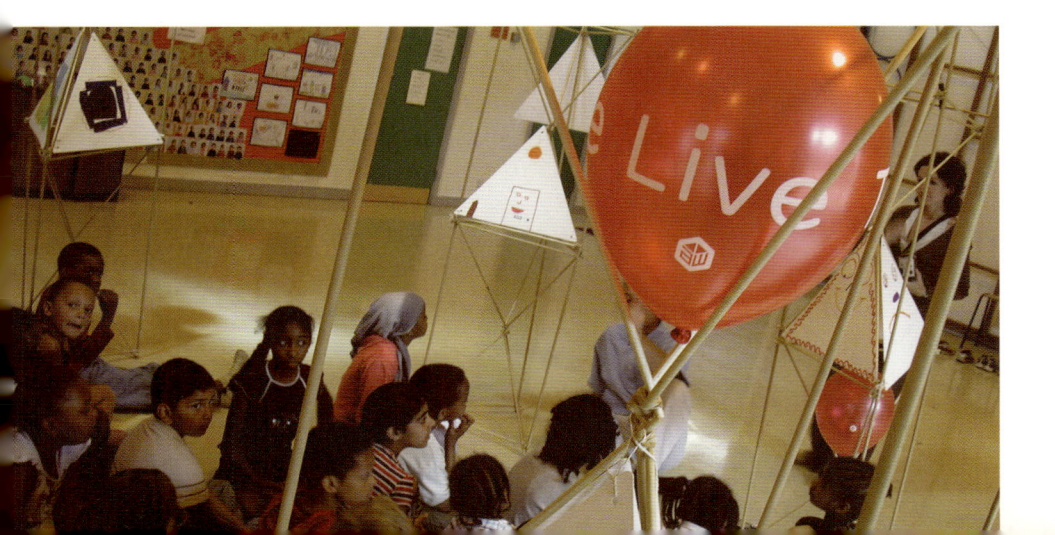

136 PLETTS HAQUE

Pletts Haque specialises in interactive design and research projects, exploring the ways that people relate to each other and to their surrounding space. We design both physical spaces and software and systems that bring them to life. Recent commissions include a global interactive tourist node, funded by the Interaction Design Institute Ivrea and the development of interactive elements for London's bus shelters. Our current research explores the concepts of 'hardspace' and 'softspace' and proposes ways in which architects can act as designers of 'spatial operating systems'.

'Scents of Space'
Interactive smell installation
Prototype installed in UCL Portico August 2002, final project built at Fabrica Gallery in Brighton
August 2002
Pletts Haque: design, construction

Scents of Space is an interactive smell pavilion. Visitors enter an enclosure, and experience zones of fragrance that define and demark spaces without physical boundaries. The installation is a carefully orchestrated sensory environment: smells are emitted singly or in 'chords' in response to people's movements, in combination with a visual cue in the form of glowing cubes. Smells travel slowly through the interaction zone in straight lines until visitors choose to mingle the fragrances with the movement of their bodies. Pleasant and unpleasant, recognisable and unfamiliar, natural and artificial fragrances are used.

Smell helps to alter our perception of a space: its size, openness and intimacy; but artists and architects have been slow to pick up on the potential for developing evocative and memorable experiences using our sense of smell. *Scents of Space* posits that if architecture could be precisely 'tuned' with scents, it would be possible to create completely new sensual ways of experiencing, controlling and interacting with it. The installation was constructed with the help of Jon Voss (Bartlett Diploma 2003) and Rayhan Omar (Westminster University).

PRINGLE BRANDON ARCHITECTS

Upon graduating from my Diploma at the Bartlett, I was awarded a TCS Research Scholarship Partnership with the Bartlett and Pringle Brandon. This was a fantastic opportunity to continue the research into intelligent interactive installations and environments that I had undertaken during my diploma, and to develop these projects for real-world applications. As a UCL Research Fellow I had access to many University resources, in particular the excellent staff and equipment at the Bartlett workshop, and Pringle Brandon was very supportive.

Andrew Whiting

EDF Trading Interactive LED Wall, Mid City Place, High Holborn, London
Interactive architectural installation
Budget: £40,000
Completed: March 2002
Andrew Whiting: designer/research fellow

The EDF Trading Interactive LED wall is located in the new headquarters of a multinational energy distribution company. Made up of 5,000 super-bright white LEDs behind a glass screen, it is inspired by graphics of national grid networks. The LEDs are mounted on bespoke white-lacquered circuit boards with all the electronics on show and are linked to 28 secreted movement sensors. Software creates a pseudo-random pulsing of light along the length of the wall, until human presence is detected, when light begins to 'shoal' like fish around the source of the input.

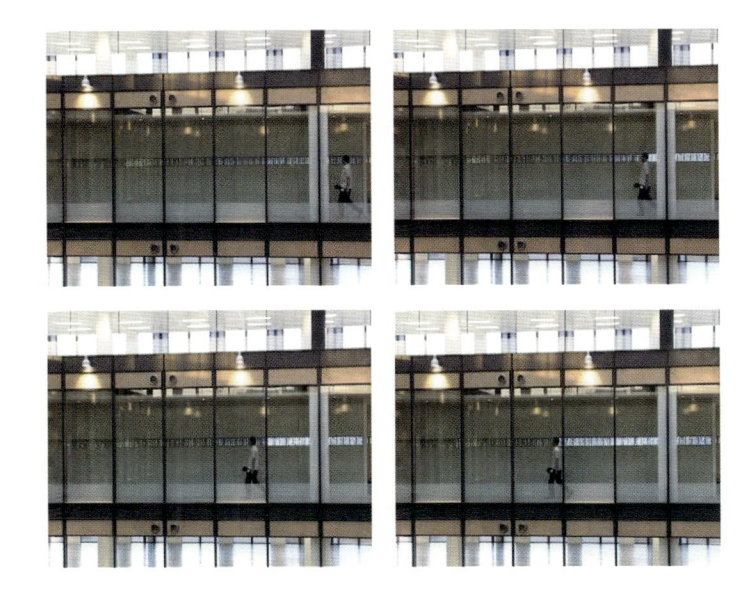

138 PROJECT ORANGE

After completing my diploma during the transition from 'old' Bartlett to 'new', I joined Conran Roche working on architectural and interior design projects. After ten years it was time for a change and in 2001 I left to join Christopher Ash full-time at Project Orange, which we had set up in 1997. We believe in narrative architecture that allows a thematic reading of outsides and insides. Our work embraces vigorous use of colour, texture and materials, resulting in playful spatial collages. For the past two years I have been running the Serious Glamour Unit at the Bartlett.

James Soane

Delhi Deli ▶
Takeaway restaurant fit-out
Budget: £105,000
Completed: December 2002
James Soane: architect

Delhi Deli is a new concept in Indian food, a top quality delivery and takeaway service, with shops designed to delight the passer-by with arresting patterns, abstracted from traditional Indian textiles but subverted to capture the spirit of colourful kitsch associated with a more youthful India.

The first unit in Battersea has a handcrafted façade of zinc sheet scales, cut to Moghul design profiles, around a frameless glass window. A pink neon sign pronounces 'Delhi Deli'. It can't be missed! Inside, there is a riotous lining of fuscia and green, with brick tile floors and cast-concrete counters, street-vendor style. At the heart of the shop the freestanding cooking station brings the theatre of preparation to centre stage. The food is dispatched in cute branded packaging via liveried scooter-vans. For those drawn in off the street there is a lime leatherette bench from which to watch the world go by.

Bolton Gardens, London SW5 ▲
House refurbishment
Budget: £250,000
Completed: February 2001
James Soane: architect

We rebuilt this house for Brad, Australian bachelor venture capitalist, around a journey up the staircase through a vertical daylit slot. At the top of the staircase is Brad's private realm, with a library/study opening into his bedroom – an extruded section reminiscent of the upper deck cabin of a jumbo jet. On a clear night you can see the stars through the glass roof over the stone-clad shower: just like back home.

The house was published in *FHM Magazine* July 2001.

JOHN PUTTICK

139

I am interested both in how buildings are resolved physically, and in the ideas that surround and inform architecture. My own work (which I continue in parallel with direct involvement in construction projects in practice) began with *Land of Scattered Seeds*, and is concerned with creating contemporary tales that evolve self-contained realities that reflect our world. All the complex relationships of life – be they social, ecological, economic – are studied and developed in miniature. These relationships are then played out through space and structure, revealing surprising connections between the most disparate things.

Land of Scattered Seeds
Artwork/book
John Puttick: artist

Land of Scattered Seeds is an architectural narrative presented in the form of a book. The story follows the daily lives of a small group of characters inhabiting the city of Graz, Austria, with the events being played out through the development of structures and gradual urban change. The work has been exhibited in London, Coimbra and Munich, and in 2002 a copy was purchased by the Museum of Modern Art, New

Stefan & Helga were delighted by the Pergola they had insisted that Franz construct. The space enclosed will be perfect for our Cocktail and Conasta parties, they agreed. Fifi loved her new space too.

JOHN PUTTICK

Hermann the birdman.

For some time wild birds have stolen the grapes that Franz has cultivated. Gathering his courage, the timid bird lover suggests one solution - an aviary.

York, for their Art and Architecture collection.

The story begins with two brothers, Franz and Jorg, who have lived on Sackstrasse at the foot of the Schlossberg all their lives. Depressed by the emptiness of their working routine and desperate to add to their income, the pair dream of becoming farmers. Utilising the only space they have available – the exterior of their apartment buildings – the brothers go into production. Franz establishes a vineyard, while Jorg grows pumpkins to refine into Kurbisol. The two maniacally compete.

Across the street live Olga and Florian, who retired from the civil service five years ago. Horrified by the vegetal chaos erupting in the area, the couple cultivate formal gardens on the façade of their building as an act of floral defence. Lola, owner of the local hairdressing salon, proves more enterprising – taking the petals shed from Franz' vines to produce an enriching shampoo.

As time passes the area flourishes – the farmers exploit the terrain to provide irrigation, and Franz has to use all his resources to persuade other local characters (Stefan, Helga, Hermann, Hugo and Wolf) of the merits of his scheme. All the while wild plants and birds continue to invade and so the struggles of Franz, Jorg, Olga, Florian and Lola continue. . .

PEG RAWES

I teach History and Theory at the Bartlett and Critical Studies in the Visual Arts Department, Goldsmiths' College, University of London. Having studied Art History and Philosophy and Literature I am completing PhD research into philosophical concepts of geometry and modernist art practice, at Goldsmiths'. This research proposes a series of aesthetic geometric methods in philosophy and contemporary visual arts practices.

Alice's pillow-books: adventures in immanence
This text is an essay to accompany the exhibition 'Species of Spaces' held at The Danielle Arnaud Gallery, London in August 2002.

Georges is most well known for his predilection for inventing the world through lists, but he also desired 'space as invention'… So, take a leap from Georges' bed into the 'fresh horizons' that are to be discovered in the pillow-books of Alice. In the oneiric space between Alice's head and her pillow a continuum of other worlds, empirical and imagined states of difference are to be found…

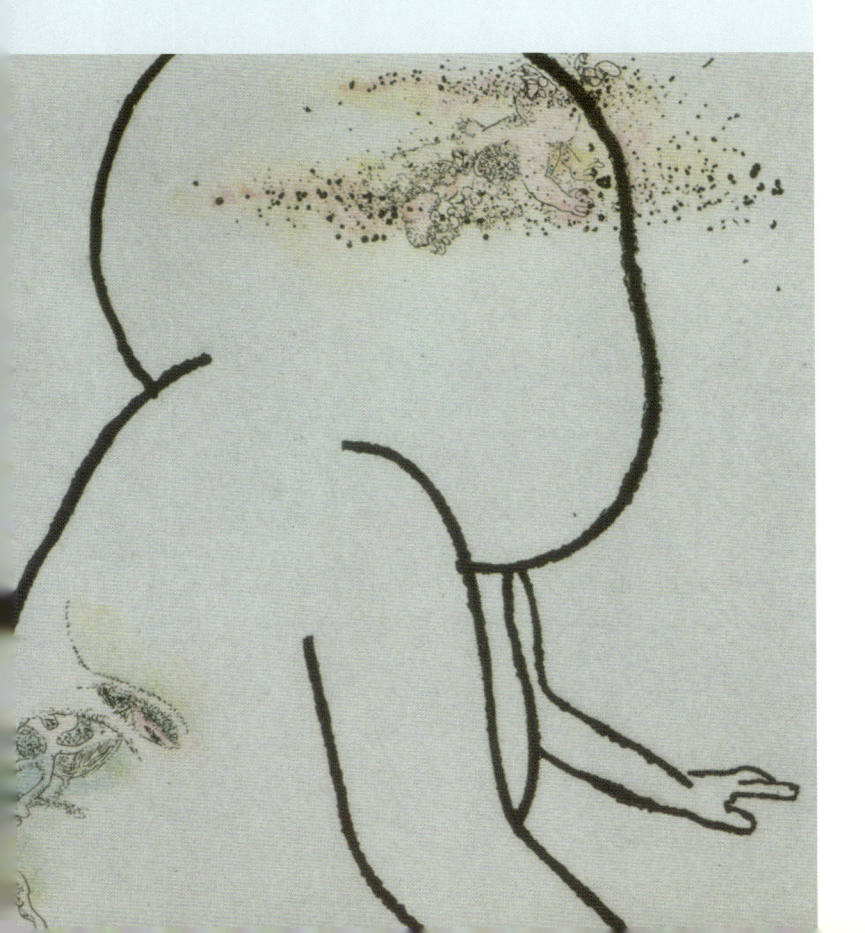

THE CANOPY > A figure can be seen travelling at high speed, leaping through the deep, dense but capacious canopy of the forest. Feral and agile, this singing figure calls out her way as she traverses between the precarious uppermost plane of this canopy, gradually spiralling her way down into the deeper topology of trees… Circling high above the canopy, the Kite has watched Alice settle and now she guides herself gently down on the thermals to alight in a slender White Poplar nearby… Alice had heard of kite-riding, derived from the practice of securing a human to the frame of a kite to ride the winds to become an embodied bit of sky, between the Gods and the secular world…

Minutes later, on the back of the kite she understands the meaning of the mixture of magic and technology that this raptor embodies as they rise up through the canopy which seems impossible to leave… they have been flying for some time, and still they are immersed within the iridescent patina of the canopy. Finally, however, she realises that this space is not empty air, but a mist of dense vapours and light, so highly reflective of the vibrant plateau that it sustains the qualities of the canopy…

THE HOLLOW > They descend into the midst of the forest, and Echo lands lightly onto the boughs of a small Pomegranate tree to find that the sonorous voice which emanated through the foliage belongs to an earwig, Persephone, whose affinity for sound is registered in the homophony between her mythical name and 'pierce-orielle,' the ear-piercer. Persephone's singing accompanies her construction of a space that is neither inside or outside – a hollow… This hollow, at the centre of the tree, becomes a den, lined with moss that will allow them to emerge as if from a fur-lined sleeping bag suspended between the trees. Later, Alice is still covered in bits of moss, having rolled around in the giving greeness until it has hollowed out a reflection of her girlishness that yesterday seemed unremarkable, but today gives her a flexibility that makes negotiating the space between the canopy and the ground so much easier…

THE ESTUARY > Below, in the river, there is another figure, Villanelle, whose appearance disguises her digital webbedness that enables her to get to the depths of things… Gliding up under Alice, Villanelle invites her into the broad base of her boat to go in search of another guide whose colourful dance is at its most imperceptible on the margins of land and sea… Alice takes to the water to follow the octopus's shifting, chimeric movements as she negotiates her way through the shallow depths. Ariadne's intelligence doesn't just stretch to the imitation of predators… but gives her the possibility of continuous invention within the diverse ecology of the estuary… And, gradually, Alice finds that the waves feel less resistant to her movements and become a continuous envelope of the pulsing ebb and flow that she creates until she is unclear of the boundary between her body and the materiality of the sea…

142 JANE RENDELL

In my work as an architectural designer, historian and writer, I explore the relationship between architecture and other disciplines – feminism, fine art practice and writing – published in books such as *Gender Space Architecture* (Routledge, 1999), *Intersections* (Routledge, 2000), *The Unknown City* (MIT Press, 2000) and *The Pursuit of Pleasure* (Athlone Press, 2001). I am currently completing a book for Reaktion Press, *A Place Between: Art, Architecture and Spatial Theory*, and developing a project with site-specific writings. At the Bartlett, I have established history/theory courses at MA and Diploma level where practice-based processes inform the production of site-specific writing. At PhD level some of my students work between the PhD by Text and the PhD by Architectural Design, exploring the creative potential of critical writing as a form of spatial practice.

'Les Mots et Les Choses'
Text-based installation
2003
Jane Rendell: Artist/Author

This piece is set in threes: one object and two texts describe three places. 'Moss Green' describes a derelict house in the green belt, where, on a Sunday walk in early March, we found photographs of a brave new world of modernist high rise housing. Later that year, just after the autumn equinox, just after her death, I dreamt of the home of my Welsh great aunt. 'White Linen' recalls this dream, while 'Bittersweet' remembers an abandoned cork factory in Catalunya visited the following spring where we found the names of colours scattered over the floor.

For an expedition to Seoul, as 'what is the colour of memory?' (April 2002), a Korean vocal translation was added to each text and object pair. The texts were translated back into written English from the Korean audio recordings for their journey to Los Angeles as 'the voice one cannot control' (November 2002). In moving, the words have been translated from English to Korean and back again, from writing to speaking and back again, yet the objects appear unchanged.

In *'Les Mots et Les Choses'* (1966), translated into English as 'The Order of Things', Michel Foucault explores the ordering of systems of relationships between different cultural elements (for example, those that are real, those that represent, those that resemble, those that can be imagined). Between words and things, between writing and speaking, between one site and another, this triptych consists of three objects positioned in the slippage of language that occurs through translation and displacement.

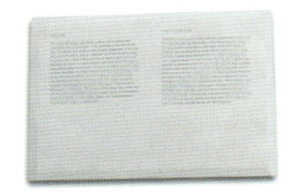

MOSS GREEN

It's a beautiful house – one storey building, with a square plan – born at the birth of modernism in the aftermath of the First World War. It embodies the values of early English modernism, of the arts and crafts movement: 'truth to materials' and honest craftsmanship.

From the road it looks a little un-loved, in need of some care and attention. Up close it is clearly derelict, almost in ruins. We enter a room with windows at each end. Curtains are falling away from the runners. The fabric has been soaked overnight and is drying in the spring afternoon sunshine. On the window sill and spilling over onto the floor are piles of old magazines. The pages are stuck together and disintegrate if you pull them apart. There are some photographs of buildings. One is particularly damp, the corners are soft, the surface is wrinkled. It shows a tower block, just completed, empty and pristine, a moss green utopia, the modernist dream dispersing as it soaks up spring rain.

WHITE LINEN

I dreamt of the house last night. My mother's house in Cwmgors, south Wales,
a place where it always rained in the holidays, that as a kid I resented, but now,
as it is being taken from me, I already begin to miss. I was in the dining room;
the rest of the house was empty except this one room.
The furniture was far too big and covered in linen. The air was thick and still, silent.
With the curtains drawn, it was very dark, but the linen glowed white.
I went towards the mantelpiece to take a look at myself in the mirror,
and I saw for the first time in the reflection, that the room was full of plants;
so alive I could smell moisture still on their leaves.

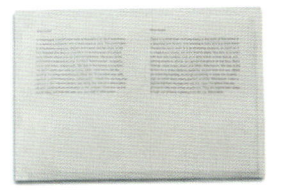

BITTERSWEET

In Palafrugell, a small town north of Barcelona on the Costa Brava is a derelict
cork factory with a clock tower in front. The clock tower is a handsome structure,
elegant and robust, but the clock on top has stopped.
The floor is covered in dust and pieces of furniture, lamp-stands, chairs and old printing
machinery. There are words everywhere scattered all over the floor:
'burnt orange', 'turquoise', 'black and white', 'bittersweet'.
We stay in the factory a long time. We don't speak, just walk and look. Later, once we've left the
building, he brings something to show me. It is a white sign with carefully painted black letters:
'bittersweet'. I reach into my bag and pull out a clear square section rod;
along one side of it letters printed onto cardboard are embedded in the perspex.
From the top it is out of focus, but from the side I can read it: 'Bittersweet'.

RIBA JOURNAL

'Back from the brink'
Magazine article
Budget: my time and train fare plus the cost of photographs
Published: *RIBA Journal*, October 2002
Eleanor Young: architectural journalist

Bradford has no grand project under construction and no architectural superstars rooting for it. So it could seem an unpromising start for a feature on physical regeneration, but when I suggested writing it I already knew Bradford had a great Victorian heritage and that it would be on priority lists for government money following riots in 2001. I also knew that Bauman Lyons had recently built some crazy red bus stops there. Surely these were encouraging signs?

So I started my research: over the last few years there had been lots of new projects announced. Architects and those preparing Bradford's 2008 Capital of Culture bid were upbeat about the city's future. Then the story broke that Bradford's rejected masterplanners were calling for a boycott of the city council. Contacting critics of the council I was told that local government was indecisive and lacked the skills to regenerate the city.

On my train ride north I sat over a map, circling the sites I wanted to visit. I was going to familiarise myself with the city, to suggest some shots for the photographer and to confront the council with some of the criticisms. Then wandering around the city there were some puzzling vacant sites. Local architects later filled me in on numerous schemes that had come to nothing.

At the council I stood looking over the city with various regeneration and planning heads while they pointed out various developments. I put some of the problems to them, and they admitted it was a tough job. Modest ambitions for call centres in the area are at least realistic. The real story that emerged is one of powerlessness. It is one we forget in the age of government promises.

Brought up on a parental diet of obsession with stones, trees and land-surveys, engaging with my environment has always been important to me. Walking the city I have to suppress my desire constantly to point things out. So when my first job in journalism came to a full stop, and I had time to think about my next step, I dreamt of writing about architecture – about what makes the city. An apprenticeship sub-editing at the *Architects' Journal*, learning how to write about buildings and design, under generous editors who also allowed me the flexibility to study the MSc in Architecural History at the Bartlett, gave me the chance. Now I can point things out more knowledgeably, and even get some of them into print in the *RIBA Journal*.

Eleanor Young

RICH MARTINS

At the Bartlett I focussed on the incorporation of issues related to race, culture and identity into architecture. Rich Martins Associates, comprising architects Peter Rich and Walter Martins, was established to implement a series of projects that will form a tourism route through Alexandra Township. During 30 years of practice, Peter has produced a body of work that seeks both materially to enrich and culturally to empower Black South Africans. His designs key into the spatial patterns of vernacular architecture, producing environments that are in harmony with indigenous cultures. Working with Peter and Walter is equipping me with a vocabulary of built form with which to pursue the agenda in which I first became interested at the Bartlett.

Jonathan Manning

Mandela's Yard Museum, Alexandra Township, Johannesburg, South Africa
Museum and community facility
Budget: ZAR 2.8 million (£240,000)
Completion: late 2003
Jonathan Manning: assistant architect

The Mandela's Yard Museum will be built close to the yard and single room in Alexandra Township where Nelson Mandela lived as a young lawyer during the 1940s. The building bridges the road between two corner sites. The design refers both materially and spatially to its rich context. The steel structural grid follows the dimensions of the single room spatial grid of Alexandra, and the convoluted layout mimics that of the surrounding network of yards, with an added verticality facilitating views across the township. Non-structural infill panels made by members of the community use materials echoing the surroundings, including corrugated steel, concrete blocks and recycled beer bottles.

IAN RITCHIE

Ian Ritchie Architects have realised major new works throughout Europe: including the Reina Sofia Museum of Modern Art in Madrid, the Leipzig Glass Hall, the Louvre Sculpture Courts and Pyramids and La Villette Cité des Sciences in Paris, and the Jubilee Line Extension and International Regatta Centre in London. The practice has received many national and international awards, and our work has been widely published in books, reviews and journals, and featured in several films and exhibitions.

Ian Ritchie enjoys being an external examiner at the Bartlett where he has been involved on and off since 1990.

146 IAN RITCHIE

Alba di Milano, Piazza Duca d'Aosta, Milan, Italy
New monument
Budget: €1 million
Completed: 2001
Robin Cross: project architect

Ian Ritchie Architects was announced the winners in January 2000 of an open international competition for Milan 2001 III Millennium Segno Luminoso. The new light monument was officially inaugurated by Milan's mayor, Mr Albertini, twelve months later in January 2001.

Alba di Milano is at the centre of Piazza Duca D'Aosta, directly in front of Milan central station, and faces south to Via Vittor Pisani, the main promenade leading to the city centre. Steel foundations support two curved and tapering steel beams that cantilever towards the station at an angle of approximately 60°, and are clothed in light-emitting fabric, made from randomly fractured optical glass fibre woven with fine stainless steel wire. The piazza is a point of orientation within Milan – from it journeys to and from the city begin and end. Springing like the water from the ground, Alba di Milano will raise the profile of the Piazza within the city, and communicates Milan's world renown as the centre of fashion and design style, quality and innovation.

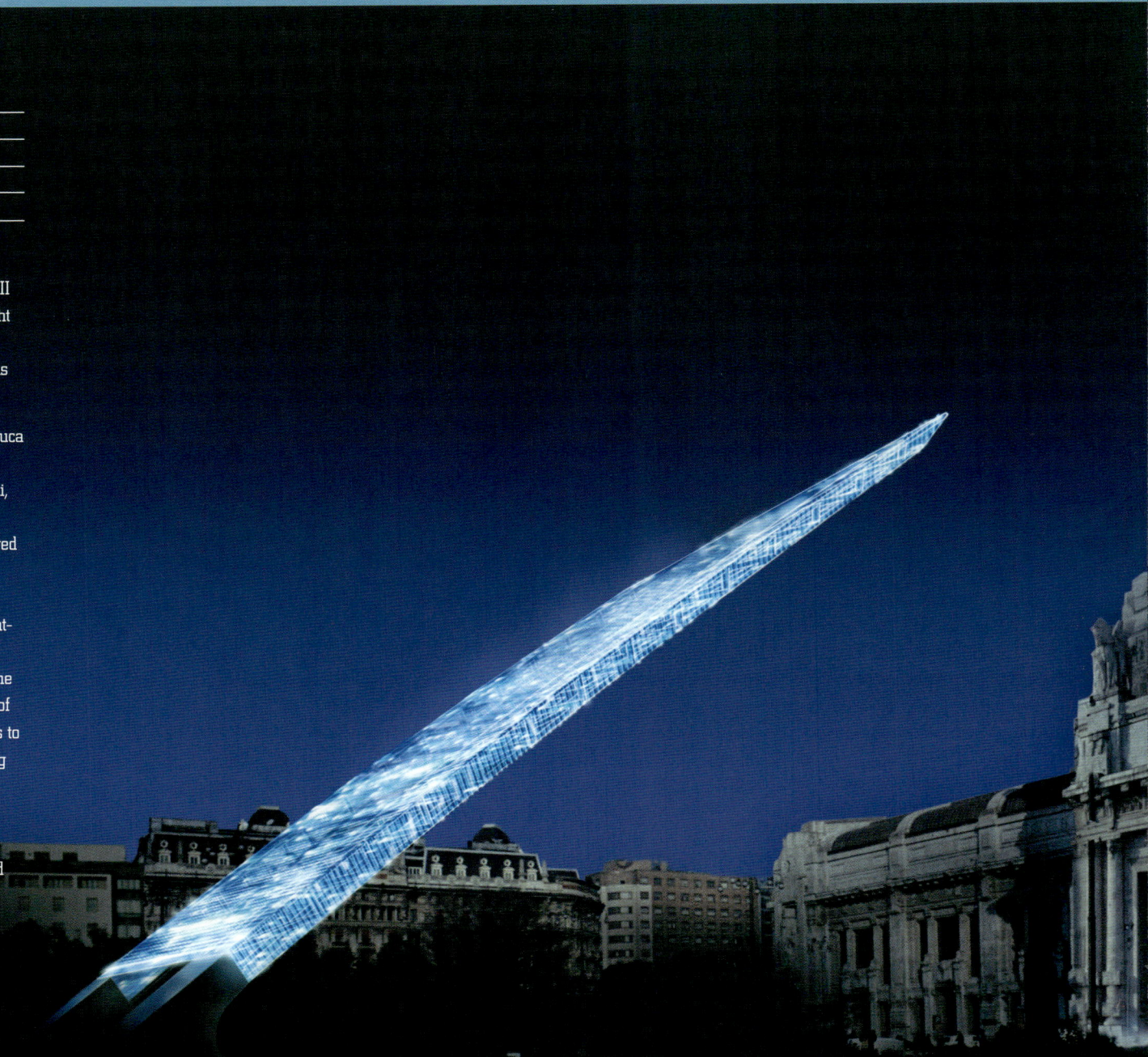

Shepherd's Bush Green, West London
Urban landscape design
Budget: £7 million
Phase 1: 2003
Phase 2: 2005
Anthony Boulanger: project architect

We were commissioned in 1999 to analyse the existing conditions of Shepherd's Bush Green and its immediate surroundings and to develop a design vision for its improvement. The Green is a significant public open space and an important local landmark, and will be central to the regeneration of the area.

As well as widening pavements, planting new trees to create 'avenues' to the south and west, improving lighting and creating wide pedestrian crossings to increase accessibility, we introduce water for childrens' play and certain shifts in the existing topography of the Green to change the way it is used and perceived. We foresee the creation of the Shepherds Bush Contemporary Art Space, which would become a new cultural hub in the capital, an outdoor urban gallery without walls. An ambitious programme of contemporary art by local and international artists, ranging from sculpture to installation and film, will be curated specifically for the space.

148 IAN RITCHIE

The Spire of Dublin, O'Connell Street, Dublin, Ireland ▶
New monument
Budget: £2.9 million
Completed: 2003
Robin Cross: project architect

Won in an international competition, this monument is the flagship project in the wider improvement of the centre of Ireland's capital city. 120 metres high and three metres in diameter at its base, the tapering spire rises above O'Connell Street, breaking above the roof line in as slender and elegant a movement as is technically possible. It responds to the character and climate of the Irish landscape: swaying gently in the wind and by day softly reflecting the light of the Irish sky. From dusk, the tip is strongly illuminated to provide a beacon over Dublin.

The bronze base incorporates a spiral, alluding to the continuity of Ireland's history and an expanding future. Bronze's historical role in the development of Irish art is augmented in the future as the base acquires both a patina from the Irish climate and a golden polish from human contact.

Plymouth Theatre Royal Production Centre, Cattedown, Plymouth ◀
New cultural building
Budget: £5.85 million
Completed: October 2002
Toby Smith: project architect

The new Production Centre centralises all production activities of the Plymouth Theatre Royal, including making sets, costumes and props; and rehearsal, education, and communal spaces. It can support the demands of two simultaneous full productions. The architectural concept is developed from complementary themes and strategies: 'driftwood' – parts of the building are designed as if washed up by the tide; 'cardboard theatre' – overlapping layers present a montage of activities; 'veils' – naturally weathering enveloping skins filter light; 'Yin and Yang' – the principal activities of manufacture and performance are organised by rotational symmetry around routes that encourage chance encounters and a sense of community.

RICHARD ROGERS PARTNERSHIP

Richard Rogers Partnership has offices in London, Barcelona and Tokyo. The practice is now some 130 strong, including twelve directors and 20 associates. RRP is committed to designing schemes that create successful public space and enliven inner-city areas.

The projects included here give a good overview of our recent work – three major European law courts – including Antwerp and Bordeaux; the Millennium Dome in Greenwich; Lloyd's Register of Shipping in the City of London; education buildings in Japan and the UK; major airport projects, such as Barajas Airport in Madrid; a new library for Birmingham; and the new National Assembly for Wales in Cardiff.

Masterplanning represents about one third of our output – major schemes include the South Bank Centre in central London and Convoys Wharf in Deptford. Sustainable planning is a key feature of our work, most notably on the Greenwich Peninsula, for which we have produced a masterplan and redevelopment strategy.

Antwerp Law Courts, The Netherlands
New build
Construction cost: £65 million
Completion: June 2005
Ivan Harbour: project director

Won in a public two-stage competition, Antwerp's new law courts have been conceived as a symbolic gateway to the city, as well as a bridge connecting adjoining neighbourhoods. Straddling a major motorway interchange leading into the centre, it forms the catalyst for the regeneration of the area southwest of the city. The new building will accommodate a number of disparate judicial functions, including 36 courts, hearing rooms, offices, a library and dining room. The focus is a grand public hall, the Salle des Pas Perdus, covered by a series of dramatic, sail-like roof forms, visible from vantage points all over the city.

150 RICHARD ROGERS PARTNERSHIP

Minamiyamashiro Elementary School, Japan
New build
Construction cost: £11.8 million
Completed: 2003
Ivan Harbour: project director

In 1995 RRP was approached by the mayor of Minamiyamashiro to design a relatively low-cost school, planned as the core of a new educational and welfare zone in the village. A double-height multi-purpose hall forms the heart of the building, with views from its mezzanine over the playground and to the mountains. Flexible spaces are framed by the 8.1-metre-square structural grid, and classrooms can be joined to allow larger group activities. Colour is used to express circulation zones and to define the character of spaces, with neutral tones for adult areas, warmer colours for younger children and cooler colours for older pupils.

New Area Terminal, Barajas Airport, Madrid, Spain
New build
Construction cost: £448 million
Completion: 2005
Ivan Harbour: project director
Andrei Saltykov: project architect

The New Area Terminal, which will be the biggest in Spain, will provide improved facilities for the existing Barajas International Airport to enable it to compete with other major European hub airports. The terminal consists of a series of parallel linear buildings, separated by long slots allowing the landscape and daylight to penetrate deep inside. Oversailing arching roofs extend over all of the main structures, including the arrivals and departures forecourts, parking and railway and metro station, and thereby encompass the entire sequence of transit activities from drop-off to gate.

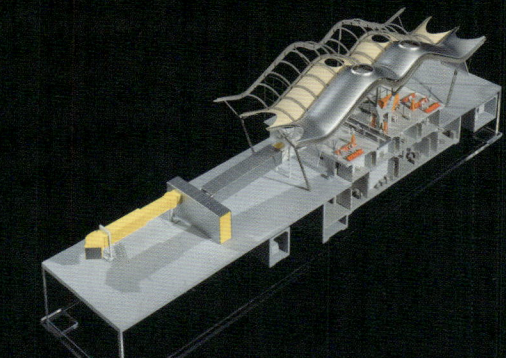

Lloyd's Register of Shipping, City of London
New build
Construction cost: £70 million
Completed: 2000
Carmel Lewin: design team, final stages project architect

The new Lloyd's Register of Shipping headquarters comprises six storeys of office space stepping up to 14 in the centre of the site. The tapered floorplates, fitting the awkward geometry of the site, create a fan-shaped grid composed of vaults formed around two dramatic atria spaces. This design allows daylight penetration and provides thermal buffers between the offices and the external environment.

Service cores are expressed as towers: two primary circulation cores at the front with secondary cores at the rear housing toilets, goods lifts, staircases and main service risers. The steelwork of the cores is colour-coded: blue for main structure, yellow for stairs, red for lifts and silver grey for secondary elements. Highly transparent glazing allows instant legibility, and people using the fully glazed wall-climbing lifts and stairs animate the exterior.

152 RICHARD ROGERS PARTNERSHIP

Tribunal de Grande Instance, Bordeaux, France

New build law courts

Construction cost: £27 million

Completed: 1998 (landscaping 2003)

Stephen Barrett: site architect

Ivan Harbour: director in charge

The transparency and openness of the new Bordeaux Law Courts meet the French Ministry of Justice's request that the building should promote a positive perception of the accessibility of the justice system. Public access is via a grand stairway over a water pool, leading to the *piano nobile* of the Salle des Pas Perdus, a large glazed public ambulatory beneath the seven round conical courtrooms. The building's silhouette is sympathetic to the gothic profile of the cathedral it faces, while the form of the courtrooms echoes the mass of the adjoining mediaeval towers. Supported on pilotis, the courts stand behind a near-invisible glass curtain wall, and penetrate the lightweight undulating copper roof above to facilitate natural ventilation.

An atrium divides the public *piano nobile* from a five-storey wing housing offices for the judges, magistrates and their support staff. Judges enter the courtrooms via open bridges across the atrium from their offices. The legibility of vertical circulation is a direct expression of the various judicial processes housed within the building.

National Assembly for Wales, Cardiff
New build
Construction cost: £41 million
Completion: 2005
Ivan Harbour: project director

The new National Assembly for Wales sits on the waterfront of Cardiff Bay, facing towards a spectacular panorama of sky and water. As the home for the Welsh Assembly the building comprises a debating chamber accommodating up to 60 members, committee and meeting rooms, offices, IT/media facilities, a members' lounge, education and exhibition spaces and a public concourse, gallery and café.

The building sits on an impressive stone-faced plinth which steps upwards from the water, and is cut away to allow views and daylight into the administrative spaces below. The building is completely transparent at the public level, to symbolise democracy by encouraging public participation in the democratic process. A lightweight, gently undulating roof, pierced by the protruding extensions of the debating chamber and public hall, shelters both internal and external spaces.

Ourtown Story exhibition zone, Millennium Dome, Greenwich, London
Exhibition stage
Construction cost: £400,000
Completed: 1999
Tosan Popo: project architect

The tailored form made of ripstop fabric (usually used for sails) was constructed without structural cables or stiffeners – the seams did all the work. The enclosure was suspended off the main dome cable net and housed a stage for children from around the country to perform for a day at the Dome.

1&2 Waterside, Paddington Basin, London
New build offices
Construction cost: £52 million
Completion: 2003
Maurice Brennan: architect
Daniel Wright: detailing, site supervision

1&2 Waterside is a robust twelve-storey high building comprising served spaces – the main flexible occupied floorplates – and secondary service elements that are expressed as corner towers. The principal vertical circulation towers contain the main passenger lifts and give a strong dynamic identity to the development. The floorplates are cut back on plan to create simple external spaces fronting onto the canal that benefit from increased levels of sunlight. A full-height atrium with circulation bridges allows daylight to penetrate into the building.

Torro Espacio Tower
Competition entry
Budget: €110 million
John McElgunn: architectural assistant

This proposed new building, supported by a pair of giant A-frames, is one of a cluster of four towers in the Madrid Arenas, a redevelopment of part of the Real Madrid Training grounds north of the city. The 215-metre high tower has 45 storeys providing a gross floor area of 56,250 square metres. Structure and support cores, including glazed lift shaft towers, are located on the east and west ends of the tower, allowing unimpeded views of Madrid to the south and the hills to the north from the main office spaces between, which are arranged in a series of flexible rectangular floorplates. Double-height spaces located at strategic levels accommodate plant and communal facilities, as well as restaurants, cafés, sky gardens, health clubs and conference rooms, characterising the building as a series of 'vertical villages'.

Library of Birmingham
New build
Construction cost: £130 million
Ivan Harbour: competition stage design
Carmel Lewin: project architect
John McElgunn: architectural assistant

The most dramatic feature of the new Birmingham library is its great oversailing roof, independently supported on structural 'trees' – simple, elegant and powerful forms that also provide interior flexibility. Its concave top surface defines a sky park for quiet study and contemplation. The floors sheltered below are conceived as clear, flexible structural systems. The reference library occupies the upper three levels above the lending library, exhibition areas, foyers and auditorium.

A simple linear bar of accommodation wraps around one edge of the library, introducing complementary cultural and social activities, as well as providing shade for the library and protecting it acoustically from the neighbouring elevated railway viaduct. A vibrant public pedestrian street with cafés and shops runs between the two. A new park adjoins the library, and a further circular 'satellite' building could provide debating areas and an auditorium.

SATELLITE DESIGN WORKSHOP

Formed in 1995, Satellite Design Workshop embraces opportunities to work in varied creative fields, encouraging a conceptual discourse within the studio. We structure our time to allow for teaching and research, enabling us to form a continual critical appraisal of our ideas and practice. The resulting body of ideas and our concerns with site, form and occupation set the framework for our approach to all projects.

Waterford Riverside Community, Ireland
International architectural and urban design competition entry (selected for public exhibition)
2000
Sarah Allan, Stewart Dodd, Neil Wilson: design team

In 2002 the Office of Public Works in Ireland launched an international competition to create a new riverside community on a derelict site on the north bank of the River Suir in Waterford. By interweaving different scales and programmes we set the framework for an environment that can evolve through its occupation. Through the articulation of the open spaces, an invented landscape evolves along the waterfront creating a continuum, linking the site together while allowing a hierarchy of spaces to exist as independent structures. By seeking a new dialogue between the infrastructure and public space, a distinct transformation in scale occurs between the industrial and human, which has been utilised to counter homogeneity within the masterplan.

The Cross Workspaces, Kings Cross Road, London
New build workspace facility
Construction cost £1.4 million
Completed: July 2002
Stewart Dodd: project architect
Neil Wilson, Sarah Allan: design team

The radical form of the Cross Workspaces was set by the 'rights to light' angles for the west windows of the adjacent Welsh Chapel. This feature was carried though as a conceptual driving point to achieve an exterior that masks the simple cellular office layout within.

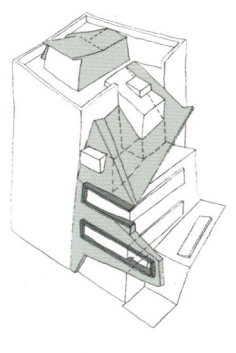

SCOTT BROWNRIGG

Established in 1910, Scott Brownrigg is now a fourth-generation architectural practice that covers the spectrum from large-scale masterplanning to crafting intimate tactile spaces on a small scale. Constantly moving between scales and capturing and utilising light always inspires me, and this I would directly attribute to some of the experiences and tutoring I had at the Bartlett. In smaller projects my focus might be the detailing of what will be beneath your feet, what you will touch, or how seats will gently flex as you drop onto them; in larger schemes it might be on the enclosure of space and creating environments that many people can occupy.

Darren Comber

Veritas Headquarters campus, GreenPark, Reading
Project Value: £22 million
New build offices
Completed: 2002
Darren Comber: designer and project director

The three Veritas buildings are set in a 'collegiate' landscape setting by a lake. They are arranged to benefit from the natural aspect of the park, with main façades orientated towards the best views, and internal gardens creating a heightened sense of space and openness. With a restricted number of primary materials the buildings present a crisp appearance. Stainless steel mesh solar-shading banners are hung vertically along the façades, and move gently in the wind: a vertical reinterpretation of the waves of the lake.

SHEPPARD ROBSON

Sheppard Robson is a long-established, award-winning practice that provides an integrated range of architectural, urban design, planning and interior design services. With over 240 staff and 14 partners, we are one of the largest UK-based practices. Our extensive breadth of experience, allied to the practice's design profile, allows us to bring technical and commercial innovation to any project.

95 Queen Victoria Street, London ◂

New build speculative office

Contract cost: £24.5 million

Completed: May 2003

Claire Haywood: Site Architect and Lead Architect Interiors

The main façade of this new office building in a prominent location in the City of London, built for Legal & General with Stanhope, follows the curve of Queen Victoria Street. The roof, with its externally expressed structure, rises to a peak at the northeast corner, its form determined by restrictions imposed by the proximity of St Paul's Cathedral. A restricted palette of materials inside and out (black granite, polished stone, opaque green glass, brushed stainless steel, white painted plasterboard and 'Bleue de Savoie' grey marble) creates an elegant and unified appearance, and blurs the boundary between external and internal space.

A series of multi-coloured panels made of tessellated glass pieces, by artist Alex Beleschenko, form a pattern of curves and hoops at eye level along the length of the main façade, creating a strong presence on the streetscape.

158 SHEPPARD ROBSON

Centre of Engineering and Manufacturing Excellence, Rainham, Essex ▶
Education and urban regeneration project
Budget: £20 million
Completion: September 2003
(Dominic) Chi lok Choi: architectural assistant

The Centre of Engineering and Manufacturing Excellence is the flagship project in the Heart of Thames Gateway strategy to improve opportunities for local people and revitalise the area. Phase one consists of a central teaching spine, housing lecture rooms, technology workshops and meeting spaces. Along its northern side the spine opens up into huge motor vehicle and mechanical workshops. Passers-by on the adjacent A13 trunk road are given a theatrical view of the processes within. To the south of the spine is the 'Street', a 150 metre long interactive zone with information points, IT hot-desking areas and a restaurant.

350 Regents Place Euston, London ▲
Speculative 'landmark' office building
Budget: £36 million
Completed: December 2002
Sylvian Hartenberg: external envelope architect (concept/elemental designer)

350 Euston Road replaces a series of slab blocks from the 1950s and 60s. The new urban concept for the site treats it as a plateau on which buildings and landscaping are arranged to reinforce the typical city language of streets, vistas, squares and arcades. The depth of floor plates is restricted to provide flexible workspaces and to enhance personal interaction. The continuous double-skin glass façade along the front of the building allows natural light and ventilation in, while reducing heat gain and acoustic transmission, and maximises occupants' awareness of the surrounding city. From outside the building presents itself as a transparent environment without barriers.

Salvation Army Headquarters, Queen Victoria Street, London
New build
Budget: £35 million
Completion: 2004
Anthony St Leger: architectural assistant

The Salvation Army required that their new international headquarters in Queen Victoria Street, where they have been based since 1881, should be religious but modern in spirit. In response we have designed a contemporary but frugal building comprising two blocks: one for the Army, and one with lettable office accommodation. Curtain walling relates the two and maintains the proportions of the street, while distinct dynamic elements within each result from their different uses. Around the perimeter of the Army's block the lower-level floor plates are cut back from the glazed façade, creating an atrium slot and allowing views into the lower ground floor café and exhibition spaces. Six raking double-height structural concrete H-frames standing in the atrium increase its drama.

160 SHEPPARD ROBSON

Project Phoenix, Experian Data Centre, Nottingham ▸
Electronic data storage facility
Budget: £18 million
Completion: December 2003
Roy Naughton: architectural assistant

The design of this electronic data storage facility was driven by the need for high security and environmental control. A 170-metre long wall, its appearance inspired by digital data storage codes and the aesthetics of natural-stone walls, screens a 'street' zone for circulation and support spaces, with technical areas, offices, primary plant and the 'Command Bridge' behind. Its relatively heavyweight construction provides thermal mass to assist in stabilising the internal environment. A reed bed creates a wetland habitat that will enhance the establishment of wildlife in the adjacent country park.

Project Renaissance, Experian Office Headquarters, Nottingham ▸
Office headquarters and conference facility
Budget: £12.2 million
Completion: July 2004
Roy Naughton: architectural assistant – responsible for cladding and curtain walling

The project has a glazed central thoroughfare that serves as a circulation and meeting area. The 'street' is the focus for a rich weave of activities, and accommodates the transitions between public, shared and private areas. It is pierced with offices, service pods and suspended meeting and conference pods. The skin of the 'floating' conference pod is randomly patterned with fritting of varying transparency, affording shifting experiences of the space. Large areas of clear glazing maximise daylight in the offices and offer largely uninterrupted views of the magnificent surrounding landscape.

DEBRA SHIPLEY MP

It was a bit of a struggle to get onto the Masters in Architectural History course at the Bartlett – my first degree had been in History of Art and Anthropology, and as a mature student I had joined a Masters in Art History at Birkbeck. The Birkbeck course was excellent, but very much painting based, whilst my interest was architecture, and one year in I wanted out! So off I went to put my case for a transfer to the Bartlett. Adrian Forty, the Masters course Director, heard me out and said 'no'. A few weeks later I was back pleading with him. The first interview had served to convince me that the Bartlett Architectural History course was exactly what I wanted to do. Again Adrian said 'no'. So I wrote to him pleading my case again. Again the reply was 'no'. Then, out of the blue, Adrian rang and offered me a place. Perseverance had paid off.

To say that the Bartlett course was rigorous is something of an understatement – but that was what made it worth doing. Luckily I thrived on challenging ideas. Naturally stroppy and argumentative! – though I met my match with other students and tutors. Evenings spent poring over text after text were rewarded by mornings of argument. Eventually I learnt how to construct my dialogue and to substantiate my argument. It was fun! My dissertation was on MARS – the Modern Architecture Research Group of the 1930s – which entailed delving into dusty boxes in the RIBA and interviewing key figures such as John Summerson and Berthold Lubetkin: definitely a privilege.

Before doing the course I was an established author, having published a range of non-fiction books. After completing the Masters I wrote a book on Durham Cathedral looking at how religion, politics and mythology combined to influence the architecture of this powerful building. Some years later I was elected as Labour MP for Stourbridge in the West Midlands – seemingly a complete change in direction. The Bartlett had however made its mark on me, and architectural history did, in fact, include much material that a Labour MP holds dear, such as the development of social housing. I have recently pressed the minister responsible for construction to require new buildings funded by the government, including social housing, to have a large environmental element. The rigour of argument at the Bartlett has also served me well when scrutinising legislation (and indeed when pulling apart other people's arguments) and more recently architecture itself has again become an important focus for me.

My first term in office was dominated by my Act of Parliament. Unusually for a backbench MP I succeeded in getting a large Act on the Statute books, the Protection of Children and Vulnerable Adults Act. I have since become parliamentary ambassador for the NSPCC and much of my work in Westminster is to do with child protection issues. However, when I was elected for a second term, I felt able to develop a second parliamentary focus, the built environment. I am currently joint chair with Richard Rogers of the all-party parliamentary architecture group. I recently hosted a large reception in Westminster with over 50 MPs, which three ministers and around 100 architects from all across the country attended. The idea was to link architects with their constituency MP and to show them how to lobby for design and built excellence.

It was a step forward but architecture schools need to do their bit too, they need to teach their students how to lobby MPs effectively. The vast majority of architects are not politically active. Their professional body has failed to shape political opinion and as individual practices they don't realise how important their influence can be. I passionately believe that architecture impacts on us all. I want that impact to be positive. Doing my bit to help bring that about should be enough to keep me occupied until the next general election!

162 SIXTEEN*(MAKERS)

We established our methodology of design through making as students at the Bartlett in the early to mid 1990s. Since then the school has remained a host to many of our practices, which involve teaching, research, design and fabrication. Rather than submit any one project, as many have been published previously, in *Bartlett Works* we wish to illustrate the range of work we have explored over our history – something which has never been put across before, and is especially important to us as a small diverse enterprise.

sixteen*(makers) was set up from a light industrial workshop in Shoreditch in 1994 at a time when the practice of architecture was undergoing great upheaval. The 'stability' of a professional career and its underlying status within a fragile industry was under exceptional pressure. As graduates in transition from education to the 'real' world, our momentum led us to establish an alternative definition of practice based upon a long-held and exercised commitment to 'the making of things'. The motivation behind this decision and its action in bridging the gap between education and practice has remained a core foundation in all our work. From the outset sixteen*(makers) was intent on evolving its knowledge base through change in its membership, technology, and by forming collaborations with a broad range of disciplines engaged with processes of manufacture and design.

To date sixteen*(makers) has evolved through projects in furniture, interiors, exhibitions, installations, refurbishment, responsive objects, CAD/CAM methodology and database systems, commissioned in the private and public sector.

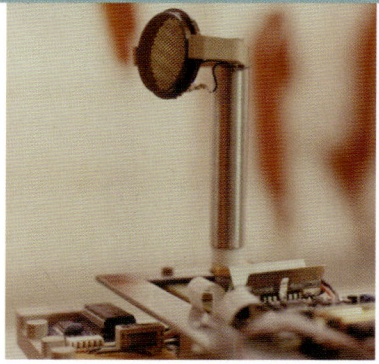

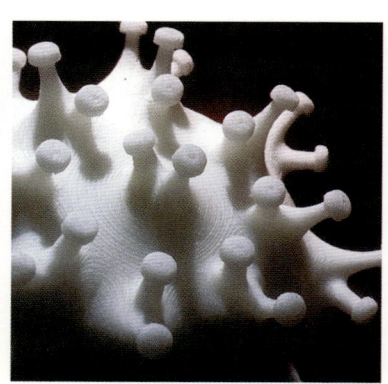

163

164 SOM

I wanted to work for SOM, renowned for their serenely rational office buildings, in order to hone my understanding of practice and the construction process, and developed a good working relationship with Nic Jacobs, a design director. Our similar design approaches culminated in producing the Jordan House. I always try to have a rigorous approach to design – in which the Bartlett has influenced me greatly. Special thanks to Neil Spiller, who helped me realise my potential.

Davin Torch Benning

Jordan House, Bellas, Portugal
€2 million
New Private Residence
In-progress (Designed 2001-2002)
Davin Torch Benning: design development, 3D design-modelling

The Jordan House takes its form from the geometry and materiality of its peninsula-shaped site, its roof like an outcrop of rock carved and polished to form a smooth domed surface. Beneath, it is as if the rock has been hollowed out and inhabited by a dramatic sequence of overlapping curvaceous spaces – from the traditional Portuguese entry courtyard, enclosed by sloping rockery walls, to the viewing platform/lounge with panoramic views of the surrounding landscape. At the centre is the pod – a service core with a spiral glass staircase encased by glass library shelves, washed with natural light and descending to a wine cellar.

SOFTROOM

Softroom, established in 1995, is headed by Bartlett graduates Christopher Bagot and Oliver Salway. Based in central London, our work has been published and exhibited worldwide. Softroom are registered architects as well as acting as a design consultancy and conducting conceptual research. Our award-winning work is innovative and diverse – projects encompass a growing portfolio of public, residential, retail and commercial buildings and interiors; transport, exhibition and set design; virtual spaces; advertising and editorial imagery.

Selfridges, London and Manchester stores
Retail design
Completed: 2001-02
Softroom: architects

Selfridges operates a rolling programme of refurbishment works, and views high quality design as an essential catalyst to increased sales. Their stores' departments are subdivided into branded concessions (Gucci, Ralph Lauren etc.) and 'generic' areas that carry a variety of labels under Selfridges' direct control. We have been contracted on several occasions to 'masterplan' departments, determining the layout and lighting strategy, developing unique items of shopfitting for the generic areas, and liaising with the concessions to ensure their smooth integration into the whole.

The largest of these projects has been the 'Spirit' ladieswear department, occupying 2,300 square metres on the ground floor of the London store. The task was thoroughly to reorganise a bustling, noisy space, introducing a theatrical mezzanine of brightly coloured changing rooms, a nail bar, and a vibrant 'marketplace' of small stalls. As is often the case, the work had to be rigorously programmed to allow the majority of the department to continue to trade during the installation period.

166 SOFTROOM

Floating Retreat and Treehouse
Concept designs published in *Wallpaper* magazine
1997-98
Softroom: architects

In the late 1990s, Softroom developed a series of concept projects for the lifestyle magazine *Wallpaper**. In each case, we wanted to communicate theoretical architectural ideas to a wide audience in as direct a way as possible. The designs were deliberately tongue in cheek, using computer graphics to suspend disbelief.

'Floating Retreat' proposed a private tow-away desert island, complete with inflatable beach: the design is very much a concept, but several people have expressed an interest in building one. The first prototype would of course be quite expensive, but as a mass-produced product it would probably cost about the same as a medium-sized yacht.

Responding to a one-word brief calling for a 'treehouse', we designed a lightweight structure that could be attached to a large tree with minimal impact on its host. The framework would accept a variety of drop-in living components, such as a picnic table and fly-away bed.

Like all the projects we did for *Wallpaper*', these designs were developed extremely quickly, and as such certain liberties with regards to structural analysis and construction were necessarily taken. However, with the proper resources there is no reason why the idea, or something similar, could not be implemented. Furthermore, the formal language of 'Treehouse' paved the way for a real-world Softroom project, the award-winning Kielder Belvedere.

168 SOFTROOM

Kielder Belvedere, Kielder Forest National Park, Northumberland

Public arts project

Completed: 1999

Softroom: architects

Softroom were chosen to design a lakeside 'belvedere' in Kielder, one of the largest forests in Britain – the first architectural commission to form part of an ongoing public arts programme developed by the Kielder Partnership. The structure functions as a shelter for walkers who find themselves overtaken by the elements and, from spring to autumn, accommodates passengers waiting to board the ferry across Kielder Water.

The Belvedere takes the form of a truncated triangle. On approaching from the land, two etched-steel mirror walls reflecting the forest flank a doorway set beneath a richly-coloured glass canopy. Inside, a circular golden chamber is lit by soft daylight filtering through the coloured skylight. A bench faces a single slot window in the curved far wall, which offers a panoramic view of the Water. In contrast with the flat flank walls, the exterior face of the third wall is a dramatic convex curve, in whose reflective mirror-polished stainless steel surface the vista is drawn in towards the curving slot window and those within.

The Kielder Belvedere was awarded the RIBA Stephen Lawrence Prize 2000 for the best building under £250,000, and received a Royal Fine Art Commission Jeu D'Espirit Building of the Year Award in 2000.

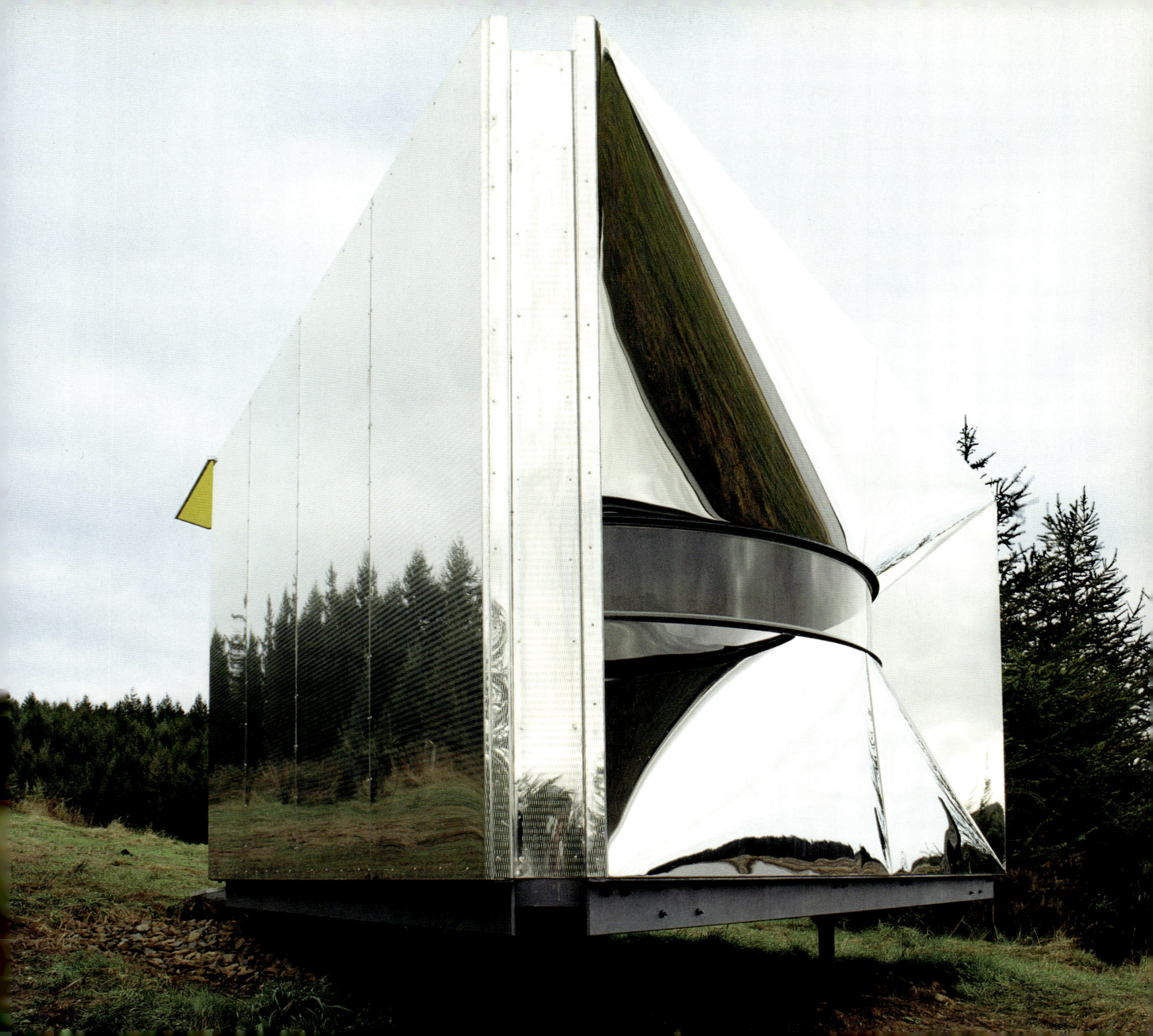

170 SPACE SYNTAX

Space Syntax is an international consulting company providing property and design services to public and private agencies. We offer strategic design, evaluation, monitoring and forecasting services in a wide range of fields, including urban regeneration, transport, retail design, workplace interaction, residential planning and urban safety, addressing the design factors that most influence performance.

We have a close working relationship with the Space Syntax Laboratory, the world-leading architecture research team and part of the Bartlett's highly renowned Space research group. Space Syntax members also teach on the Bartlett's MSc Advanced Architectural Studies, MSc in Urban Design and MSc in Building and Urban Design Development courses.

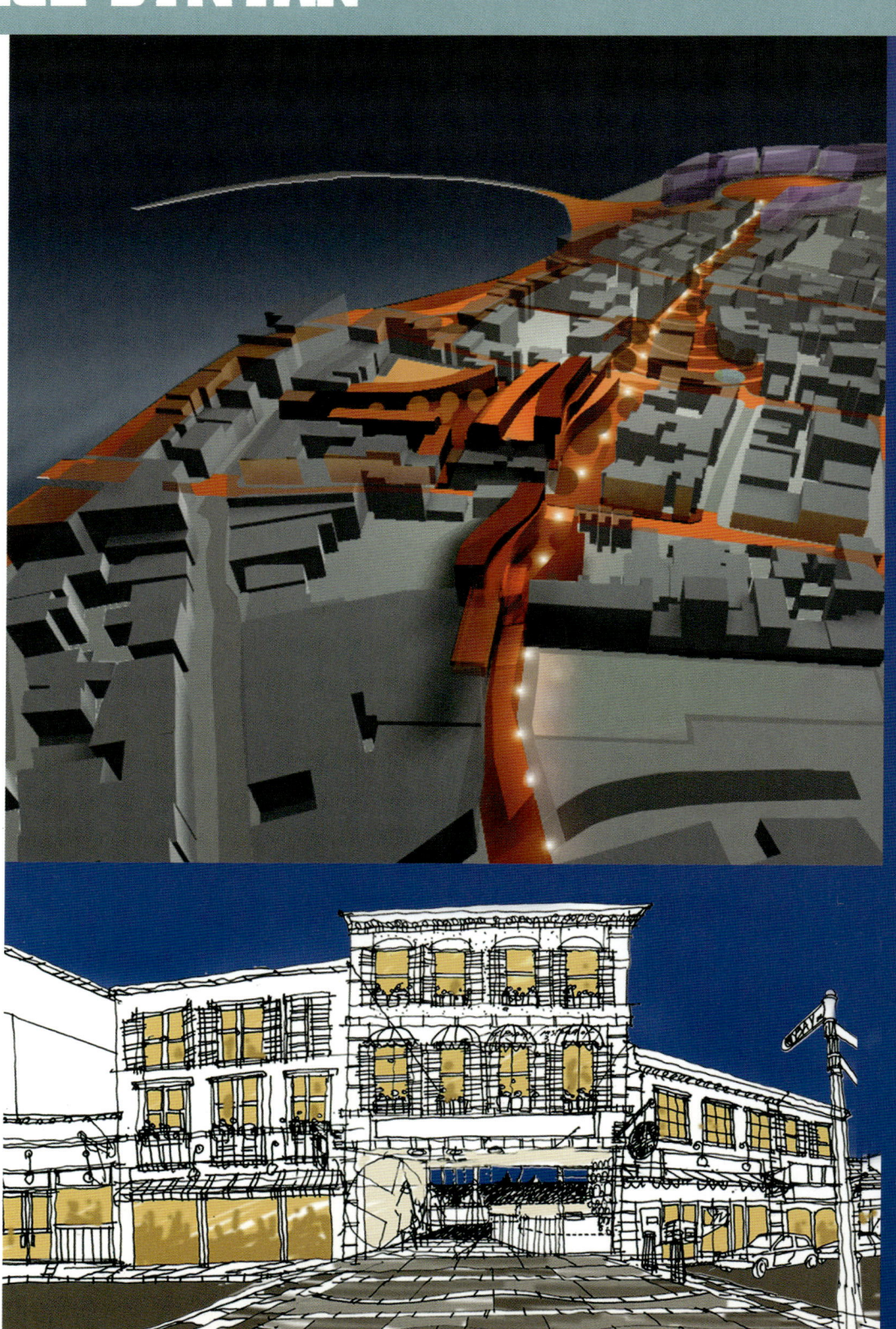

Old Town Masterplan, Margate
Urban regeneration proposal 1999

Polly Fong, Maria Zerdilla: field observations, data analysis, design and report writing
Kayvan Karimi: project leader
Tim Stonor: coordination, analysis and design

In 1999 we were appointed to develop a regeneration strategy for the historic core of Margate. After a careful analysis of the historical evolution of the town and its patterns of economic activity and pedestrian movement, we found that, while the historic core is locally permeable and inter-accessible, it is segregated from the rest of the town. To reach it, you have to know that it is there. In a town that depends on tourist newcomers to sustain its economy, this layout is untenable.

We used a spatial integration computer model to identify ways to make it easier to move from one part of the town centre to the other within a network of pedestrian routes, activated and animated by ground-level activities. The next step was to develop a physical regeneration strategy in line with the pattern of pedestrian movement potentials.

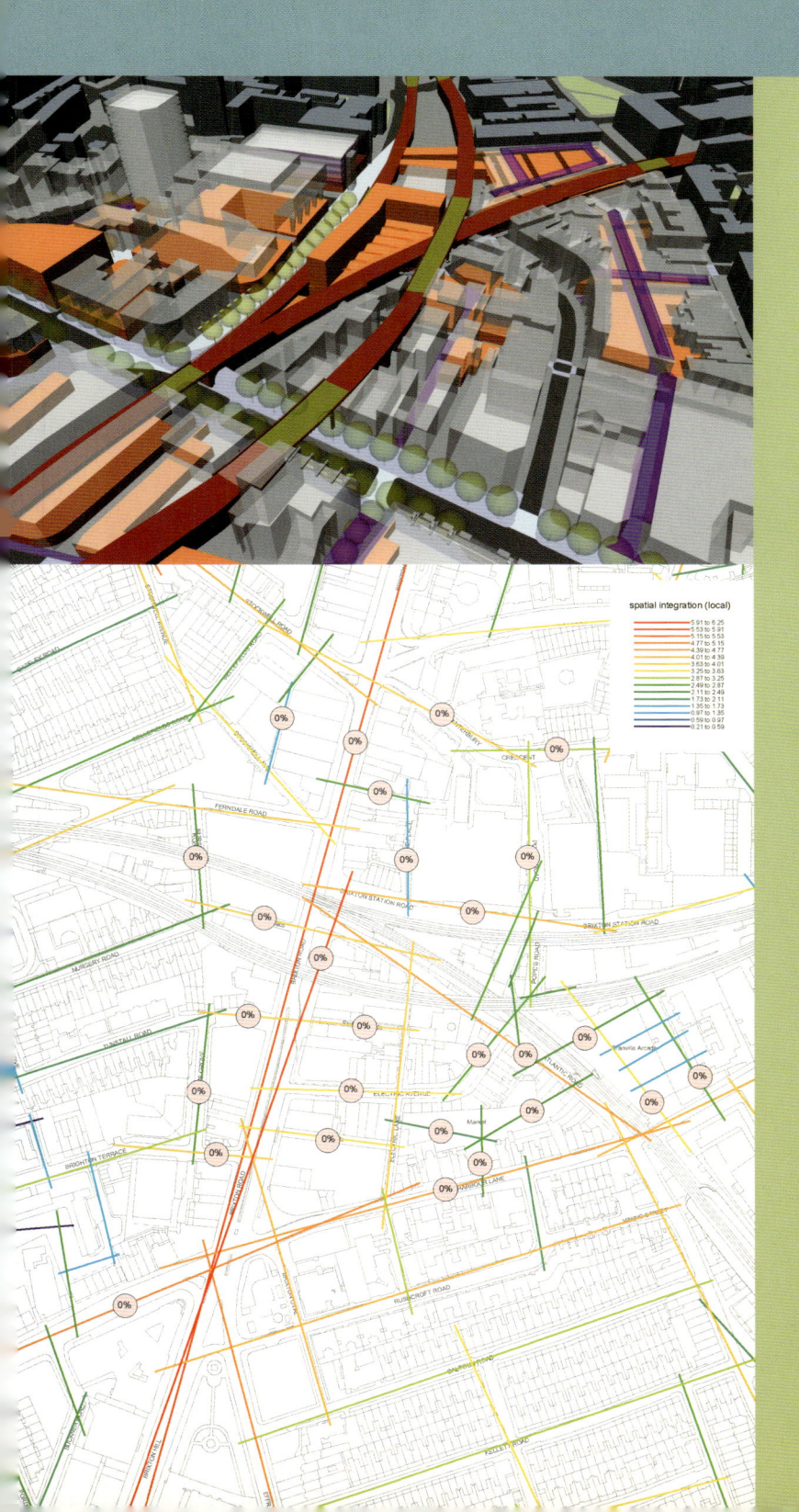

Town Centre Vision, Brixton, London
Urban regeneration proposal
2000

Beatriz Campos: field observations and data analysis
Biljana Savic: project leader, analysis and design
Tim Stonor: coordination, analysis and design

We were appointed by the London Borough of Lambeth in 2000 to develop a design-led investment strategy for Brixton. Analysis of its land use, movement network, and property values shows that the town centre is highly fragmented, and north-south and east-west linkages are poor. Only Electric Avenue and the central part of the High Street are easy to move around.

Our strategic design proposals include opening up arches beneath the railway lines to allow people to flow north-south; removing railings in the High Street that prevent people from crossing east-west; and widening footways to provide more space for pedestrians and to 'calm' through traffic. Pedestrian modelling studies indicate that these new linkages will encourage movement throughout the town centre to reduce pressure on the High Street and Electric Avenue and release the value of development sites elsewhere.

Princes Circus, London
Urban regeneration
2001

Tim Stonor: coordination, analysis and design
Biljana Savic: project leader, analysis and design proposals
Beatriz Campos: coordination and design of fieldwork and data analysis

Our design strategy includes a major new pedestrian link that runs diagonally across the site, making a direct connection between north Covent Garden and south Bloomsbury, and is created by rerouting northbound vehicular traffic. Pedestrian approaches are re-modelled with wider footways and direct pedestrian crossings, located on 'desire lines' identified in a diagnostic study.

Movement forecasts – made using a 'spatial integration' computer model developed specifically for this project – show that the proposals would generate high pedestrian flows through Princes Circus. The new north-south route would be well used by tourists, local residents and office workers. Princes Circus would thus be integrated with its surroundings and movement on foot through the area encouraged.

NEIL SPILLER

I like architecture that is mythic, enigmatic, oblique and encrusted with decoration. I like it to suggest worlds, essences and supernatures. I despise the white, the simple and the tediously functional. I cannot bear the self-righteous minimalist or the cynical post-modern ironicist.

I started to study as an architecture student in the late 1970s, a low point in architectural optimism. Thatcher's grip was tightening around our throats and the Yuppie was being created from the primordial filth. Neo-vernacular stalked the English sensibility and carbuncles where about to erupt on the faces of old friends.

My work of the last 15 years, such as the books *Digital Dreams* and my monograph *Maverick Deviations* together with projects such as 'Hot-Desk' – the first architectural project to deal with nanotechnology and 'communicating vessels' – deals with space-time vectors, and hypersensitive remote ecological sensing. I have always sought to push the envelope of architectural discourse, creating new spaces where architecture might dwell. This quest first started with a reassessment of architectural ornament and narrative. A sound body of intellectual points of departure have always, for me, had to accompany projects. I value very highly the work of others that does not pander to current fashion and does not seek to be either popular or trendy.

My search has taken me through all manner of terrain, from seeing the way architects are educated as a microcosm for society via the issue of the representational column with its millennia of histories, large city masterplans about time and duration and their impact on the city, the mystical and cyclic process of alchemy, the virtual topologies of cyberspace, to the magic power of nanotechnology. All these researches have left me convinced of a few crucial notions and these ideas I try to communicate to my students. These are: there are no rights or wrongs, no guilt or shame, no honours awarded for faceless competence, no stars for the expected. Students have to firstly regain their self-respect, this enables them to adopt a polemic and informed theoretical position and this in turn will allow them to create a personal architectural lexicon.

Fifteen years ago, sites were real and unassailable, architecture was simple and the architect's skills were less numerous. Architecture and architects looked relatively safe. One had only a few clues about how the onslaught of technology would blow the doors off architecture's Mini Minor. I started experimenting with an encrusted architecture, a series of filters, an architecture beyond the starkness of functionalism, an architecture whose way of representing itself was a combination of extravagant prose and a graphic gambit that was as powerful as it was invigorated, energetic and loose-limbed. It owed very little to the established protocols of the prevailing modernism. My architectural language was honed by years of experimentation, with technology, with mythology and with shifting aesthetic preoccupations.

If we consider your or my back garden, superimposed over it is a massively complex world, an ecology always rearticulating itself. Next door's back garden is different but similar. Your kitchen is planned differently to your neighbour's and you use the space differently. Different things are important to you and to your neighbour, you may like Monet, he may like the ball-game. People are very different, yet still have a demand for a personalised architecture to call home, be it a rucksack or a mansion. Is it possible to create an architecture that stitches this tapestry of philosophy, aspiration, interest, movements, both seen and unseen, into a whole new landscape of enclosure and exposition, that changes in time and makes no distinction between art and architecture, no matter what 'code' of aesthetics is being used? Can we create architectures that slip into other locations and spaces and return to show us what they've found and 'plant' a notation of this event in our environment? These 'plantings' might exist for some for a long time, sometimes for shorter periods. Such ideas are capable of producing a sublimity of space that grows and decays, changes and rearranges, that speaks of the human condition as the actor in a series of linear, non-linear and quantum events. The torsions of everyday existence, small expansions, minute stresses and strain and stains, vibrations in the World Wide Web, tigers caged in the quantum zone, and many more, all have the potential to invigorate elements in this architecture.

These ideas are critical to the centrality of architecture to society, anything short of this just won't do and will leave us ill-prepared for the future.

Bread-hurdened Dalinian Leg
Slamhound 2002

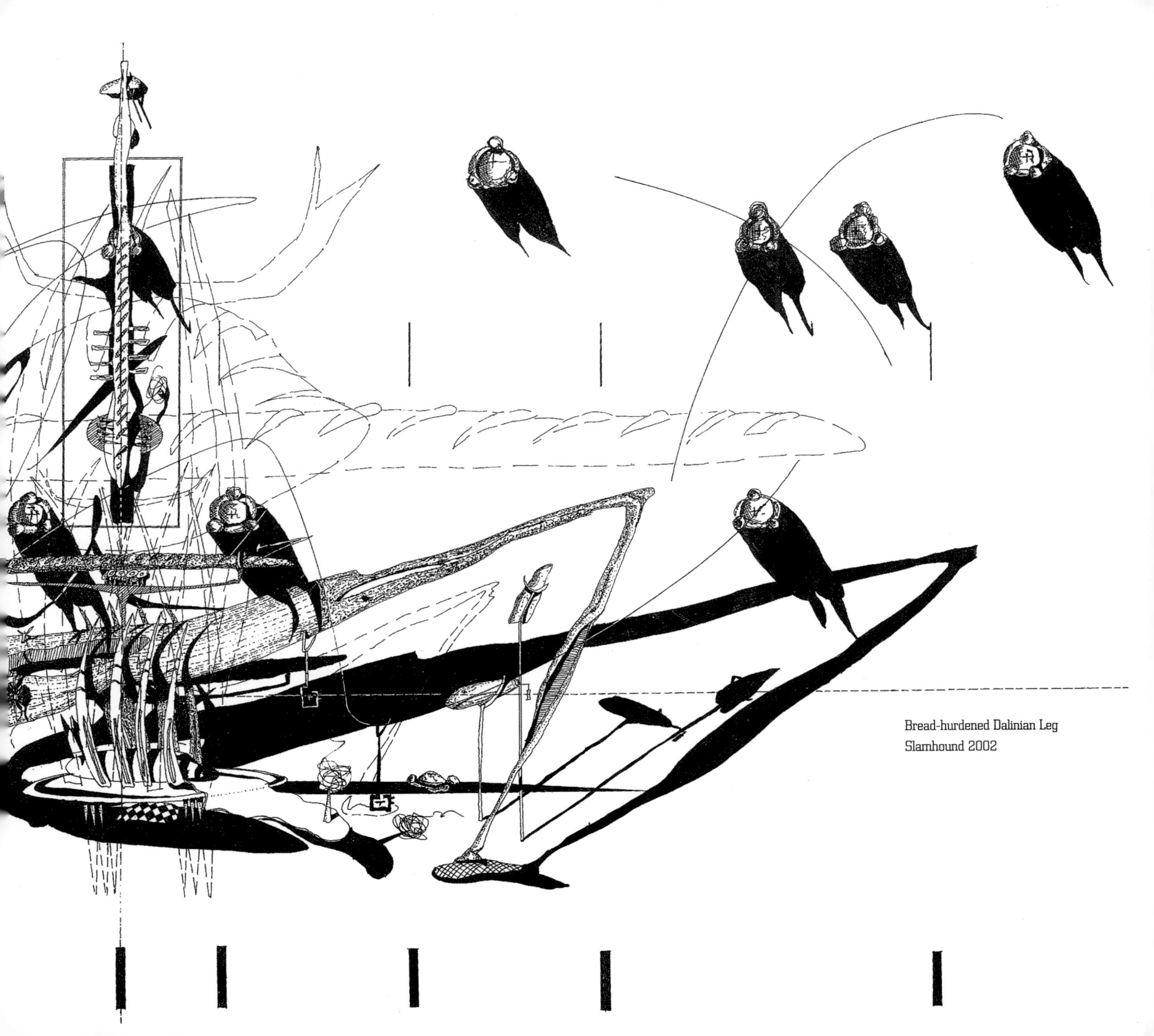

174 SPRINGETT MACKAY ARCHITECTURE

We formed a close working relationship as undergraduates whilst studying at the Mackintosh School of Architecture in Glasgow, and then worked together on a series of urban interventions in New York and on a number of competitions after our Diplomas (at the Bartlett and Royal College of Art respectively). Springett Mackay Architecture was formed in 2000. We have been involved in a mixture of domestic conversions, private new builds and workplace research. Our work is sensitive both to materials and the occupier's needs, with wit and pragmatism of equal importance.

Matthew Springett and Kirsteen Mackay

Kingstown Street Mews House, Primrose Hill, London
New build private house
Budget: £525,000
Completed: summer 2003
Springett Mackay: architects

This new house is set within a mews in Primrose Hill, London. It is the last of a series of 'back garden' sites to be developed. The clients once lived in the house that adjoins the site, and their understanding of the local area helped our design to be harmonious with the townscape. The house is set within a split-level site and sits stealthily between its neighbours. Its modern open aspect is stepped back in line with the other houses in the street, mimicking the existing grain and fabric. Bedrooms and bathrooms are on the ground floor. The first floor with its L-shaped plan appears to hover above, supported by a rendered steel frame. It is devoted to living and working, and incorporates a central opening rooflight which creates an 'outside room' at the heart of the building.

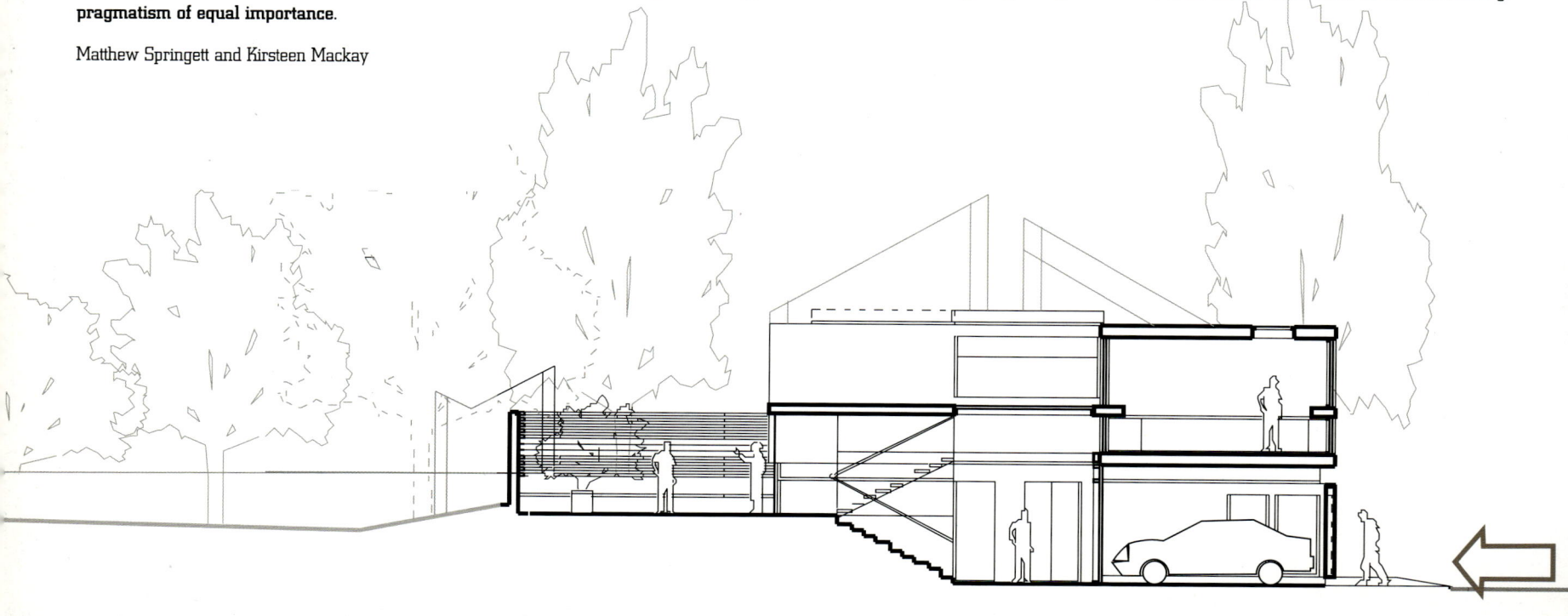

SQUINT/OPERA

We are Bartlett architecture graduates Oliver Alsop, Martin Hampton, Alice Scott and Edinburgh history graduate Julius Cocke. Our interests lie within film and architecture. We aim to push the medium of film to gain new perspectives on architecture. From the documentary which tells the story of an architectural process, to the installation which attempts to explore spatial concepts, the uses of film in architectural practice are many. All four of us share roles in the scripting, shooting, producing, directing, animation and post production of projects.

Urban Renaissance Programme films, Yorkshire
Documentary films
March–October 2002
squint/opera: film makers

In March 2002, we were commissioned by Yorkshire Forward, the Regional Development Agency for Yorkshire and the Humber, to produce a series of films documenting the pilot phase of their Urban Renaissance Programme, in which a panel of international architects, economists and urbanists were commissioned to tackle the problems of towns in the region. The films are considered an integral part of the regeneration process.

We gathered sounds and images to reveal the towns' fabrics; their beauty, decay, potential, past and future. We recorded hundreds of images, comments, conversations and arguments; interviewing, getting people talking, encouraging participation, stirring it up...

The finished product is a DVD containing four films: *urban renaissance*, *all Barnsley might dream*, *green around the gills* and *kissing sleeping beauty*.

The films were shown to encourage debate at community planning events, as trailers in local cinemas, in local schools and libraries as well as in national institutions (the RIBA and the Commonwealth Institute), internationally (Toronto), and at conferences (Urban Summit 2002).

176 STORP_WEBER_ARCHITECTURE

storp_weber_architecture (s_w_arch) was set up with my partner Sabine Storp in London in 1998. After receiving the commission to design a house on the edge of the Rhine valley and the Black Forest we worked on a range of projects from a wardrobe in Kilburn, to a series of delicatessen shops, to a large distribution centre in Germany. We use every possibility to explore architectural design – the creation and manipulation of space. Everything is possible, there should be no limits or constraints – we try to see problems as possibilities for reinventing and reinterpreting both our approach and the rules of the game.

Patrick Weber

House33/28, Buehl, Germany (designed with Sabine Storp) ▶
New build house
Completed: January 2001
Patrick Weber: architect

A three-dimensional skin wraps itself through this house, encapsulating spaces and separating communal and more private areas without the need for separating walls and doors. The skin emerges at the top of the house as a curved zinc roof.

The house is orientated to give controlled views in each direction towards the Rhine Valley and the Black Forest. We have used materials whose colours alter according to the light, and so seem to alternate throughout the day – redwood façades, reflective glass that becomes more transparent as it becomes shaded during the day, and the zinc roof that appears cold blue in the morning but turns to a warm gold in the evening sun.

The design tries to exploit fluctuating levels of light and shadow and their effects to make the inhabitant very aware of the changing seasons and to make them feel as if they occupy somewhere between outside and inside.

Unit 63, Canal Building, Shepherdess Walk, London (designed with Eduardo Rosa) ▲
Apartment fit-out
Completed: June 2000
Patrick Weber: architect

This design was conceived as a flexible living space for a young urban professional couple, their first joint property. The assignment was to fit a shell loft into a former warehouse building overlooking the canal in Islington, London.

The project takes shape with the placement of a single large structure, a freestanding storage element, which generates different areas for possible activities within the space. This structure also allows unconstrained movement of people around the 80 square metre loft, and natural light to reach all areas. Curved and sculptured, it connects adjacent spaces and provides for multiple overlapping functions around it. A raised oak platform defines the sleeping area. The oak is a contrastingly soft surface compared to the concrete floor and original concrete structure. A linear bathroom acts both as a connecting/interrupting element in the loft. A striped colour scheme on the back wall wraps around the central element and unfolds a series of different scenarios within the space.

Placing such an independent element within the existing structure reaffirms its context and reflects domestic life as a series of overlapping time and functional zones. Living is based in a relationship to these different spaces and the movement between them.

MARK SWENARTON

I first arrived at the Bartlett (in those days, still next to the Slade in the front quad) on 1 September 1974 to work on my PhD thesis under the supervision of Reyner Banham. It wasn't an auspicious start, because the school admin had misplaced my forms, Banham was away and nobody knew who I was.

But after that rocky start things improved markedly and I had a happy relationship with the school for some 15 years. Banham's subsequent departure to Buffalo ('changing sinking ships in mid-ocean', as he put it) created a vacancy and in 1977 I was appointed to teach history alongside Adrian Forty (with Bob Maxwell providing professorial cover for us, in characteristically genial fashion). In 1981 Adrian and I launched the MSc in History of Modern Architecture. Nowadays practically every school has a history Masters of some sort but in those days it was a great innovation – ours was the first Masters in History of Architecture in the UK and we had to justify it not just financially but also (in some quarters) as an academic discipline. Graduates from the early years of the course included Murray Fraser, Ruth Owens, Colin Davies, Bill Menking, Iain Borden and many others who have since made their mark.

Meantime I had completed and published my thesis, *Homes fit for Heroes*, which looked at the politics and architecture of the state housing programme introduced after the first world war; and I followed this up with a study of the English socialist tradition in architectural thought, *Artisans and Architects*, which was published in 1989. By this point however I had grown restless in British academia and considered a move to the US but – encouraged by a Bartlett alumnus of a very different generation and eminence, Sir John Summerson – found a new challenge in a different area, namely architectural publishing.

In 1989 with Ian Latham I set up the monthly magazine *Architecture Today*, which we continue to edit and publish. In the magazine (which is sent free to some 20,000 architects in the UK) we seek to review the best current projects from the UK and Europe, with many of the critiques written by practising architects. In this way we aim to steer a reasoned course between on the one hand the tabloid mentality of the architectural weeklies and on the other the theoretical preoccupations of the academic architectural journals, focusing on the more substantial issues in the developing art and profession of architecture.

JERRY TATE   TECHNIKER

I believe that design should be informed by the poetry of motion and activity, demonstrating and glorifying the practice of everyday life. Under Nat Chard at the Bartlett, designing for everyday life was a prime consideration, as was ensuring that a design enabled as diverse a range of functions as possible through static and kinetic structures. In our built environment the range of activities is widening, and the space available is contracting. In response I would like to produce efficient, yet wonderful, architecture.

Carthew Road House, Hammersmith, London
Complete refurbishment of a Victorian terraced house
Budget: £80,000
Completed: September 2002
Jerry Tate: architect

This was my first private job of any decent size. I had to design and administer it all in my spare time, which was a real headache!

We opened up the ground floor of our client's Victorian terraced house, and inserted a 'multi-functional' panelled wall along one side. This serves variously as a drinks cabinet, wine rack, book store, home cinema and entertainment centre, display area, furniture store, plan chest, CD rack and computer terminal; and with an integrated new sandstone fireplace brings everything the clients wanted out of a living space into one, tightly packed location. The one piece missing from the jigsaw was to continue the wall into the kitchen, thereby bringing all the house's living functions into one linear element. The client is currently considering the idea...

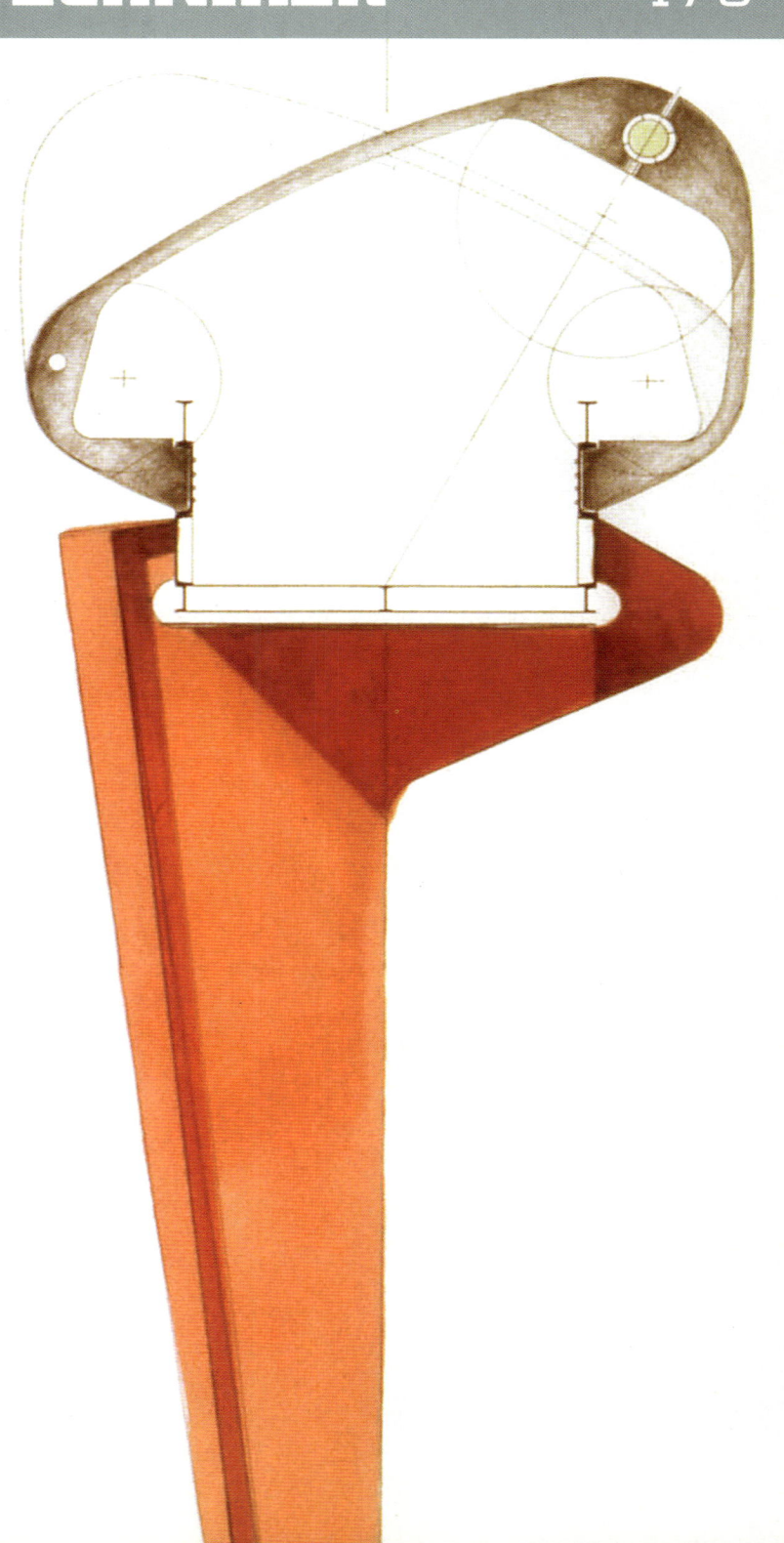

180 TECHNIKER

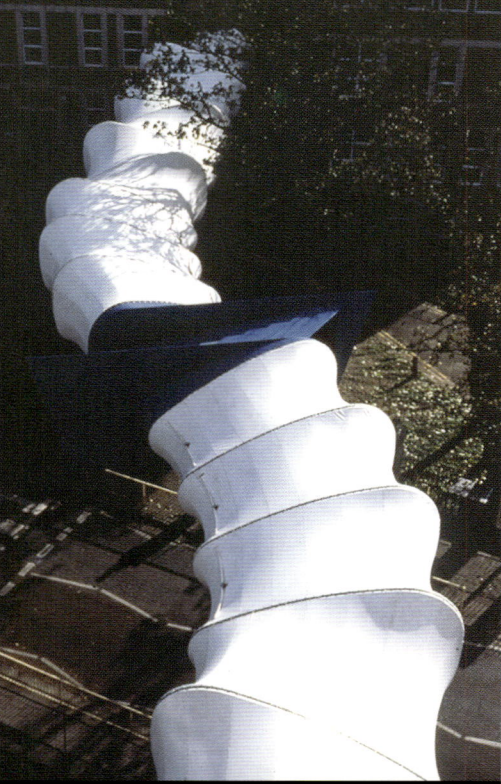

Techniker Ltd is a firm of structural engineers. Over the past ten years our staff have regularly contributed to technical teaching at the Bartlett. Through tutorials we direct the production of technical studies to meet the educational requirements of the RIBA and other professional bodies. This study process enables us to extend our research and to maintain an overview of contemporary concerns in the application of technology to architecture. We continually review our strategies of structural design in order to develop alternative processes for use in practice. Our objective is fully to understand the relationship between engineering and architectural enquiry.

Plashet Lane Bridge, London
New enclosed footbridge
Budget: £600,000
Completed: November 1999
Matthew Wells: project director

Twenty years ago a grammar school and secondary school on either side of Plashet Lane in Plaistow were amalgamated within the comprehensive system. This covered bridge, designed with architects Birds, Portchmouth and Russum, links the two precincts.

The simple steel sections of the bridge's girders are rolled to curve on plan around the site's mature trees. Differences in level are handled with a transitional profile made by heat bending. Free-form canopies of Teflon veneered glass fibre fabric are computer modelled to make a balanced continuum which restrains an array of supporting rings. Rainwater collectors are integrated into the membranes and main structure. Details of the sculptural heavy plate pier are deliberately crude and mannered to draw attention to the bridge's simplicity and materiality.

The entire structure was pre-fabricated and assembled in the factory, before being cut and delivered in segments. Everything had to be put in place during a single weekend when the road beneath the bridge was closed.

Royal Victoria Dock Bridge, London
New footbridge
Budget: £4.5 million
Completed: September 1998
Matthew Wells: project director

Working on the structural design of this long-span footbridge with architects Lifschutz Davidson, we sought to explore the limits of an engineer's concerns. The premise was straightforward: to produce a crossing with the minimum intrusion into the physical environment, with the least inhibition to pedestrian movement and with something of the quality of its dockland surroundings, which led us to considerations of historicism. The design suggests a history of reconstituted parts taken from the steel grain clippers that once occupied the dock. The provisional and transitory nature of dockyard equipment is reflected in our detailing, with junctions devised so that the structure could be erected without bolting or on-site welding.

Wind tunnel studies influenced form and details. The degree of perforation of the balustrade panels is precisely determined to ensure that they act as aerodynamic dampers, and the myriad joints produce a high degree of intrinsic damping, so tuned dampers were not required.

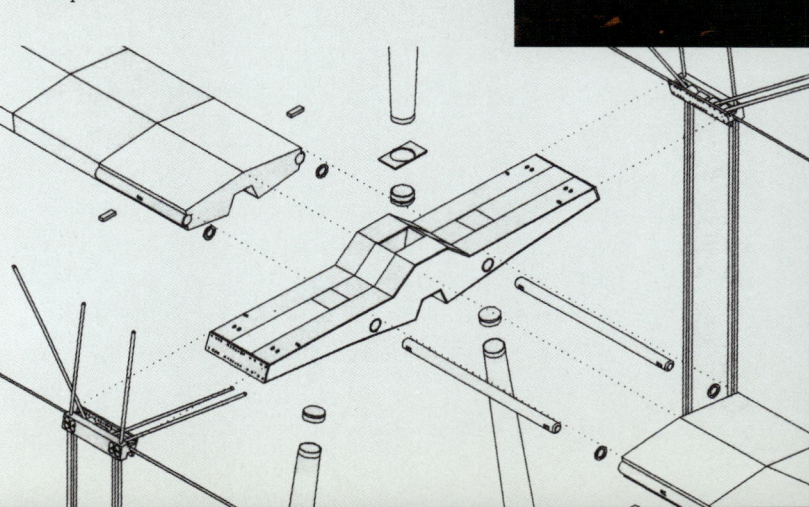

TEMPLETON 181

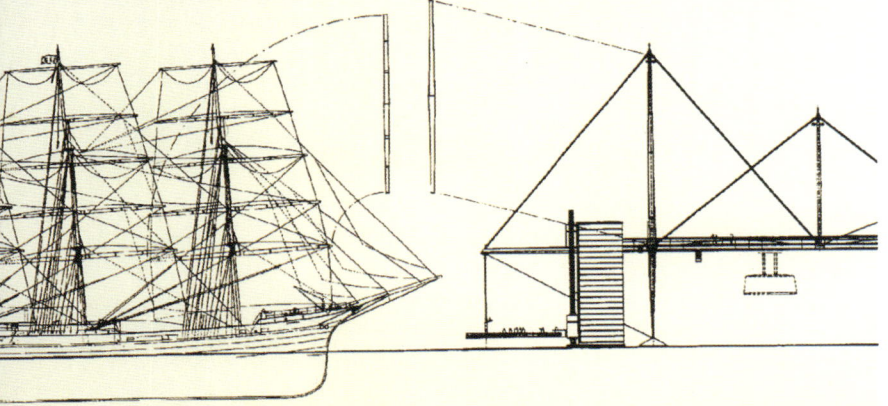

I founded Templeton Associates in 1994 in Belfast, and relocated to London in 1998, where we have been very successful working on large-scale residential projects. I think that it is hard for an academic environment to prepare one for private practice, and that business and marketing qualifications would have helped. I learnt most from the eight years I spent working with Nicholas Grimshaw before setting up my practice, though the people I met studying at the AA and then at the Bartlett continue to influence me – not a day goes by when I don't ask the question 'what would he or she do in this position'.

Simon Templeton

Wimpole Street, Marylebone, London
New build/refurbishment of private house
Completed: 2000
Simon Templeton: project architect
Bernd Felsinger, Jonathan Rowley: design team

Our client, a family with three young children, embraced the idea of living in a listed building built for gracious living with servants occupying the lower and upper floors, but also wanted a large open kitchen, playrooms, media room, pottery room, photographic darkroom, workshops and swimming pool! An enormous new glass roof connects the five-storey town house with a mews building to the rear, creating a contemporary space juxtaposed with the refurbished historic structure. A new stair links the ground floor to the basement: a more 'gentlemanly' route down than the narrow steps built for staff some 200 years ago.

182 TESSERA

Founded in 1999 by Anthony Boulanger, Penelope Haralambidou, Yeoryia Manolopoulou and Eduardo Rosa, *tessera* is an architectural collaboration involved in practice, research and theory, intersecting architecture and the visual arts. Our projects reflect primarily on issues addressing contemporary public space. We have taken part in international competitions and exhibitions and our work has been published in Greece, France, Britain and Spain. All four members came to the Bartlett to pursue the MArch Architectural Design, and we maintain a very close relationship to the school through teaching and developing academic research.

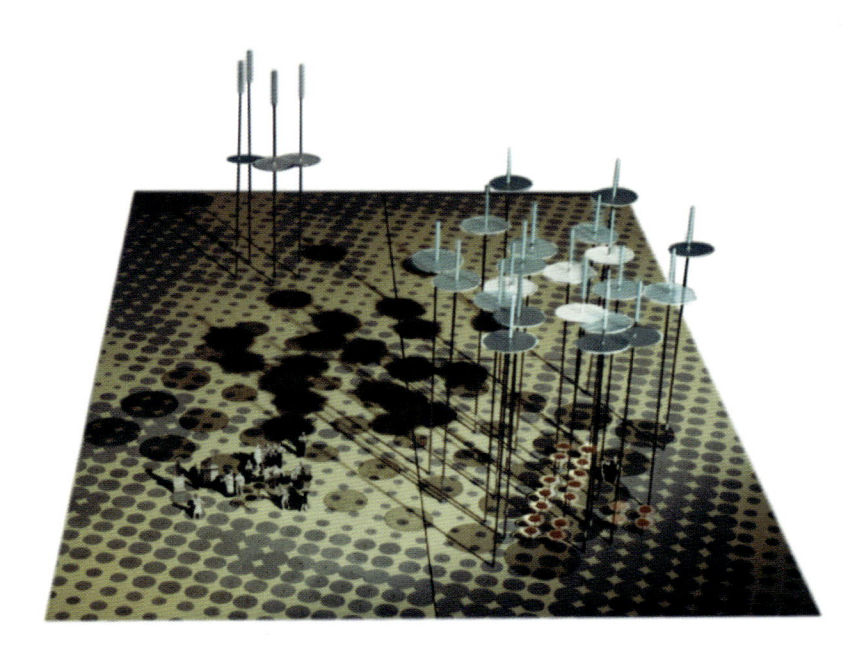

Urban Forest, Syntagma Square, Athens, Greece
Urban design competition entry
1998
tessera: architects

Based on the spatial experience of the natural forest, we proposed a flexible space that continuously transforms the public function and image of Syntagma square in Athens. Through performance, the square 'self-composes' various spatial configurations and thus always creates an element of surprise. The design consists of vertical linear elements, 'the poles', which support a number of floating light covers, 'the hats'. The pole and hat configuration changes depending on the seasons, events and celebrations of the city. The hats cast shadow patterns during the day and glow with artificial light, illuminating the square, by night. The poles are arranged, as desired, on a grid of sockets that relates to a half-tone typographic image, enlarged to the size of the whole surface of the square. The image isolates an anonymous film-still from 1950s Greek cinema, illustrating the typical Greek 'saloni', a symbolic icon of the 'public' life of the interior of the Athenian house.

'Drawing Fix'
Participation in exhibition
2002
tessera: architects

'Drawing FIX' was commissioned especially for the exhibition 'Big Brother: Architecture and Surveillance' held at the National Museum of Contemporary Art (the former FIX brewery) in Athens in the summer of 2002. The FIX brewery, designed by Takis Zenetos, one of the most distinguished architects of Greek modernism, stood as an exemplary piece of architecture and a dynamic landmark in the centre of Athens for more than three decades. In the 1990s half of the building was dramatically demolished to facilitate works for the new metro.

Drawing FIX is conceived as an urban apparition, a 'ghost image' of the lost building. Re-tracings of the original two long elevations are merged to create a thin diaphanous structure, an inhabited elevation, where visitors wander in its narrow ramps and decks. The concrete and glass zones of Zenetos' design are now translated into strips of sweeping electronic images. When the handrail along the top deck is touched the transmission of data is broken, and the building fills with 'noise' or disappears in parts.

Transient Field, Bellevue-Stadelhofen Square, Zurich, Switzerland
Urban design competition entry
2000
tessera: architects

During World War Two the exposed earth of the Bellevue-Stadelhofen Square in Zurich allowed the cultivation of potato and rape crops, an image deeply engraved in the collective memory of the city. Up to this day it facilitates traditional events such as the burning of the snowman, the installation of the circus and the alternation of seasonal markets. Our project keeps and reinterprets this rural character. We propose the construction of a sliding floor that enables the transformation of the square into an even surface for contemporary urban use. The new floor is composed of panels arranged in long parallel strips which slide, creating various configurations between the two extreme conditions: absolutely empty, revealing the field, and fully covered. The panels can fold up producing adaptable equipment: benches, low walls, playgrounds etc. At night the floor becomes a luminous horizontal screen, with the coloured panels constituting the pixels of the screen, rendering images of past memories or advertising future events.

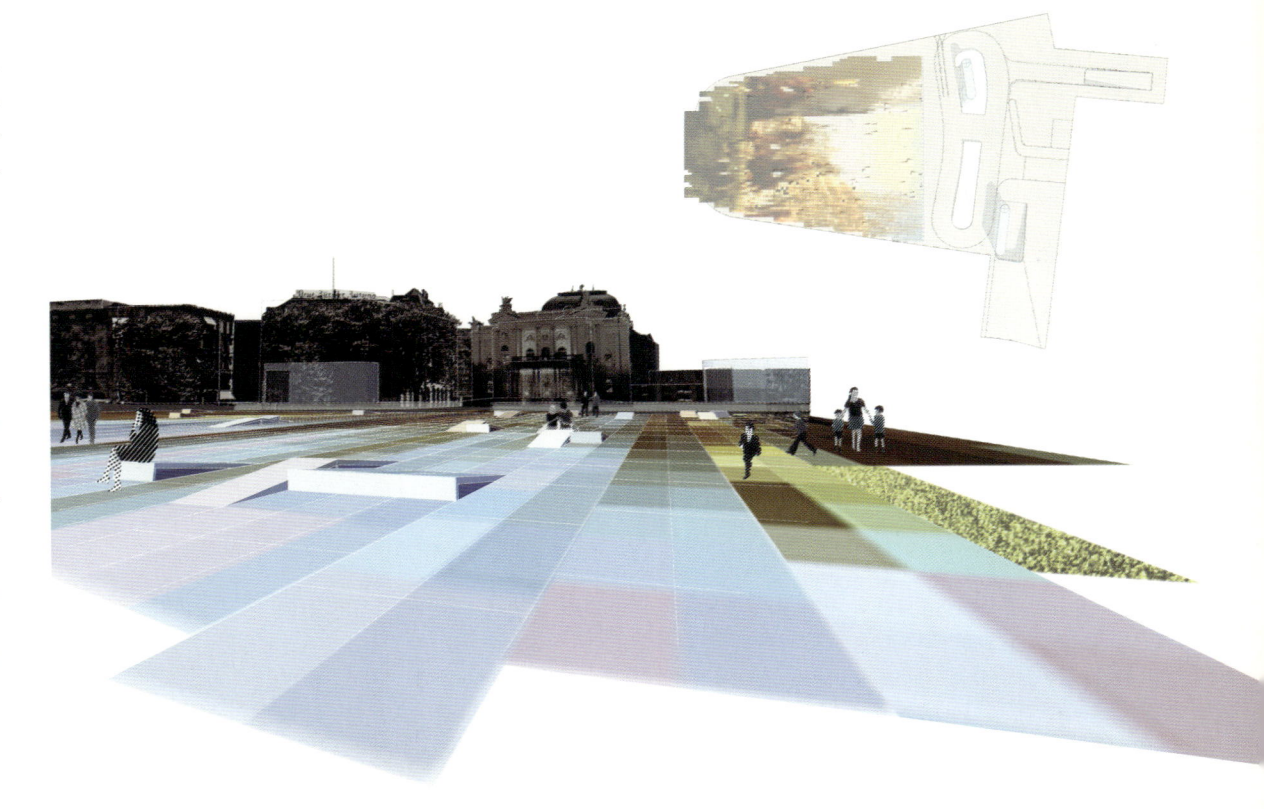

184 THARANI ASSOCIATES

In my time, in the 1970s, the Bartlett did not promote any one particular design approach, but encouraged exploration, which allowed me to realise the primary importance of place – the nature of a site and its context. For me design is a collusion between place, programme, and one's memories, observations and obsessions. This is particularly the case in the tropics where theoretical (and ideological) questions of modernity and appropriateness and are all the more acutely posed – although such things as the way a sand crab moves are just as important.

Like all small practices, our work ranges in scale from coffee tables to hospital design. Perhaps the only difference between practice in Britain, where I worked till the early 1990s, and here in Tanzania, is the non-availability of manufactured materials (and smaller budgets) – but then this can be a welcome restriction.

Nadir Tharani

House, Mwanza, Dar es salaam, Tanzania ▶
New build house
Completed: 2002
Nadir Tharani: architect

This large house is built among the rocky outcrops that are a feature of Mwanza, retaining and incorporating the landscape into the architecture. Accommodation is strung along the east-west axis, the split section allowing views of Lake Victoria from the pool, living and dining areas and from the master bedroom. The east-west alignment, a prerequisite in the tropics, minimises solar gain, while wide overhangs protect the walls from the sun and tropical downpours. Security, a secondary but critical consideration, determined opening window sizes, and retractable grilles are used wherever possible. The house has withstood two minor earthquakes so far.

Crab Stools and Maua Meeting Table, Tanzania ◀
Furniture design
Completed: 2000
Nadir Tharani: designer

The Crab Stools were inspired by small sand crabs on the beach. Made of coconut timber, they can be arranged in six different configurations. They are made in Zanzibar. The 'Maua' Meeting Table can seat five, but its shape allows an intimate group of two or three to be seated. The projecting shape allows incidental items (calculators, files, ashtrays, etc) to be positioned on one side. The top is maple veneer (a version in solid coconut was also made), and the support is part of a tree trunk (muhuhu, a local hardwood).

STEPHEN TIERNEY

I presently work for James Gorst Architects, London, designing large private houses. Previously with Ian Ritchie Architects I worked on the Spire of Dublin. I teach undergraduate design, Unit 7, at the Bartlett with Christian Groothuizen. I am married with a son aged two, Joseph.

Before Architecture I did a BA in History of Art and History at University College Dublin. An interest in landscape, history, and lightweight materials influences my design and teaching.

Donkey Shelter, Tipperary, Ireland
New build residential
Cost: £1,800 to build (excluding labour)
Completed: 1998
Stephen Tierney: design and build

Sally and Snowball, my Mother's two donkeys, are both around 40 years old and like to shelter from the sun and the wind. The brief was to create a simple shelter in the corner of a field for them, that would also act as a focus at the end of the garden path.

There were several ideas behind the shelter's form. In plan it is similar to a donkey's hoof in mud. In elevation the overhanging roof frames the distant lake view much like the boughs and roots of the surrounding oak trees. The slate for the walls was taken free from a local abandoned slate quarry, and the roof is tarred canvas over laminated beams, similar to west of Ireland curraghs. The shelter was built over four summers, starting in 1995, with help from college friends.

Eel class racing canoe, Lough Derg, Ireland
Boat-building
£8,000 budget for prototype
Development: 2002–present
Stephen Tierney: Design and build

Lough Derg in Ireland is a lake famous for its perfect sailing conditions – steady winds, small waves and varied geography. In 1921 Morgan Giles, a well-known yacht designer, created the One-Design class of racing dinghy specifically for Lough Derg and the Shannon lakes, which is still very popular.

The intention of the Eel was to design another boat specially for this ideal location but with younger more agile sailors in mind. It will be a difficult, unsteady and wet boat for two people to sail. The long narrow canoe hull makes for fast, weatherly upwind sailing. The high aspect, low area rig reflects the low drag hull form. The hull is to be made from cold moulded veneers using the West system and all spars and outriggers are carbon fibre. The centreboard will initially be steel as a small concession to stability. The prototype is currently being prepared.

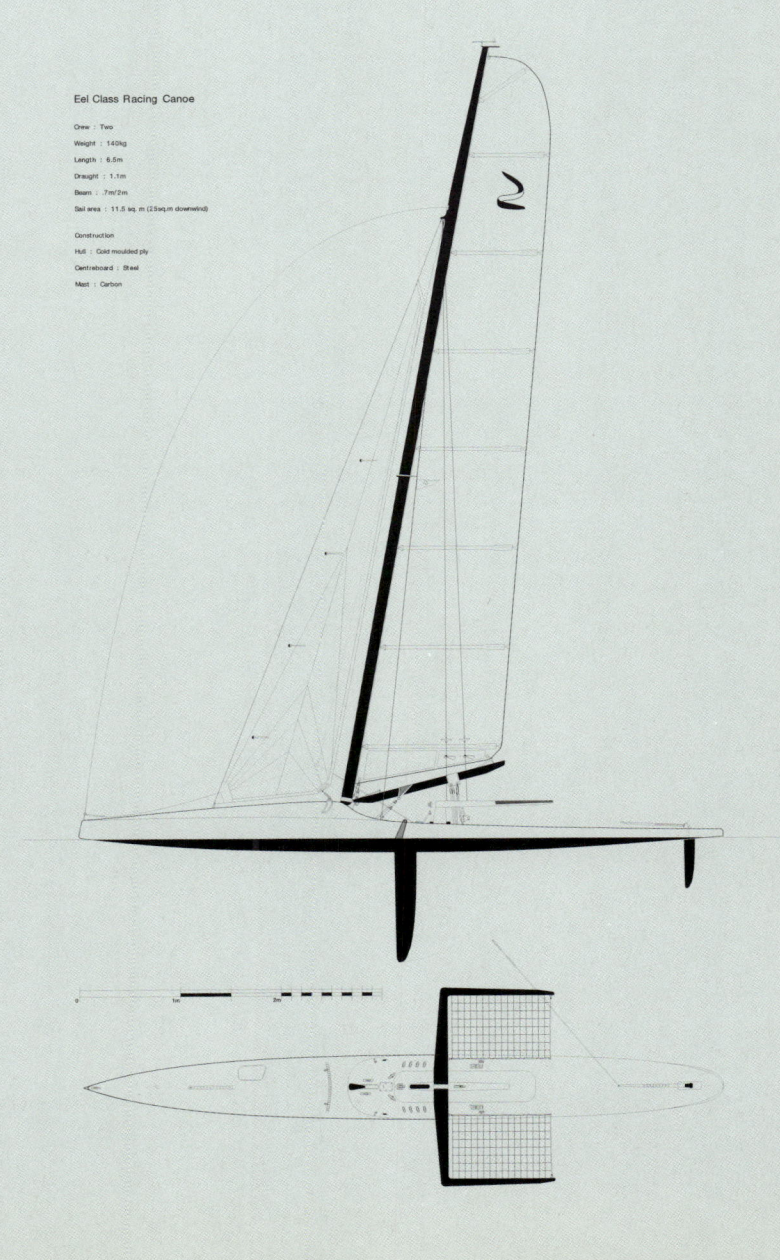

Eel Class Racing Canoe
Crew : Two
Weight : 140kg
Length : 6.5m
Draught : 1.1m
Beam : .7m/2m
Sail area : 11.5 sq. m (25sq.m downwind)

Construction
Hull : Cold moulded ply
Centreboard : Steel
Mast : Carbon

186 TRANSIENT

I established Transient in London in 1997 after five years living and working in Asia and several years as an associate in commercial practice in London. The practice is intended as both a conventional design studio and a vehicle for collaborative work on a diverse range of design and theoretical projects in urbanism, architecture and photography. We have collaborated in the past with composers, filmmakers and artists, and see this as an important strand of our work, pushing the boundaries of our experience and knowledge.

Jonathan Pile

Hedge-House, West Hampstead
Proposed new house
Budget: £230,000
Completion: 2004
Jonathan Pile: architect

This is a proposal for a new house on a difficult site, in a Conservation Area and only five metres deep, that was formerly a garden and is currently occupied by a dilapidated car workshop. The catalyst for the design was the pre-existence of the garden. The use of the language of garden 'infrastructure' (fences, hedges, treehouses) meets the demands of contextual sensitivity, and creates the opportunity to experiment with unusual materials and to treat the dwelling as a hidden retreat, even though it is built hard onto the street edge.

Sedum planted in a system of geo-textile mat trays grows over the upper floor elevations, irrigated with rainwater from adjoining roofs. Thus the parasitic new 'growing' house takes its sustenance from the 'host' buildings. Internal spaces are largely top-lit, with funnel windows protruding through the 'hedge' to peer at the 19th-century neighbours.

The design, described by Camden's Conservation and Design Department as 'an obvious case for outright refusal' was initially turned down, but successfully taken to Appeal, with support from CABE. Work will start on site in 2004.

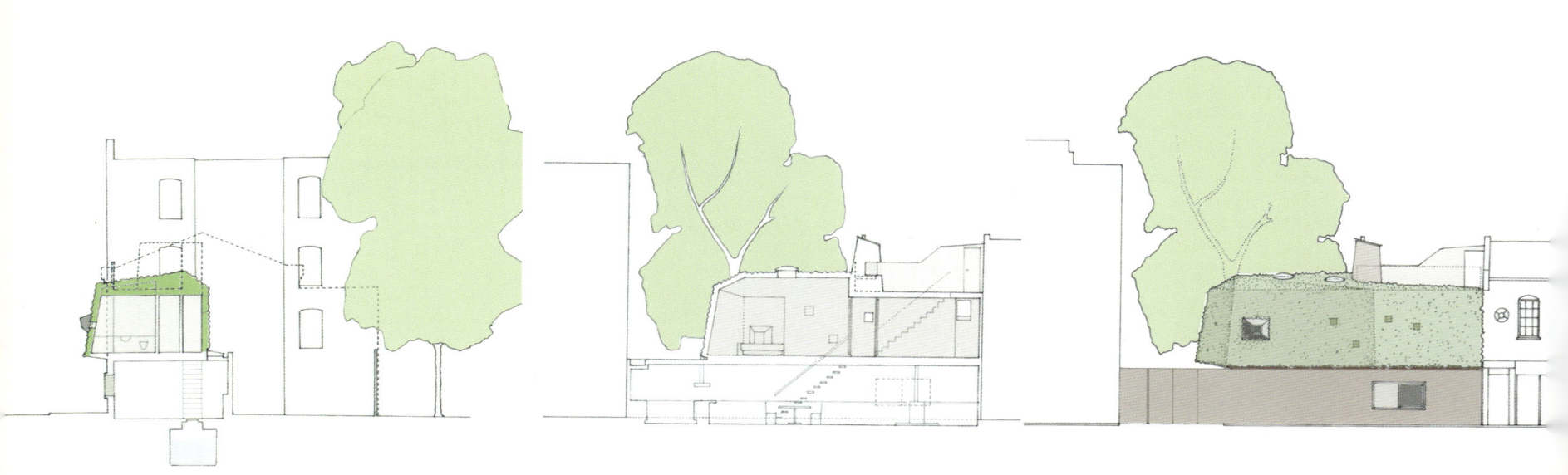

Spun Yarn
RIBA 'Future-City' Exhibition
2000
Jonathan Pile: designer/author

Part invented allegory, part serious urban proposal, part provocation, this work, combining photography, collage, drawing and text, was made for a collaborative exhibition held at the RIBA in 2000. Participants were asked to speculate on urban futures within the Thames Gateway development area. Our work centred on Beckton and Creekmouth, home of Europe's largest sewage treatment complex.

The North London Line will be extended approximately three miles east following the river edge, to serve a new dense, car-free settlement based on rail and river transport. London's sewage is treated by being filtered through vast reed beds and bamboo groves extending for miles, the latter providing a renewable supply of scaffolding for the construction industry.

Treated sludge is pumped alongside rail-lines and used to irrigate and fertilise pleasure gardens, allotments, market gardens and orchards. Towering vertical greenhouses suck up nutrients from the sludge-lines for the production of cut flowers. Produce is transported by rail and barge to the West End and the villages of North London, retracing the route of Bazalgette's sewers, completing the cycle.

The layers of industrial archaeology remain, the bamboo rustling against the rusting gasometers. The new greening of East London and beyond continues for decades, many acres of deep fertile new soil are created every year, dwarfing Richmond Park, reaching out to the suburbs, a register of the consumption of the metropolis. The East prospers at the unwitting expense of the West, redressing an ancient imbalance.

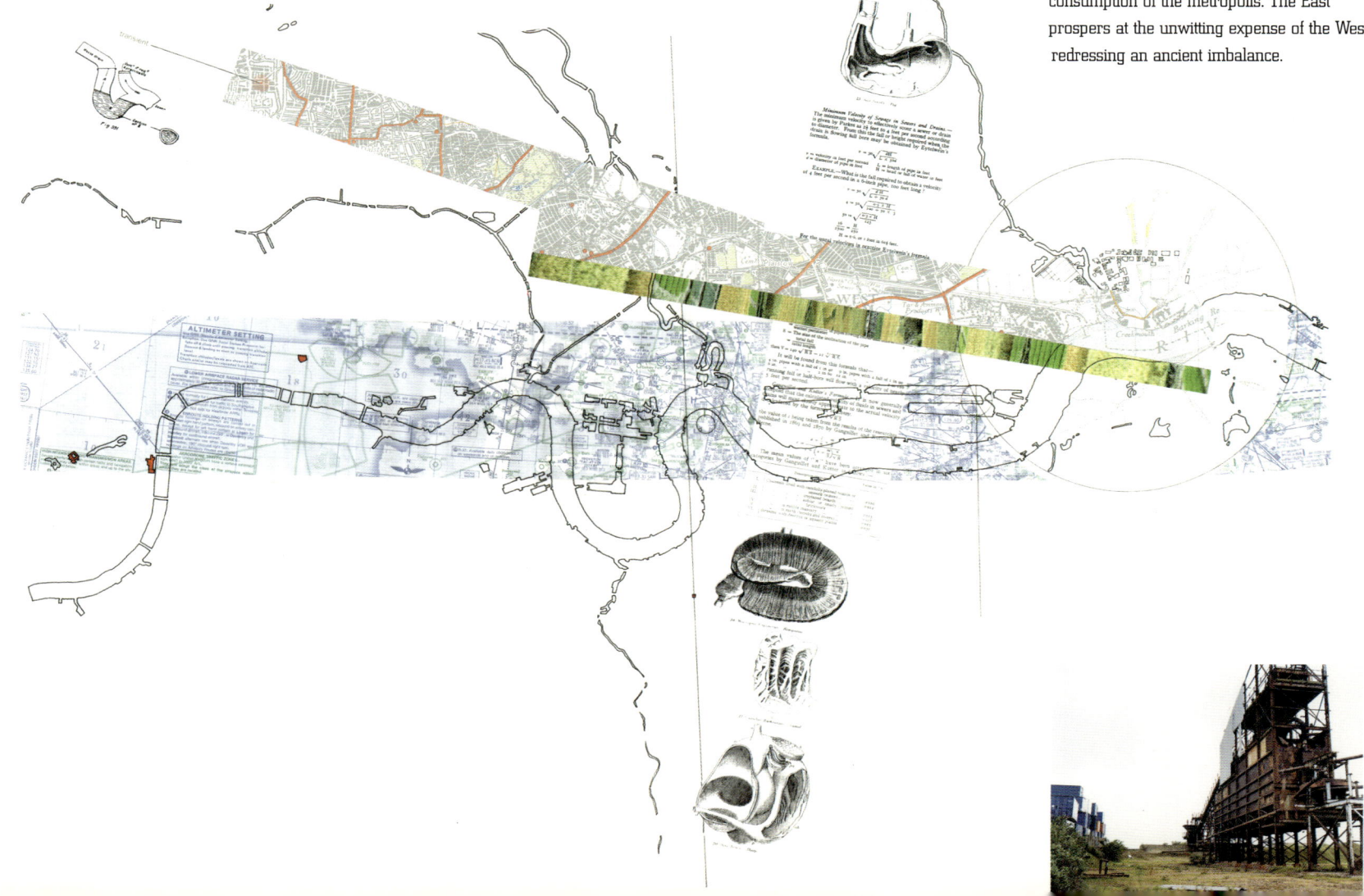

188 UNIVERSITY OF SOUTH AUSTRALIA

The Line of Lode Miners Memorial and Visitors Centre, Broken Hill, New South Wales, Australia
New build
Budget: AU$1.95 million
Completed: April 2001
Chris Landorf: project architect with David Manfredi, leading a team of recent graduates and undergraduates (Angus Barron, Steve Kelly and Dario Paulumbo)

The Line of Lode Miners Memorial and Visitors Centre is the result of an ongoing collaboration between the University of South Australia and the mining community of Broken Hill that culminated in the awarding of the Walter Burley Griffin Award for Urban Design in 2001. The Miners Memorial commenced as a student project in 1996 and following the awarding of a $3.65 million Federation Grant, the Memorial became the cornerstone of a larger development of the historic Line of Lode mining precinct and Broken Hill Living Museum. The Memorial commemorates the lives of over 800 men who have died along the Line of Lode since its discovery in 1883 and offers a place of remembrance for the community. A Visitors Centre forms an integral but subservient companion to the Memorial. Using aggressively fractured planes and a strong sense of journey, both structures seek to express the powerful industrial nature of the mining industry in contrast to the lighter and more tenuous nature of the surrounding city.

I joined the University of Newcastle (Australia) in 2002 following twelve years at the University of South Australia, including a three-year appointment as Head of the School of Architecture and Design. I have also been President of the South Australian Chapter of the Royal Australian Institute of Architects. The Broken Hill Line of Lode project is a good example of my commitment to both academia and practice. The Diploma in Facility and Environment Management I did at UCL has contributed greatly to several industry-based research projects that I am engaged in, including the sustainable management of complex heritage sites (PhD in progress) and the impact of design on organisational effectiveness, particularly in relation to health care facilities.

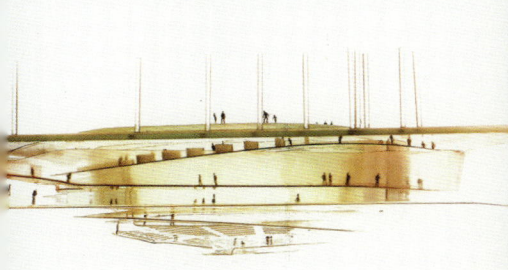

URBAN FUTURE ORGANIZATION

Founded in London in 1996, urban future organization operates as a network of independent architectural offices, each office responding to its own locale whilst being able to draw on the resources of a global collective. To date, this includes offices in Italy, Netherlands, Greece, Korea and the UK.

Sarajevo Concert Hall, Bosnia i Herzegovina
New build concert hall
Budget: £28 million
Completion: (estimated) 2008
Steve Hardy: design team member

Won in an international architectural competition that attracted more than 450 entries, the proposed Sarajevo Concert Hall is currently being publicised to generate support and promote fundraising.

The building, with a 1,500-seat hall for symphonic and choral concerts, and a 500-seat hall for chamber, contemporary and popular music, will be built in a park in the Marijin Dvor area in the core of the city, near to the Parliament and State Museum. The concert halls are buried into the earth, extending the public realm of the city beneath the ground. Surrounding surfaces meld into the underground spaces in a whirlpool movement, giving access from several critical urban connections and bringing daylight inside. The parkscape continues above, allowing indoor and outdoor spaces and events to blend, and an unobstructed flow of people through the site.

Museum of Contemporary Art, Castelmola, Sicily, Italy
New build museum
Budget: £4 million
Completion: 2008
Steve Hardy: director

The hillside town of Castelmola in Sicily annually invites artists to stay, who in exchange donate artworks to the town. A competition was held for the design of a new museum to accommodate the resultant expanding collection of art. We were joint winners and were awarded the commission. The majority of funding for phase one of construction is now in place.

Our proposal is inspired by the way traditional terraced local farms work with the steep landscape. The museum emerges as subtle undulations from the ridge of the hill, with a series of cascading sections controlled by the contours of the site. The sections vary in size, height and relationship to each other, providing multiple conditions for exhibiting works of art, and can be added or removed over time – like the local houses, which are in a state of continual formation flux, always evolving.

190 USHIDA FINDLAY

Ushida Findlay has worked on a range of projects, including arts venues, listed buildings, commercial property and varying scales of private residential commissions. We believe that buildings should acknowledge their surroundings, and have developed a design language that creates a fusion between natural landscape and architecture. Our work has progressed naturally to involve indigenous crafts, climate and culture as both formal generators and as a source of practical methods to aid construction. This sensitivity to, and re-appraisal of, the environment and craft techniques develops with each project.

Grafton New Hall, Cheshire
New country house
Completion: 2005
Paul Madden: concept design, design development
Matthew Potter: design development

Grafton New Hall was the winning scheme in an RIBA competition to reinterpret the English country house on an estate in Cheshire. The ultra-modern 3,500-square metre house breaks with the tradition of dominating the landscape and instead reflects and positively embraces nature. The building extends like fingers into a low-lying surrounding meadow, creating a series of ridges and furrows, which reflect, enhance, and frame the contours of the mediaeval landscape. It appears to grow/evolve like a stone outcrop; rough at its base, smooth at its top, as if it had spent many decades obtaining the patina of weathering.

Internally, spaces are laid out in a fanning spiral, feathering at its edges, creating a strong and open relationship between inside and outside. The concept is one of continuity; floors, walls and ceilings are one, both structurally and aesthetically. Grafton New Hall is orientated such that the pattern of daily activity loosely follows the path of the sun.

SECTION BB WING 2-LIVING WING

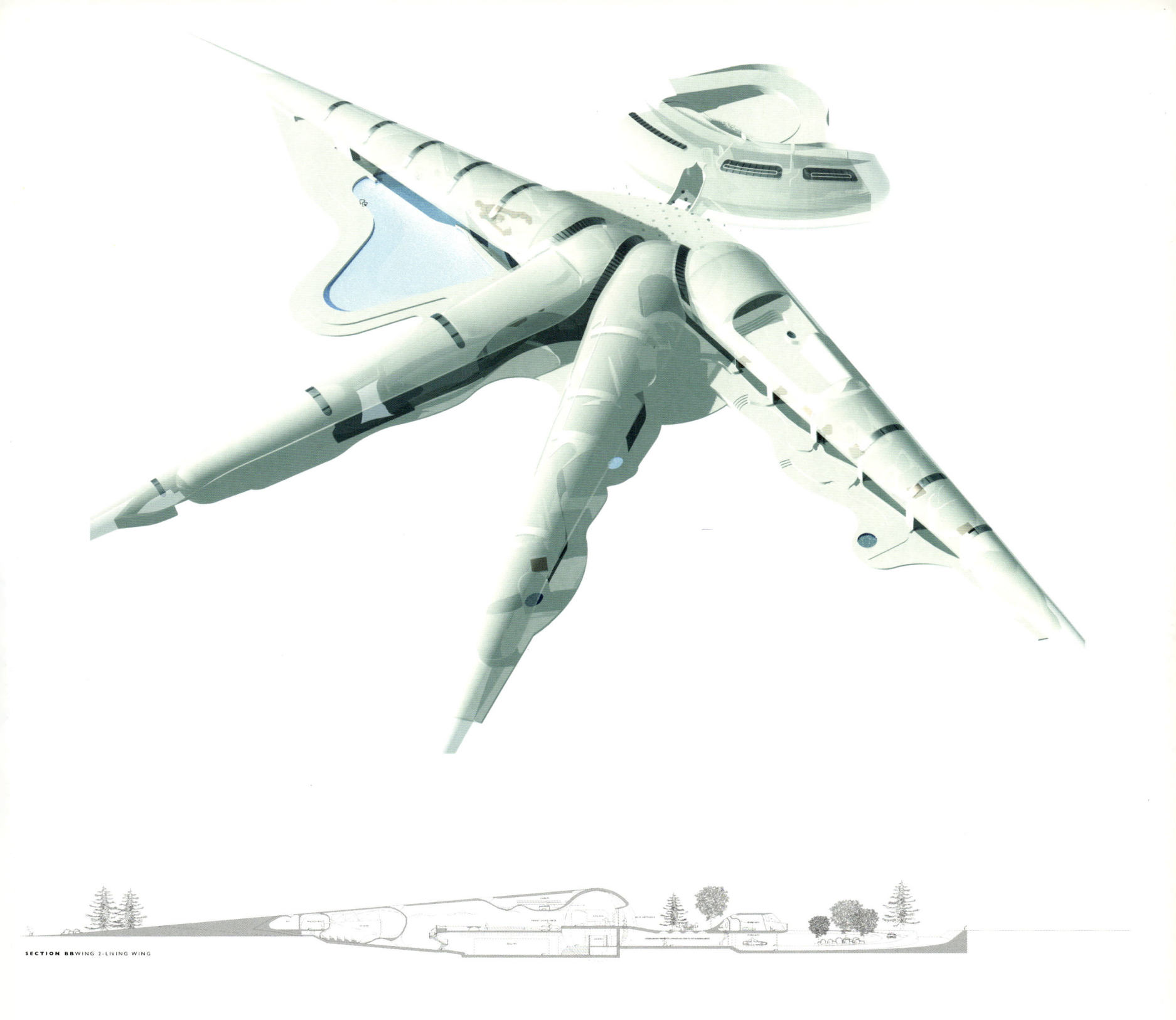

192 USHIDA FINDLAY

Armada Way, Plymouth
Competition entry (phase two shortlisted)
2003
Anne Maria Galmstrup: worked on design and concept development

This pavilion is a competition entry for the development of Plymouth's Armada Way. Through a careful understanding of the social and commercial nature of the context we formulated a proposal that creates a number of continual activities (on a 24/7 basis) throughout the site which help to sustain a truly economically viable solution.

A series of grass waves flow and undulate through the site, inspired by the textures of the surrounding moorland landscape. A limited palette of stonecrops, gorse, grasses, mosses and silver birch will intensify the experience of the changing seasons. Different activity levels are created by the waves, whilst the design comfortably caters for a range of new high-quality retail outlets. The 'Armada Waves' will become an invigorating urban landmark for the local community.

Hastings Visitor Centre

Visitor and tourist information centre/fish restaurant

Budget: approximately £3 million

Completion: estimated 2004

Kate Francis: concept design, design development

Matthew Potter: design development

This new building on the seafront in Hastings was commissioned through a two-stage open competition. The site is in a unique corner of Hastings between the historical winding closes of the Old Town, and the living heritage of the beach fishing fleet, net shops, and museum. The centre forms a gateway to the Stade Maritime area, orientating visitors to Hastings, with a new public plaza, exhibition space, coffee shop and high-profile fish restaurant. The design was inspired by the curve of fishing boats' hulls nestled amongst the net shops and winch huts.

I worked on the design of the structure, which was based on research I began at the Bartlett into biomimetics. This was an excellent chance to develop ideas, with Arups and artist David Ward, of flows, traditional boat building technologies and tidal organic forms, particularly the sea anemone.

Kate Francis

194 VELVET AIR

So who are we? "We come not from Heaven but from Essex", to quote William Morris. Partners Simon Herron and Susanne Isa studied at the Architectural Association, London and Städelschule, Frankfurt. Practising as Herron Associates with Ron and Andrew Herron, built works include three projects for Toyama Prefecture Japan. Herron Associates was closed in 1993, and the practice renamed Velvet Air.

We have taught at the Bartlett since 1991 in both undergraduate and diploma school, and are currently running Diploma Unit 16. Collaborative works include international workshops in Miami, Moscow, Hamburg, Taipei and Finland.

We have no formal manifesto and believe that it is better to have attitude than to be trapped by style.

☐ Known America
■ Unknown America
● Location

'Laboratories for architecture'
Photographic project
Ongoing
Simon Herron and Susanne Isa: location scout and photographer

In a letter to Le Corbusier dated 22 April 1936, Albert Frey wrote:

'The California desert continues to charm me, continues to nourish me, to give me an opportunity for modern architecture... our efforts are not hindered by building codes regulating size, style or materials. The result of this freedom is that parcels of land look like laboratories of architectural and materials research.'

For the past ten years we have undertaken journeys of between 2,000 and 3,000 miles traversing the American West, exploring unexpected corners, technologically maintained sites, supposed cultural backwaters. Imagining ourselves as detectives, forensic investigators, archaeologists of everyday life: our tool the camera.

Sites are established as a scene of crime, or archaeological dig: a table, a discarded magazine, stale beer, an abandoned shack, a collapsed trailer, a shot up sign, a shopping mall, suburban subdivision, the interstate, a gas stop, daytime TV, rolling news, the weather channel.

These photographs are part of a series in search of fragmentary evidence, residue traces of the *American Dream*. They are momentary perceptions, disassociated memories, collectively experienced as disconnected filmic fragments. Forgotten histories, folk stories, discarded inventions, lost utopias; montaged together, as collaborative scenes from the cutting room floor, outtakes from nowhere.

'A man went looking for America and couldn't find it anywhere' – billboard ad for 'easy rider'.

Illustrated here are Salvation Mountain, by Leonard Knight, Slab City; and 'Hunting Season' – both Nihland County, Imperial Valley, California, USA. 33n115w

KEEPER

ROAD
CLOSED
AHEAD

LOVE
JESUS I'M A
SINNER PLEASE
COME UPON
MY BODY
AND INTO
MY
GOD
IS
LOVE
A SINNER PLEASE
COME UPON MY
BODY AND INTO
MY HEART

196 WAG ARCHITECTURE

WaG Architecture is a design practice and spatial ideas consultancy, founded in 2001 by Cordula Weisser and Jon Goodbun. Extending and where possible realising our teaching and research interests (based in the new Polytechnic research group at SABE, the University of Westminster), our work currently ranges from small building projects to writing, from spatial art projects to interface design, new media and urbanism. An important strand of our work is a constant questioning of the ways in which CAD and technological developments affect the production of social space – both in individual and collective experiences of use and inhabitation.

Towers of Wind
Competition entry
2002
Jon Goodbun, Cordula Weisser: design team

This project is a response to a competition brief that asked for 'ephemeral' and 'parasitic' structures to be sited within the city of Athens during the 2004 Olympics. The Tower of Winds (named after a first century BC Athenian structure) rethinks, through these terms, the way in which architecture works to construct social space. We identified cool clean air and shadows as our architectural materials.

The 60-metre high fabric tower is suspended from a floating ring of helium. Water is pumped up the tower through small high-pressure tubes, and runs down inside it. As the water evaporates it cools the air within the tower, the cool air sinks and draws clean air in from above low-lying pollution. The tower can be delivered to site by car, and erected within an hour, and will produce a breeze of one metre per second and a temperature drop of eleven degrees Celsius.

The walls are a pattern of transparent kevlar and opaque PV fabric (which powers the water pumps). The patterning produces shifting fields of 'event shadows' across the streets and buildings of the city. After the Olympics, the Tower can be erected to provide protective envelopes of clean air around historic monuments during periods of heavy pollution.

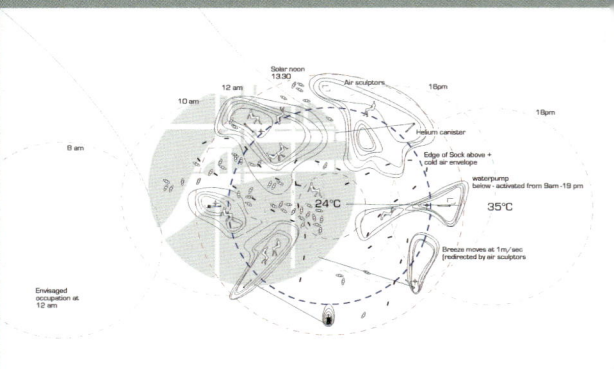

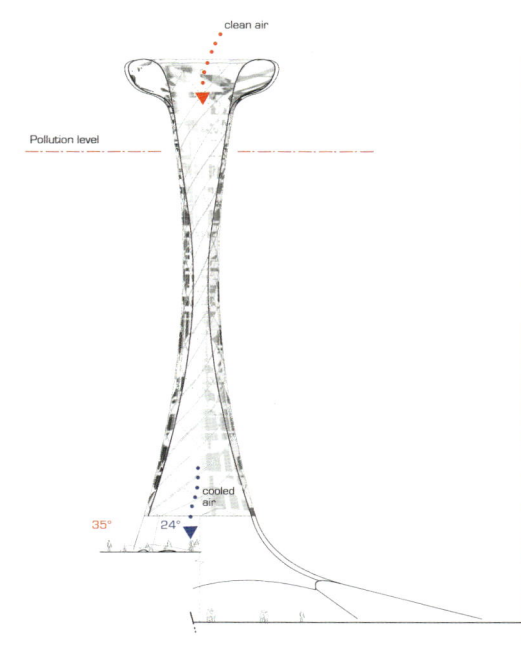

INGALILL WAHLROOS ARCHITECTS

I established my practice, Ingalill Wahlroos Architects, in New York in 1999 and currently work in the United States and in London with my partner Roland Wahlroos-Ritter, on residential projects, exhibition designs and competitions.

I combine architectural practise with teaching design studios and courses in materials technology – particularly glass in architecture – at Cornell University and Yale University in the US, and with Roland at the Oxford School of Architecture and at the Bartlett. Our interest in materials has led us to develop a course at the Bartlett that is based on the assumption that materials carry with them potential implications for form, function, meaning, programme and appropriation.

Ingalill Wahlroos-Ritter

The Summer Stage, Corning, New York
Outdoor theatre
Construction budget: US$1.9 million
Completed: June 2001
Ingalill Wahlroos-Ritter: project architect

The Summer Stage is an outdoor theatre for glassblowing demonstrations, located adjacent to the Museum of Glass in Corning, a small town in New York State. The project consists primarily of a glass roof sheltering an aluminium seating-platform. The design not only celebrates such familiar properties of glass as its reflectivity, transparency and lightness; but also its slipperiness, thinness and weight. Glass surfaces are alternately smooth or textured, carefully choreographed to be transparent or reflective depending from where they are seen.

The roof consists of two glass planes tilted diagonally away from each other. Viewed at an oblique angle they are purely reflective and appear as huge single planes of glass, uninterrupted by mullions and sliding free of the supporting steel structure. The glass edges are unframed where possible, heightening the expression of their thinness. The seating platform below is raised above the courtyard to the level of the tree canopy, giving it a surprising intimacy.

I also helped design a custom-made mobile stage, which when not touring the country is docked at the western end of the platform. The first of its kind, it is a fully functioning hot-glass workshop and classroom.

198 WHAT ARCHITECTURE

If one premise for architecture has been to ground space to place, then WHAT value does site-specificity hold in these contemporary times of easyJet travel and liquid mobility? Has the banal anonymity of the *generic* meant that the *locale* has risen in value? WHAT_Architecture, founded by Anthony Hoete and Gerrit Grigoleit, is an office whose design strategies are guided by the oscillations between global and local spaces. The city today is a place of immense instability generated by flow: the transience of its tourist-citizen demographic; the rapid exchange of information, goods and services; the sensitising resonance between phenomena foreign and familiar.

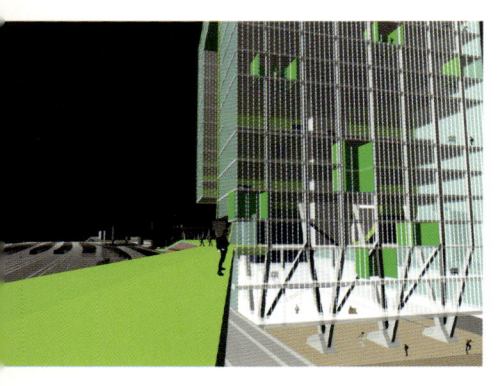

'Burol', Vlaams Administratie Centrum, Leuven, Belgium
Proposed new build office building
Ongoing
WHAT_Architecture: architects

The Belgian city of Leuven is notable for two reasons: students and beer! The city hosts one of Europe's oldest universities as well as the headquarters of Stella Artois. Given its large student population (30% of citizens) and the logistics of a major brewery, Leuven is a commuter concentrate within Flander's mobilised landscape. An urban residue of adjoining ringroads and railways, the site for this government administrative centre was considered a traffic island. In response to the surrounding commotion a tranquil workplace was desired – a hybrid desert-island/traffic-island. The office programme needed to shift seamlessly between control and accessibility. The VAC was thus organised – indeed rolled – to create configurations with good public access at lower levels ceding to high control (and limited access) above. Where one cannot enter, one can see: a vertical pedestrian roundabout! The state also gets 'four buildings for the price of one' as landscape, tower, bridge and hanging buildings are rolled into a single continuous mass.

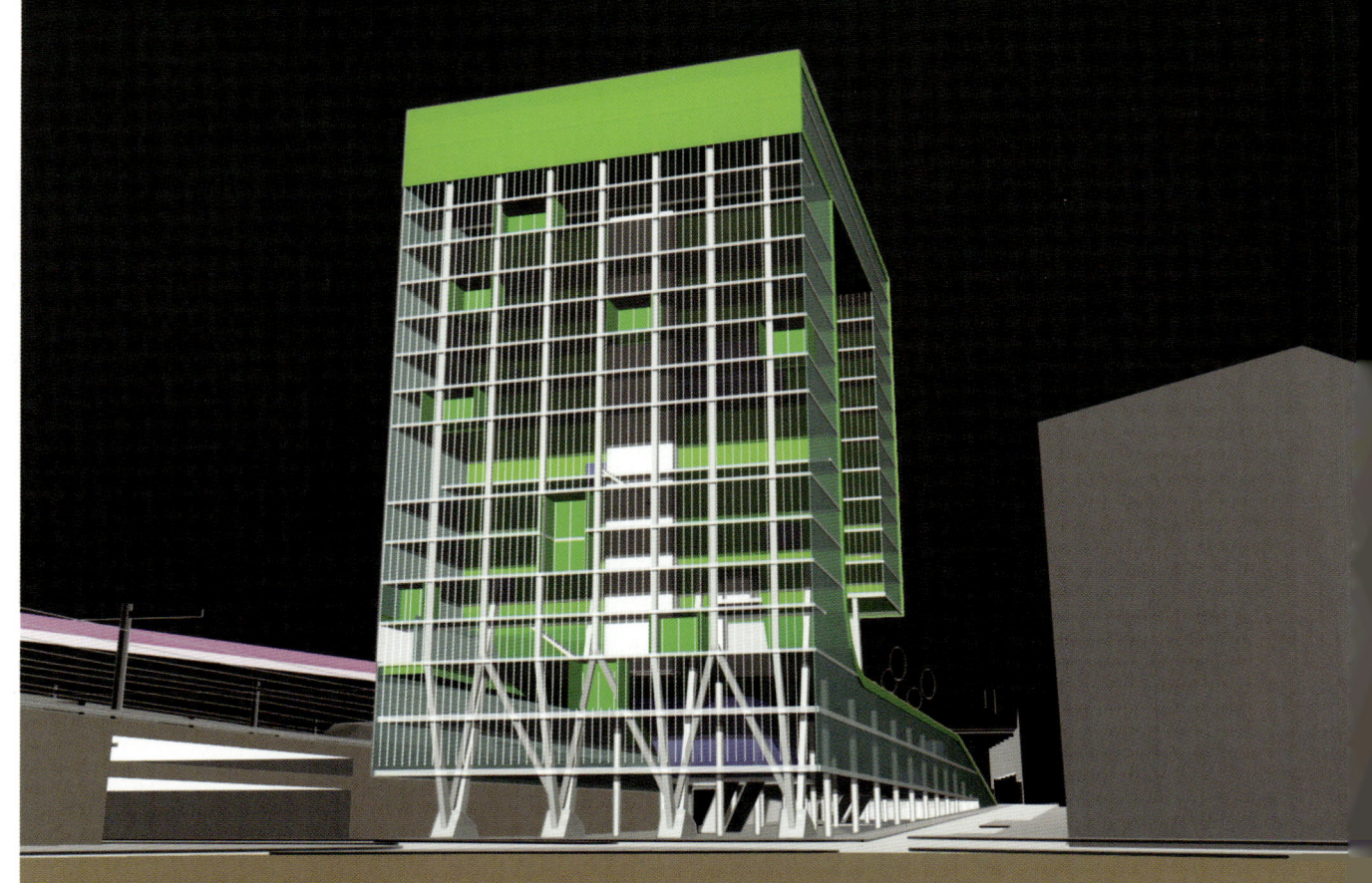

WHITE PARTNERS

If you're working in a large practice and you're not sure how to deal with your client, or how to approach a project, what do you do? Probably ask your boss. But what to do if you're running your own firm, who do you turn to? That's where we come in – to give architects a wider view and advice on managing projects and contracts.

What do architects produce? – ideas, concepts, design solutions – i.e. intellectual property. Many architects fail to recognise the value of their intellectual property; our first area of activity is advising them on how to capitalise on it – gaining it, refining it, protecting it, selling it. Key to this is setting projects up properly, which includes recognising what clients want from the architect, properly understanding the work to be done, recognising risks and of course negotiating fees.

Our second area of expertise is knowledge management, that is, how architects can use their knowledge base to enhance their working processes. How is a practice's accumulated information store accessed and used? Why and when are decisions made in projects? This knowledge manifests itself in the production of drawings, images, models etc., but many architects are not clear about the route by which they produce this material, and it is much better if they can map it as it is happening.

And third, we advise on the external value of architects' work: copyrights, archive value, use of imagery and legacy value. Very often architects will design façade systems or furniture products, for example, the rights over which they fail properly to control.

I like to work with architects from the inception of projects and to meet regularly as designs develop to influence the processes followed as they are happening, rather than trying to tie up loose ends later. It is also only as a project develops that the potential gains and risks crystallise.

So how did I come to do this kind of thing?

I've always been fascinated by invention and problem-solving, and so when I first went to university I studied Applied Physics at Durham. Applied Physics wasn't 'applied' enough for me, and so I left to study architecture at the Bartlett instead. Under David Dunster, the Bartlett taught a very structured approach to designing the built environment, and this application of process to architecture fascinated me. After five years working in practice I joined Hanscomb as a project management consultant, and later I saw the opportunity to set up White Partners.

People sometimes ask if I miss working as an architect, or imagine that my interest is simply in finding ways to cut corners and costs to produce cheaper buildings and maximise profits, but I see my work as contributing to the process of creating good architecture. I'm an architect; I like good design and I understand what motivates architects – I want to help them achieve their aspirations. It isn't only a question of financial gain – if an architect's expertise is recognised and valued they will get more control over decision making and will do more rewarding work. Good business practice and creative design benefit each other.

Another misconception is that our advice is only applicable to larger more corporate firms, but we work with a whole range of practices. We do not seek to impose one standard-fit approach on all our customers, but to help them appreciate the value of what they particularly do, and to capitalise upon it.

I've worked as an architect, but to be honest I'm too much of a perfectionist to make the kind of compromises in the design process that one must in practice. I'm still working in architecture, only I've realised that my specialist interest lies in the process by which architects can best identify and apply their knowledge and skills.

200 MICHAEL WILFORD & PARTNERS

After working in some rather frenetic offices, the calm, studious environment of MWP at Fitzroy Square was striking. Everyone sat quietly drawing, listening to Radio Four and absorbing the cigar smoke that filled the air. It was like being back at college. Everybody in our design team worked on independent design options, and at the end of each day we would slide our drawings under Michael's office door to discuss with him and project architect David Turnbull the next day. Normally a hybrid was agreed on.

Responsibility to develop particular aspects of the design was left with individual team members — Michael's confidence in each and every one of us was always constructive, and he was extremely supportive of the architecture at its most difficult stages. Peter Cook projects the same belief, giving you the confidence that you can and will produce work at your highest level.

Chris Matthews

The Esplanade, Marina Bay, Singapore
Arts complex
Budget: £350 million
Completed: October 2002
Chris Matthews: design development

The Esplanade project includes a 2,000-seat lyric theatre and 1,800-seat concert hall, plus various smaller studio and arts spaces. The concert hall has a huge reverberation chamber with concrete doors that can alter the reverberation time depending on the nature of the performance. The hall requires 'tuning' to the conductor's requirements, and I understand from Artec, the acoustic engineers, that it is the biggest of its kind.

The building's skins were developed with Atelier 1&10. The sunshades, the glass skin, the steel structure and the foyers themselves are physical and visual filters reminiscent of the multi-layered design of much traditional Asian architecture. Based on the building's orientation, the available views and the path of the sun, the shades' shapes gradually change depending on their position on the surfaces of the shells, making for a varying visual appearance with changing angles of view. Neither the shape of the shells nor the arrangement of sunshades would have been possible without recent computer software — both in terms of design and construction.

WILKINSONEYRE.ARCHITECTS

WilkinsonEyre.Architects' portfolio is characterised by a series of iconic civic buildings and structures that share a dramatic sense of space and provide a strong and distinctive presence through their architectural form. Several projects have acquired 'destination' status and have been hugely influential in effecting remarkable transformations in the environments with which they engage. The practice is committed to 'adding value' in the broadest sense, believing passionately that architectural design is a key component of urban regeneration.

A greater proportion of our employees have been through the Bartlett than any other school, some have regularly returned to assist in crits with their one-time units.

Port Tawe Footbridges and Walkway, Swansea, Wales
Bridges
Budget: £3.5 million
Completed: June 2003
Ben Addy: architectural assistant

This project, undertaken with consulting engineers The Flint and Neill Partnership, comprises two static spans across the River Tawe in the port of Swansea with an additional opening bridge, and associated quayside walkways. Both principal bridges connect Swansea with a redevelopment project currently under construction to the east of the city. To encourage investment, infrastructure has to be visibly in place, which has resulted in an unusually compressed programme – from design inception to completion in less than 15 months.

The North Bridge, intended to form an iconic emblem for the regeneration of the Port area of Swansea, adopts a classic symmetrical cable-stayed configuration, but in cross-section the deck is held along only one edge. The simplicity of the overall form is belied by the apparent precariousness of the asymmetrically suspended walkway.

Poole Harbour Bridge,
Bridge
Budget: £14 million
Completion: 2006
Ben Addy: architectural assistant

Won in competition in late 2002, the Poole Harbour Second Crossing is a new opening road bridge connecting the towns of Poole and Hamsworthy on the South Coast of England. The bridge spans the entrance to Hole's Bay and its in-shore marinas, and so will have to open around 15 times a day, 365 days a year. This requirement provided the basis for the initial design.

Whereas most such bridges comprise two lifting rectangular sections, the new Poole Bridge has two lifting triangular sections that are each longer than the span between them. This affords a number of benefits: the centre of gravity of each leaf is brought closer to the bearings, allowing for more efficient and lower-rated hydraulics; bridge users can see past one open section to traffic moving through the channel; in the closed position the leaves can be simply supported at both ends, removing the need for complex interlocking mechanisms; and most notably, with each 35-metre leaf crossing the other, the process of opening becomes an unexpected theatrical event.

TIM WRAY

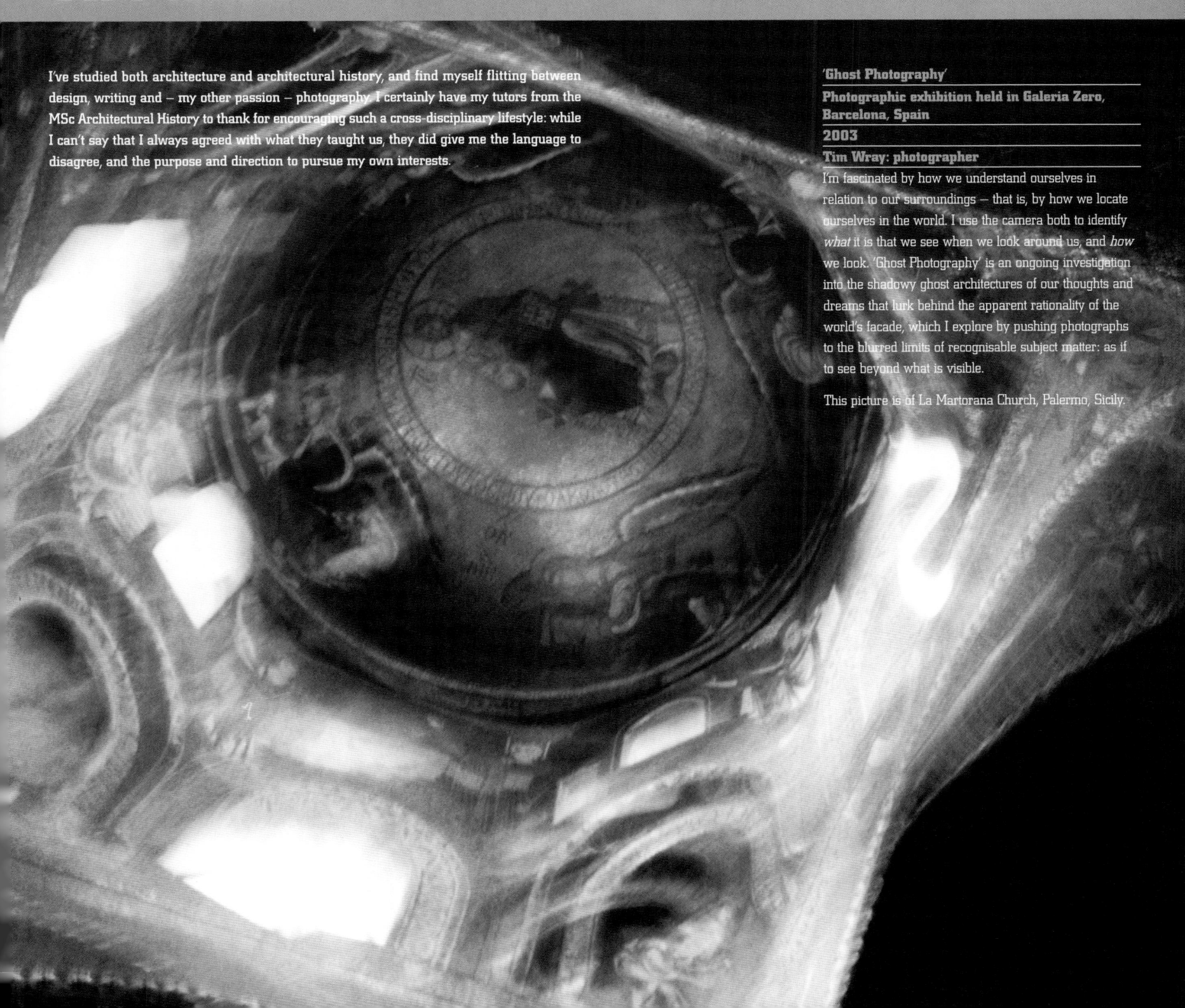

I've studied both architecture and architectural history, and find myself flitting between design, writing and – my other passion – photography. I certainly have my tutors from the MSc Architectural History to thank for encouraging such a cross-disciplinary lifestyle: while I can't say that I always agreed with what they taught us, they did give me the language to disagree, and the purpose and direction to pursue my own interests.

'Ghost Photography'
Photographic exhibition held in Galeria Zero, Barcelona, Spain
2003
Tim Wray: photographer

I'm fascinated by how we understand ourselves in relation to our surroundings – that is, by how we locate ourselves in the world. I use the camera both to identify *what* it is that we see when we look around us, and *how* we look. 'Ghost Photography' is an ongoing investigation into the shadowy ghost architectures of our thoughts and dreams that lurk behind the apparent rationality of the world's facade, which I explore by pushing photographs to the blurred limits of recognisable subject matter: as if to see beyond what is visible.

This picture is of La Martorana Church, Palermo, Sicily.

PEOPLE/PRACTICE INDEX

Practices and individuals featured in *Bartlett Works* and connected with the Bartlett are listed below. Only qualifications gained and teaching undertaken at the School are detailed.

ACQ – AGNELLI CURREY QUAZI
Hal Currey (Partner): Dip Arch 1992

ADAMS & SUTHERLAND
Graeme Sutherland (Partner): BSc Year 1 tutor 1994-present, Faculty Admissions Tutor 1996-present

ALLFORD HALL MONAGHAN MORRIS
Simon Allford (Partner): Dip Arch 1986 / BSc Unit 5 tutor 1991-93, Dip Unit 10 tutor 1993-2003
David Archer: Dip Arch 1992
Rob Burton: Dip Arch 1994
Scott Batty: Dip Arch 1997
Ceri Davies: BSc Arch 1992, Dip Arch 1995
Jonathan Hall (Partner): Dip Arch 1986, MSc History of Modern Architecture 1992
Charlotte Harrison: Dip Arch 1999
Susan Le Good: BSc Arch 1992, Dip Arch 1995
Jenny Lovell: Dip Arch 1993
Tony Martin: Dip Arch 1993
Paul Monaghan (Partner): Dip Arch 1986 / BSc Unit 5 tutor 1991-93, Dip Unit 10 tutor 1993-2003
Joe Morris: Dip Arch 1996
Peter Morris (Partner): Dip Arch 1986
Demetra Ryder Runton: Dip Arch 1997
Karen Scurlock: BSc Arch 1988, Dip Arch 1992
Morag Tait: MSc Architectural History 2002

ALLIES AND MORRISON
Jenny Lovell: Dip Arch 1993
Vicky Thornton: Dip Arch 1993
Helena Thomas: Part 3 1997

ALSOP ARCHITECTS
Oliver Blumschein: BSc Arch 1994
Isabel Brebbia (Associate): Dip Arch 1998 / BSc 'Preparing for Practice' course coordinator 2002-03
Adrian Fowler: Dip Arch 1999
Laura Guenzi: Dip Arch 1998
Alan Lai: BSc Arch 1996, Dip Arch 1999
Jonathan Leah (Director): BSc Arch 1988, Dip Arch 1991
Andy McPhee: Dip Arch 1993
Ed Norman: Dip Arch 1997
Spiros Pappas: MArch (Arch. Design) 2001
Barry Simpson: Dip Arch 1998
Max Titchmarsh: BSc Arch 1997, Dip Arch 2001
Greg Woods (Partner in RYWA): Dip Arch 1992

ARCA
John Lee (Director): BSc Arch 1986, Dip Arch 1989, MSc Advanced Architectural Studies 1990

ARCHIDESIGN
Neil Hutchison: Began studying architecture 1941, interrupted by war service 1943. Completed studies 1947-50

ART2ARCHITECTURE
Peter Fink: Dip technical tutor 1999-present
Nerma Cridge: Dip Arch 2000, MSc Architectural History 2003

ASHTON PORTER STUDIO
Abigail Ashton (Partner): Dip Arch 1994 / BSc Unit 3 tutor 1997-present, MArch (Architectural Design) tutor 1998-99
Phil Ayers: see SIXTEEN*(MAKERS)
Rachel Cruise: BSc Arch 2000, Dip Arch 2003
Tim Furzer: BSc Arch 2000, Dip Arch 2003
Tom Holberton: BSc Arch 2002
Chris Leung: see SIXTEEN*(MAKERS)
Andrew Porter (Partner): Dip Arch 1994 / BSc Unit 3 tutor 1997-present, MArch (Architectural Design) tutor 1998-99 and coordinator 2002-present

ATELIER KO / ARCHITECTS
Florence Gay: MSc Light and Lighting 1996
Akira Koyama: MArch (Architectural Design)1996

AZHAR ARCHITECTURE
Azhar: BSc Arch 1987, Dip Arch 1991

BLOCK ARCHITECTURE
Zoe Smith: Dip Arch 1996 / Dip Unit 23 tutor 2003-present
Graeme Williamson: Dip Arch 1998/ Dip Unit 23 tutor 2003-present

BLUSTIN HEATH DESIGN
Nikki Blustin: Dip Arch 1995
Oliver Heath: Dip Arch 1995

IAIN BORDEN
Iain Borden: MSc History of Modern Architecture 1986 / MSc Architectural History 1989-present, Dip history and theory coordinator 1995-2000, Professor of Architecture and Urban Culture (2002), Director of the School of Architecture 2001-present

BRANSON COATES
Guy Dickinson: Dip Arch 1996

MICHAEL BROWN
Michael Brown: MSc History of Modern Architecture 1992

JASON BRUGES STUDIO
Jason Bruges: Dip Arch 1997

BEN CAMPKIN, BARBARA PENNER AND JANE RENDELL
Ben Campkin: MSc Architectural History 2001 / BSc history and theory tutor 2000-present
Barbara Penner: MSc History of Modern Architecture 1996 / Dip history and theory tutor 1997-present, BSc Year 2 & 3 history and theory coordinator 2000-present, MSc Architectural History tutor 2000-present, BSc Architectural Studies Director 2002-present, PhD supervisor 2002-present
Jane Rendell: see JANE RENDELL

CHANCE DE SILVA ARCHITECTS
Stephen Chance (Partner): BSc Arch 1978, Dip Arch 1980
Wendy de Silva (Partner): BSc Arch 1978, Dip Arch 1980

DAVID CHIPPERFIELD ARCHITECTS
Judith Brown: Dip Arch 1994
David Chipperfield: design tutor 1985-86

PETER COOK AND COLIN FOURNIER – SPACELAB
David Ardill: Dip Arch 1997
Peter Cook (Partner): Bartlett Professor of Architecture (1990), Dip Unit 17 tutor 1990-93, Chairman of the School 1990-present, MArch (Architectural Design) Director 1995-present
Marcos Cruz: see MARCOS AND MARIAN ARCHITECTS
Jan Edler (realities:united): Erasmus exchange student pre-Dip 1994-95
Colin Fournier (Partner): Dip Unit 18 tutor 1995-present, MSc Urban Design Director 1997-present, Professor of Architecture and Urban Planning (1998)
Nicola Haines: Dip Arch 1999
Niels Jonkhans: Dip Arch 1997, MArch (Architecture) 2000
Anja Leonhäuser: Dip Arch 1998, MArch (Architecture) 2000
Jamie Norden: BSc Arch 1997, Dip Arch 1999
Mathis Osterhage: Dip Arch 1999

PETER COOK WITH PÉREZ ARROYO + HURTADO
Peter Cook: see COOK AND COLIN FOURNIER – SPACELAB
Salvador Pérez Arroyo: see PÉREZ ARROYO + HURTADO ARCHITECTS
Dr. Eva Hurtado Torán: see PÉREZ ARROYO + HURTADO ARCHITECTS

ODILE DECQ-BENOÎT CORNETTE
Odile Decq: Dip Unit 22 tutor 1999-2000

DILLER + SCOFIDIO
Joshua Bolchover: Dip Arch 2000

TOM DYCKHOFF
Tom Dyckhoff (Architecture and Design Critic, *The Times* Newspaper): MSc Architectural History 1995

EMULSION ARCHITECTURE
Yen-Yen Teh: Dip Arch 1996

EVENT COMMUNICATIONS
Gavin Robotham: Dip Arch 1993 / MArch (Architectural Design) tutor 2000-present, BSc Year 1 design tutor 2001-present

FEATHERSTONE ASSOCIATES (FORMERLY HUDSON FEATHERSTONE)
Sarah Featherstone (Director at Featherstone Associates, formerly Partner at Hudson Featherstone): Dip Arch 1994
David Appleton (Associate): BSc Arch 1993
Nicole Weiner: Dip Arch 1999

FLETCHER PRIEST ARCHITECTS
Jonathan Kendall (Associate Director, Head of Urban Design): Dip Arch 1999, PhD research 2003-present / MSc Urban Design tutor 1999-present

ADRIAN FORTY
Adrian Forty: history and theory tutor 1973-present, PhD supervisor 1976-present, launched MSc in History of Architecture with Mark Swenarton 1981, MSc Architectural History Director, Vice-Dean 1997-2000, Year 1 'History of Cities and their Architecture' course coordinator 1990-present, Professor of Architectural History (1999)

FOSTER AND PARTNERS
Angus Campbell: Dip Arch 1993
Alan Chan: Dip Arch 1999
Lord Foster: Visiting Professor of Architecture and Urban Design 1998-present
Katy Ghahremani: see KATY GHAHREMANI + MICHAEL KOHN
Richard Hyams (Project Director): Dip Arch 1994
Xavier De Kestelier: MSc Urban Design 2000
Jong-Min Kim: Dip Arch 2002
Narinder Sagoo (Project Director): Dip Arch 1999
Michiel Verhaverbeke: MSc Virtual Environments 2000

FUTURE SYSTEMS
Nicola Hawkins: Dip 2000
Rachel Stevenson: MSc Architectural History

2001 / BSc Year 1 design tutor 2002-03
Dominic Harris: BSc Arch 1998, Dip Arch 2001
Severin Soder: MArch (Architectural Design) 1998
Nicholas Mansour: Dip Arch 2001

STEPHEN GAGE
Stephen Gage: Dip Unit 14 tutor 1991-present, Director of Technology 1999-present, Professor of Innovative Technology (2000), Director of Architectural Design 2001-present
Phil Ayers: see SIXTEEN*(MAKERS)

GENERAL LIGHTING AND POWER
Nic Clear: BSc Unit 5 tutor 1993-94, Dip Unit 15 tutor 1995-present

KATY GHAHREMANI + MICHAEL KOHN
Katy Ghahremani: Dip Arch 1997
Michael Kohn: Dip Arch 1997

GLAS
Nazar Sayigh (Director): Dip Arch 199
Stas Louca (Director): Dip Arch 1995
Angus Macgregor (Associate): Dip Arch 1995

GOLLIFER LANGSTON ARCHITECTS
Mary Duggan: Dip Arch 1997

GRIMSHAW
Simon Beames: Dip Arch 1994
Jerry Tate: Dip Arch 1998

CHRISTIAN GROOTHUIZEN
Christian Groothuizen: BSc Arch 1998, Dip Arch 2000 / BSc Unit 7 tutor 2001-present,

GUSTAFSON PORTER
Peter Culley: see RICK MATHER ARCHITECTS

CHRISTINE HAWLEY
Abigail Ashton: see ASHTON PORTER STUDIO
Peter Cook: see COOK AND FOURNIER – SPACELAB
Christine Hawley: Professor of Architectural Studies (1993), Director of the School of Architecture 1993-99, BSc Arch Director 1993-99, Dip Unit 21 tutor 1993-present, Dean 1999-present
Tom Holberton: see ASHTON PORTER STUDIO
Eduardo De Oliveira Rosa: see OLIVEIRA ROSA ARCHITECTURE
Andew Porter: see ASHTON PORTER STUDIO
Patrick Weber: see STORP_WEBER_ARCHITECTURE

WAYNE HEAD
Wayne Head: see PENOYRE & PRASAD

LOUIS HELLMAN
Louis Hellman: BSc Arch 1962

JONATHAN HILL
Jonathan Hill: MSc History of Modern Architecture 1990, PhD Architectural Design 2000 / Dip Arch joint coordinator 1989-90, BSc history and theory tutor 1990-91, BSc Arch Director 1998-2001, Dip Unit 12 tutor 1990-present, PhD by Architectural Design Director 2000-present

WILLIAM HODGSON ARCHITECTS
William Hodgson: Dip Arch 1998 / digital media tutor 1998-present

ANDREW HOLMES
Andrew Holmes: Dip Unit 22 tutor 2001-present

HOPKINS ARCHITECTS
Simon Goode: Dip Arch 2000, MArch (Architecture) 2003
Tom Holdom: BSc Arch 1993, Dip Arch 1996, Dip technical consultant 1998-present
Emma Frater: Dip Arch 1999
Sophy Twohig: Dip Arch 1997

HÛT ARCHITECTURE
Scott Batty (Partner): Dip Arch 1997
Andrew Whiting (Partner): Dip Arch 1999, MArch (Architecture) 2002

IMAGINATION
Paulo Pimentel: Dip Arch 1997

DARYL JACKSON ARCHITECTS
Daryl Jackson: visiting examiner and critic 1999-2001

JESTICO + WHILES ARCHITECTS
Heinz Richardson (Director): BSc Arch 1975, Dip Arch 1978

EVA JIRICNA ARCHITECTS
Georgina Papathanasiou: MSc (Architectural Design) 1994

PATRICK KEILLER
Patrick Keiller: BSc Arch 1971, Dip Arch 1974

LUIDMLLA AND VLADISLAV KIRPICHEV
Luidmilla Kirpichev: Dip Unit 23 tutor 2000-02, MArch (Architectural Design) tutor 2000-present
Vladislav Kirpichev: Dip Unit 23 tutor 2000-02, MArch (Architectural Design) tutor 2000-present

LAB-7
Shuheng Huang (Design Principal): Dip Arch 1994

THE LIGHTHOUSE, SCOTLAND'S CENTRE FOR ARCHITECTURE, DESIGN AND THE CITY
Morag Bain: Dip Arch 1993

CJ LIM/STUDIO 8 ARCHITECTS
Rhys Cannon: BSc Arch 1999, Dip Arch (current) / Bartlett Architecture Lab research assistant 1999-2000
Michael Kong: Bartlett Architecture Lab research assistant 2000-present
cj Lim: Dip Unit 21 tutor 1991-present, Bartlett Architecture Lab Director 1999-present, BSc Arch Director 2001-present
Edward T H Liu: BSc Arch 1995, Dip Arch 1999, member of the Bartlett extension + renovation team

JOHN LYALL ARCHITECTS
Peter Culley: see RICK MATHER ARCHITECTS
John Lyall: Dip external examiner 1996-2002, Dip Unit tutor 1998-99
Morag Tait: see ALLFORD HALL MONAGHAN MORRIS
Philip Turner: Dip Arch 2001
Zoe Quick: Dip Arch 2002

LYNNFOX
Christian McKenzie: Dip Arch 2000
Patrick Chen: Dip Arch 2000, MArch (Architecture) 2001
Bastian Glassner: Dip Arch 2000, MArch (Architecture) 2001

MARCOSANDMARJAN ARCHITECTS
Marjan Colletti: MArch (Architectural Design) 1999, PhD research 2001-present / BSc Unit 5 tutor 2000-present,
Marcos Cruz: MArch (Architectural Design) 1999, PhD research 2000-present / Dip Unit 20 tutor 1999-present

RICK MATHER ARCHITECTS
Peter Culley: Dip Arch 1996

NIALL MCLAUGHLIN ARCHITECTS
Sandra Coppin: Dip Arch 1999
Hannah Corlett: Dip Arch 2000
Beverley Dockray: Dip Arch 2000
Matt Driscoll: Dip Arch 2001
Spencer Guy: Dip Arch 2000
Niall McLaughlin: BSc Year 1 design tutor 1991-92, Dip Unit 17 tutor 1993-present
Simon Tonks: Dip Arch 2002
Silko Vosskötter: Dip Arch 1999
Emma Wales: Dip Arch 2000

BRIGID MCLEER
Brigid McLeer: Dip history and theory tutor 2001-present
Katie Lloyd Thomas: Dip history and theory tutor 2000-03

ENRIC MIRALLES BENEDETTA TAGLIABUE
Karl Unglaub: BSc Unit 2 tutor 2002-present

NAAU – NEW ARCHITECTURE AND ARTISTS UNION
Rahesh Ram (Director): Dip Arch 1996

NOODLEJAM
Nina Vollenbröker: Dip Arch 2001, MSc Architectural History 2002
James Santer: Dip Arch 2001

OLIVEIRA ROSA ARCHITECTURE
Eduardo de Oliveira Rosa: MArch (Architectural Design) 1997 / BSc Unit 2 tutor 1999-2002, Dip Unit 22 tutor 1998-99

ORMS ARCHITECTURE & DESIGN
Julia Backhaus: MArch (Architectural Design) 1998 / BSc Unit 5 tutor 2000-03

PASTINA MATTHEWS ARCHITECTS
Chris Matthews: Dip Arch 1992

PATEL TAYLOR
Andrew Taylor (Founding Partner): BSc Arch 1983, Dip Arch 1986

PENOYRE & PRASAD ARCHITECTS
Wayne Head: Dip Arch 1997

PÉREZ ARROYO + HURTADO ARCHITECTS
Salvador Pérez Arroyo: Visiting Professor 1999-present, BSc Unit 5 tutor 1994-99, Dip Unit 20 tutor 1999-2003
Dr. Eva Hurtado Torán: visiting critic

PHAB ARCHITECTS
Peter Hasdell: BSc Unit 1 tutor 1999-2001, BSc Year 1 design tutor 2002-present, Dip Unit 24 tutor 2001-present, MArch (Architectural Design) tutor 2002-present

PIERCY CONNER ARCHITECTS
Richard Conner (Director): Dip Arch 1997

ALICIA PIVARO
Alicia Pivaro: BSc Arch 1988, MSc History of Modern Architecture 1990, Dip Arch 1991

PLETTS HAQUE
Josephine Pletts (Partner): Dip Arch 1997 / BSc 'Preparing for Practice' course coordinator 2001-02
Usman Haque (Partner): Dip Arch 1996 / Dip Unit 14 and Interactive Architecture Workshop tutor 2002-present

PEOPLE/PRACTICE INDEX

PRINGLE BRANDON ARCHITECTS
Andrew Whiting: Dip Arch 1999, UCL Research Fellowship 2000-02 in collaboration with Pringle Brandon architects leading to MArch (Architectural Design) 2002

PROJECT ORANGE
James Soane (Director): Dip Arch 1991 / BSc Unit 4 tutor 2000-03

JOHN PUTTICK
John Puttick: Dip Arch 2001

PEG RAWES
Peg Rawes: Dip history and theory tutor 1997-present, BSc history and theory tutor 2001-present, Dip history and theory coordinator 2003-present

JANE RENDELL
Jane Rendell: MSc History of Modern Architecture 1994 / Dip history and theory tutor 1994-present, Dip history and theory coordinator 2000-03, PhD supervisor 2000-present, MSc Architectural History tutor 2000-present, Reader in Architecture and Art 2003-present

RIBA JOURNAL
Eleanor Young (Assistant Editor): MSc Architectural History 2001

RICH MARTINS ASSOCIATES
Jonathan Manning: BSc Arch 1995, Dip Arch 1999

IAN RITCHIE ARCHITECTS
Anthony Boulanger: MArch 1997
Robin Cross: Dip Arch 1998
Ian Ritchie: external examiner 1990-present
Toby Smith: Dip Arch 1994

RICHARD ROGERS PARTNERSHIP
Stephen Barrett: BSc Arch 1988
Carmel Lewin: BSc Arch 1990, Dip Arch 1993
John McElgunn: Dip Arch 2001
Daniel Wright: BSc Arch 1996
Ivan Harbour: BSc Arch 1980, Dip Arch 1995
Maurice Brennan: Dip Arch 1993
Andrei Saltykov: MArch (Architectural Design) 1998
Tosan Popo: Dip Arch 1996

SATELLITE DESIGN WORKSHOP
Sarah Allan: Dip Arch 1995
Stewart Dodd (Director): Dip Arch 1994 / BSc Year 1 design tutor 1995-2000, Dip technical consultant 1995-2000
Neil Wilson (Director): Dip Arch 1995

SCOTT BROWNRIGG
Darren Comber (Main Board Director): Dip Arch 1990

SHEPPARD ROBSON
Claire Haywood: Dip Arch 1997 / Dip 'Learning from Practice' course tutor 2001-present
Sylvian Hartenberg: MArch (Architectural Design) 1996
(Dominic) Chi lok Choi: MSc Urban Design 2000, Dip Arch 2001
Anthony St Leger: Dip Arch 2000
Roy Naughton: BSc Arch 1998, Dip Arch 2001

DEBRA SHIPLEY MP
Debra Shipley, MP for Stourbridge: MSc History of Modern Architecture 1990

SIXTEEN*(MAKERS)
Phil Ayres: Dip Arch 1998 / BSc Year 1 tutor 2000-present, Dip Unit 14 tutor 1998-present, electronics consultant 1998-present, CADCAM and info systems developer 2002-present
Nick Callicott: BSc Arch 1991, Dip Arch 1995 / Director of Computing 2000-03, BSc Unit 6 tutor 1995-2003
Chris Leung: BSc Arch 1995, Dip Arch 1998
Bob Sheil: BSc Arch 1991, Dip Arch 1994 / BSc Year 1 technology lecturer 2000-present, BSc Unit 6 tutor 1995-present, Web Info Systems Director 2000-present

SKIDMORE, OWINGS & MERRILL
Davin Torch Benning: Dip Arch 1998

SOFTROOM
Christopher Bagot: BSc Arch 1991, Dip Arch 1994
Daniel Evans: BSc Arch 1991, Dip Arch 1994
Oliver Salway: BSc Arch 1991, Dip Arch 1994

SPACE SYNTAX
Tim Stonor, Managing Director: BSc Arch 1989, MSc Advanced Architectural Studies 1991
Biljana Savic, Associate Director: MSc Advanced Architectural Studies 1994
Kayvan Karimi, Associate: PhD Architecture 1998
Beatriz Campos, Associate: PhD Architecture 1999
Polly Fong, Consultant: MSc Advanced Architectural Studies 1998, PhD Architecture research 1988-present
Maria Zerdilla, Consultant: MSc Advanced Architectural Studies 1998, MSc Building and Urban Design in Development 1999

Myrto Zirini, Consultant: MSc Advanced Architectural Studies 2001

NEIL SPILLER
Neil Spiller: Dip Unit 19 tutor 1992-present, Dip Director 1994-present, Reader in Architecture and Digital Theory 2000-present, Vice-Dean 2001-present

SPRINGETT MACKAY ARCHITECTURE
Matthew Springett: Dip Arch 1998 / BSc Year 1 design tutor 1999-2001
Kirsteen Mackay: BSc Year 1 design tutor 2000-01

SQUINT/OPERA
Oliver Alsop (Director): BSc Arch 2000
Martin Hampton (Director): BSc Arch 2000
Alice Scott (Director): BSc Arch 2001

STORP_WEBER_ARCHITECTURE
Eduardo De Oliveira Rosa: see OLIVEIRA ROSA ARCHITECTURE
Patrick Weber (Partner): MArch (Architectural Design) 1997 / BSc Unit 5 tutor 1998-2000, Dip Unit 11 tutor 2000-02, BSc Year 1 design coordinator 2001-present, Dip Unit 24 tutor 2002-present

MARK SWENARTON
Mark Swenarton: PhD 1979 / history and theory tutor 1977-89, launched MSc in History of Architecture with Adrian Forty 1981

JERRY TATE
Jerry Tate: Dip Arch 1998

TECHNIKER
Matthew Wells: Dip technical consultant 1992-current

TEMPLETON ASSOCIATES
Simon Templeton: Dip Arch 1991
Bernd Felsinger: Dip Arch 1999, MArch (architecture) 2002
Jonathan Rowley: Dip Arch 1993

TESSERA
Anthony Boulanger: MArch 1997
Penelope Haralambidou: MArch 1995, PhD research 1996-present / MArch (Architectural Design) tutor 1996-present, Dip Unit 20 tutor 1997-98, BSc Unit 2 tutor 1999-2002
Yeoryia Manolopoulou: MArch (Architectural Design) 1997, PhD research 1998-present / Unit 17 tutor 1999-present
Eduardo de Oliveira Rosa: see OLIVEIRA ROSA ARCHITECTURE

THARANI ASSOCIATES
Nadir Tharani: BSc Arch 1975, Dip Arch 1977

STEPHEN TIERNEY
Stephen Tierney: BSc Arch 1997, Dip Arch 2000 / BSc Unit 7 tutor 2001-present

TRANSIENT
Jonathan Pile (Principal): BSc Arch 1982, Dip Arch 1984 / BSc Year 1 design tutor 1998-present

UNIVERSITY OF SOUTH AUSTRALIA
Chris Landorf (Senior Lecturer): Dip Facility and Environment Management 2000

UFO – URBAN FUTURE ORGANIZATION
Steve Hardy: MArch (Architectural Design) 1996

USHIDA FINDLAY ARCHITECTS
Paul Madden: BSc Arch 1996, Dip Arch 2000, MArch (Architecture) 2001
Anne Maria Galmstrup: Dip Arch 2002
Kate Francis: Dip Arch 1998
Matthew Potter: BSc Arch, Dip Arch 2000

VELVET AIR
Simon Herron: BSc Unit 4 tutor 1991-99, Dip Unit 16 tutor 1999-present
Susanne Isa: BSc Unit 4 tutor 1993-99, Dip Unit 16 tutor 1999-present

WAG ARCHITECTURE
Cordula Weisser: Dip exchange student 1994-95, MSc Architectural History 1999 / BSc Year 1 design tutor 2001-02
Jon Goodbun: MSc Architectural History 2000

INGALILL WAHLROOS ARCHITECTS
Ingalill Wahlroos-Ritter: BSc Unit 1 design tutor 2002-present

WHAT ARCHITECTURE
Anthony Hoete: MArch (Architectural Design) 1995 / BSc Unit 7 tutor 1998-2001
Gerrit Grigoleit: BSc Architecture 1994

WHITE PARTNERS
Robert White (Director): BSc Arch 1987, Dip Arch 1991

MICHAEL WILFORD & PARTNERS
Chris Matthews: Dip Arch 1992

WILKINSONEYRE.ARCHITECTS
Ben Addy: Dip Arch 2001

TIM WRAY
Tim Wray: MSc Architectural History 2001

PROJECT INDEX

1&2 Waterside, Paddington Basin, offices, London 153
2 Newham's Row, warehouse office conversion, London 70
30D Kitchen Extension, London 90
32 Murray Mews, house, London 01
350 Regents Place Euston, offices, London 158
66-68 Sclater Street, residential conversion, London 126
7+4 Housing Towers, Asturias, Spain 129
95 Queen Victoria Street, offices, London 156

ACTION Center, customer service centre and museum, Taipei, Taiwan 97
'Adidas Predator', advertising illustration 66
Alba di Milano, monument, Italy 146
Albion Riverside, mixed-use development, London 52
'Alice's pillow-books: adventures in immanence', essay 141
Antwerp Law Courts, The Netherlands 149
Architecture Week, UK 135
Armada Way, retail development, Plymouth 192
'Asphalt Paradise', art exhibition, London 85

'Back from the brink', *RIBA Journal* magazine article 144
Bagpipe/Garden of Vessels, New Tomihiro Museum, Japan 112
Bandstand, De La Warr Pavilion, Kent 115
Barajas Airport Terminal, Madrid, Spain 151
Battersea Power Station, multi-use redevelopment, London 72
'BBC Homefront', 'BBC Changing Rooms', 'From House to Home – Channel 4', TV presenting, UK 25
BBC Radio 1 Broadcast Studios, digital studio design forum, London 72
Berkeley Tower Penthouse Flat, London 94
Bleicherweg office, Zurich, Switzerland 123
blur: the making of nothing, book 42
Bolton Gardens, domestic refurbishment, London 138
British Council E3 Electronic Entertainment Expo Pavilion, Los Angeles, USA 90
Brixton Town Centre Vision, masterplan, London 171
Broadgate Club West, health club, London 06
'Burol', Vlaams Administratie Centrum, Leuven, Belgium 198

c/PLEX, arts building, West Bromwich 15
Camden Summer Workshop, London 97
Canteen, Städel Academy, Frankfurt, Germany 76
Cargo Fleet, studio-houses, London 32
Carthew Road House, refurbishment, London 179
CASPAR Housing, Birmingham 06
Castelmola Museum of Contemporary Art, Sicily 189
Centre of Engineering and Manufacturing Excellence, Essex 158
Centro Congressi Italia, competition entry, Rome, Italy 74
Charter School, London 127
Chelsea College of Art and Design, redevelopment, London 10
City Academy schools, design illustration 56
City Hall, London 57
City Learning Centre, South Camden Community School, London 70
Clearwater Yard, offices, London 09
Clonehouse, Concept House 2000 competition entry 105
Cloth Hall Street, mixed-use building, Leeds 08
Comme des Garçons Tunnel, New York, USA 60
CowParade Interactive Cow, London 29
Crab Stools and Maua Meeting Table, Tanzania 184
Cross Workspaces, offices, London 155
Crystal Palace Park, landscape and buildings, London 106
CSIRO Discovery Centre, scientific research and information centre, Canberra, Australia 92

Delhi Deli, takeaway restaurant fit-out, London 138
Dialogue with Nature – Country House Lancashire, competition entry 102
Dominican Monastery, Lille, France 17
Donkey Shelter, Tipperary, Ireland 185
'Drawing Fix', exhibition/architectural project 183
Dream more! Demand more!, film 121
Drop House, Hertfordshire 47
Dulwich Pool House, London 01

Eden Project Education Resource Centre, Cornwall 71
EDF Trading Interactive LED Wall, London 137
Eel class racing canoe, Lough Derg, Ireland 185
'Eine Se(h)kunde', photographic documentation, USA 122
Electronic Arts European Headquarters, Chertsey 55
Elm House, domestic rebuild, Broadheath near Worcester 83
Esplanade, Marina Bay, Singapore 200
Evelina Children's Hospital, London 86
Evergreen Adventure Playground, London 03

Faith Zone, Millennium Dome, London 94
Finsbury Park Community Building, London 116
FLO houses, Velux competition entry, London 134
'Floating Retreat', *Wallpaper** magazine concept design 166
Folkestone Seafood Stall, competition entry 104
Fordham White Hair and Beauty Salon, London 48
Formation, office refurbishment, London 20

'Ghost Photography', exhibition, Spain 203
Gifu, social housing, Japan 75
Grafton New Hall, country house, Cheshire 190
Grand Central Bar, London 23
Grand Egyptian Museum, competition entry, Cairo 20
Great Glass House Internal Landscape, National Botanic Garden of Wales, Carmarthen 73
Great Notley Primary School, Essex 05

HangerHouse, Concept House 2000 prototype 68
Hastings Visitor Centre 193
'Hayling', FC Kahuna, music video 108
Health Club am Gendarmenmarkt, Berlin, Germany 125
Hedge-House, London 186
Hellman biographical cartoon 79
House 33/28, Buehl, Germany 176
House for the Future, Museum of Welsh Life, Cardiff 93
How Green is Your Garden?, publication 103

'I See You Baby', Groove Armada, pop promo 67
Imperial War Museum of the North, exhibition installation, Manchester 45
'In Place of The Page', art project 118
Inselweg 11 house, Hurden, Switzerland 124
'Inside the Whale', essay 50
Isobel's Treehouse, London 64

Jacobs Ladder House, Oxfordshire 115
Jordan House, Bellas, Portugal 164
Jubilee School, London 06

Kielder Belvedere, Kielder Forest National Park, Northumberland 168
'King's Cross Journey', arts project, London 30
Kingstown Street Mews House, London 174
Kunsthaus Graz, Austria 34

La Fromagerie, retail fit-out, London 124
Lab-7, office design, Taipei, Taiwan 99
'Laboratories for architecture', photographic project 194
Land of Scattered Seeds, artwork/book 139
'Les Mots et Les Choses', installation 142
Library of Birmingham 154
Lighthouse National Architecture Awareness Programme, Scotland's Centre for Architecture, Design and the City 100
Lightlines, light installation, Wolverhampton 18
Line of Lode Miners Memorial and Visitors Centre, New South Wales, Australia 188
Living Sites, housing, competition entry 68
Lloyd's Register of Shipping, City of London 151
London City Racecourse 54
'Love Architecture', RIBA Gallery poster campaign illustration 67
Lützoplatz Social Housing, Berlin, Germany 76

Macgregor House, Brownhill Creek, Australia 28
MACRO: Museo d'Arte Contemporaneo di Roma, Italy 40
Magna, exhibition installation, Yorkshire 44
'Maintel Telecommunications', advertising illustration 66
Maison Seynave, Var, France 17
Mancunian Way Footbridge, Manchester 16
Mandela's Yard Museum, Johannesburg, South Africa 145
Margate Old Town Masterplan 170
Marni, retail fit-out, London 62
Martello Tower Y, residential conversion, Bawdsey Beach, Suffolk 134
Mathengine Stands, CEDEC99 and GDC2000 Developers' Conferences 44
Mersey Wave Gateway, Liverpool 18
Microflat, apartments, London 132
Microlife, Selfridges shop-window installation, London 133
Minamiyamashiro Elementary School, Japan 150
Modular Offices Roof Extension, London 22
Mongrel, office refurbishment, London 19
'Moving Home!', relocating a house, Inderoy, Norway 78
Multifuctional Station, Mendrisio, Switzerland 130
Museum of Modern Art, refurbishment, Oxford 24
Mwanza House, Dar es Salaam, Tanzania 184

National Assembly for Wales, Cardiff 153
National Centre for Popular Music, Sheffield 28
'Nature is Ancient', Björk, music video 109
New England Biolabs, competition entry, Massachusetts, USA 110
New World Trade Center Proposal, design illustration, New York, USA 56
New World Trade Center Proposal, New York, USA 55

PROJECT INDEX

New World Trade Center Proposal/Ground Zero, New York, USA 129
North Greenwich Underground Station, London 107
North Osaka Station Development, competition entry, Japan 76
Norwich Cathedral refectory and library extension 87

Ontario College of Art and Design, extension, Toronto, Canada 15
Orange Imaginarium, At-Bristol Science Centre, interactive exhibition 91
Ourtown Story, Millennium Dome, London 153
Oxford School of Architecture Digital Studio 114

Paddington Central Gateway, London 18
Peabody Trust Housing, Dalston Lane, London 09
Peabody Trust Housing, Raines Dairy, London 06
Peckham Library, London 11
Plashet Lane Bridge, London 179
'Playstation', advertising illustration 67
Plymouth Theatre Royal Production Centre 148
Poole Harbour Bridge 202
Port Tawe Footbridges and Walkway, Swansea, Wales 201
'Predators', travelling exhibition, The Natural History Museum, London 91
Princes Circus, masterplan, London 171
Project Phoenix, Experian Data Centre, Nottingham 160
Project Renaissance, Experian Office Headquarters, Nottingham 160
Punctum Millennium, Pinto New Town Masterplan, Madrid, Spain 39

RIBA Headquarters, refurbishment, London 10
River of Stars, urban design, London 84
Robinson in Space, film 95
Royal Victoria Dock Bridge, London 180

Salvation Army Headquarters, London 159
San Michele Cemetery, Venice, Italy 33
Sarajevo Concert Hall, Bosnia i Herzegovina 189
'Scents of Space', interactive smell installation, Brighton/London 136
Scottish Parliament, Edinburgh 118
Selfridges Foodhall, Manchester 60
Selfridges, department store, Birmingham 58
Selfridges, retail fit-out, London and Manchester 164
Shepherds Bush Green, urban landscape design, London 147

Sidgwick Site Masterplan and Institute of Criminology, University of Cambridge 10
sins + other spatial relatives, publication 105
Skin, keyworker modular housing, London 22
SmartSlab™, interactive building product 29
Spire of Dublin, monument, Ireland 148
Spun Yarn, RIBA 'Future-City' exhibition 186
St John's Wood private house, London 05
Star Tech, office building, Taipei, Taiwan 99
Stonebridge Health and Community Centre, London 13
Stonebridge Nursery, London 13
Stratford City, masterplan, London 49
Summer Stage, outdoor theatre, Corning, New York 197

Takahata House, Yamagata Prefecture, Japan 21
Temple Quay Pedestrian Bridge, Bristol 116
Thames Barrier Park, London 126
'The Institute of Illegal Architects', in *The Illegal Architect*, publication 81
'The Pleasure of Treasure', arts project, London 30
Tomelloso Swimming Pool, Ciudad Real, Spain 128
Top Down Ventilation and Cooling in Urban Areas, technology research project, London 65
Torro Espacio Tower, competition entry, Madrid, Spain 154
Tottenham Hale Station, London 106
Towers of Wind, competition entry, Athens, Greece 196
Transient Field, Bellevue-Stadelhofen Square, urban design, Zurich, Switzerland 183
Tree House Apartment, London 23
'Treehouse', *Wallpaper** magazine concept design 166
Tribunal de Grande Instance, Bordeaux, France 152

Union Square, mixed-use development, London 07
Unit 63, Canal Building, apartment fit-out, London 177
Urban Forest, Syntagma Square, urban design, Athens, Greece 182
Urban Renaissance Programme, documentary films 175

Venus, studio/house/gallery, London 32
Veritas Headquarters campus, offices, Reading 156
Virginia Museum of Fine Arts, expansion and sculpture garden, USA 113

Vogue Table, furniture design, London 62
Voss Street House, London 48

Walsall Bus Station 05
Warehouse Conversion, apartment, London 25
Waterford Riverside Community, masterplan, Ireland 155
'Weather Architecture', in *Actions of Architecture*, publication 81
Wellcome Trust Headquarters, London 89
Wembley Stadium, London 53
'Who', *Dazed and Confused* magazine illustration 66
Wild at Heart at the Great Eastern, retail fit-out, London 62
Wildscreen at Bristol, leisure and education building 88
Will Adams Centre, education and recreation building, competition entry, North Kent 02
Wimpole Street, house, London 181
'Wittgenstein's curtains', article, Weekend magazine, *The Guardian* 43
Work/Learn Zone, Millennium Dome, London 08